GIVE ME LIBERTY

MEMOIRS OF THE

AMERICAN PHILOSOPHICAL SOCIETY
held at Philadelphia
for Promoting Useful Knowledge

VOLUME 46

Thomas Jefferson. Portrait by Thomas Sully in the Hall of the
American Philosophical Society.

GIVE ME LIBERTY

The Struggle for Self-Government
in
Virginia

THOMAS J. WERTENBAKER

Edwards Professor Emeritus of American History
Princeton University

THE AMERICAN PHILOSOPHICAL SOCIETY
INDEPENDENCE SQUARE
PHILADELPHIA

1958

*Library of Congress Catalog
Card Number:* 58-9093

PRINTED IN THE UNITED STATES OF AMERICA
BY J. H. FURST COMPANY, BALTIMORE, MARYLAND

Preface

None of the American colonies " will ever submit to the loss of those valuable rights and privileges which are essential to the happiness of every free state," George Washington wrote in October, 1774. Perhaps the British officer to whom he made this statement was startled to have him speak of the colonies as free. Yet at the time the American people were the freest in the world, freer even than the people of England. It was to defend this freedom, not to gain new rights, that the colonists rebelled against Great Britain. For decades they had been governing themselves, so when the British Ministry tried to govern them from London, they would not submit.

To understand what was in the minds and hearts of George Washington, Samuel Adams, Patrick Henry, and the other patriots, it is necessary to know how the colonies became self-governing. One must follow the political battles and hard-earned victories of their fathers, and grandfathers, and great-grandfathers in the colonial Assemblies.

This volume treats of the struggle for self-government in Virginia from the founding of Jamestown in 1607 to the Declaration of Independence. The story of the gradual lessening of the King's prerogative, of the weakening of the power of the Governor, of the emergence of the Assembly as the ruling body could be paralleled in other colonies. But it is of especial importance in Virginia, where was held the first representative Assembly in the New World, and which gave so many leaders to the American Revolution.

I wish to express my appreciation to my Alma Mater, the University of Virginia, for its award of a Thomas Jefferson Research Fellowship, without which this volume would not have been written.

THOMAS J. WERTENBAKER.

Princeton, N. J.
April 1, 1957.

Contents

Illustrations

THE CORNERSTONE OF LIBERTY

THREE little vessels—the *Susan Constant*, the *Godspeed*, and the *Discovery*—left England in December, 1606, under the command of Captain Christopher Newport, to found a colony on the distant shores of Virginia. Two decades earlier Sir Walter Raleigh had sent out a group of settlers to what is now North Carolina, and they had disappeared mysteriously. What had happened to them? men asked. Had they been killed by the Indians? Had they fallen victims to disease? Had they starved? Those who shared in this new venture must have wondered if a like fate awaited them in this strange new land.

But their spirits rose when they entered Chesapeake Bay. Landing parties were delighted with the " fair meddowes . . . full of flowers of divers kinds and colors," the " goodly tall trees," and the streams of fresh water. It was a smiling country which seemed to bid them welcome. But when they entered the mouth of a broad river, which they called the James in honor of their King, and made their way up into the country, new doubts must have assailed them. They knew that savages lived in the dense forests which lined both banks; might not strange wild beasts live there also? Might there not be fatal diseases unknown in Europe?

Possibly they wondered what type of government Englishmen would live under here. In the charter granted the Virginia Company of London in 1606 it was promised that they should " enjoy all the liberties, franchises, and immunities " of Englishmen, " as if they had been abiding " in England. Even without this promise they would have taken it for granted that they were not surrendering the freedom derived from their ancestors. This was the view taken six decades later by Francis Moryson and Thomas Ludwell, agents for the colony. If the King planted a colony of Englishmen, they and their heirs ought by law to enjoy the " same liberties and privileges as Englishmen in England." After all, the colony would be but " an extension or dilation of the realm of England." [1]

[1] *Bath papers* II, p. 44.

1

The men who came to Virginia had, in the mother country, participated in the government through representatives of their own choosing, so they insisted upon this right in their new home. They claimed, also, the habeas corpus, jury trial, and freedom from taxation save by their own consent. In England not even the King could take a man's money legally until it had been granted by the House of Commons. Upon this recognized principle English liberty was chiefly based; upon its acceptance in America depended the future of liberty there.

Yet when the first band of settlers stepped ashore at Jamestown, liberty in England still hung in the balance. At the conclusion of the Wars of the Roses the King was almost absolute. The people were desperately tired of anarchy; they were tired also of the oppressions of the barons. So long as the King put an end to both they had no desire to limit his power. The Commons ate out of his hand. Henry VIII might tear the Church from the Roman see, Mary might restore it, Edward might once more break with Rome—in each case the people submitted. Those who dared resist faced the headsman's block or the pyre.

But in time the memory of the Wars of the Roses grew dim. And the growth of the artisan class, the development of trade, the birth of a great literature, the work of the universities, the expansion of world horizons fired the imagination and awakened men to their own potentialities. Self-government is a tender plant which withers in the soil of poverty and ignorance, and it was the advance of prosperity and enlightenment under the Tudors which made possible the flowering of liberty under the Stuarts.

James I had been on the throne only three years when the little town which bore his name was founded. James has been called the wisest fool in Christendom; but he was neither wise nor a fool. His conception of the King's office was logical and simple. It was his function to rule; the duty of the people was to obey. If they did not, like bad children they should be scolded and perhaps punished, since it was not only illegal but wicked to question the King's authority. " As to dispute what God may do is blasphemy, so it is sedition in subjects to dispute what a King may do," he said. Parliament he considered a nuisance. " I am surprised that my ancestors should have permitted such an institution to come into existence," he said.

" I am a stranger and found it here when I arrived, so that I am obliged to put up with what I cannot get rid of." [2]

The House of Commons were not inclined to accept the King's theory of the relations between himself and Parliament. When James told them that they had no privileges save by royal grace, they replied that he had been misinformed. When in answer to James' demand that they refrain from meddling in foreign affairs, they entered on their journal a protestation of their right of free speech, he was so enraged that he sent for the book and with his own hands tore out the page.

The Commons considered it a precious privilege to be " governed by certain rules of law . . . and not by uncertain or arbitrary form of government." There is a general fear among the people, they told James, that royal proclamations might eventually assume the nature of laws. Then their ancient freedom would be abridged, " if not quite taken away," and " a new form of arbitrary government " brought on the realm.

The conflict between King and Parliament foreshadowed the conflict between the Governors and the people of the colonies. The provincial Assemblies were not less determined to resist any infringement on their rights than was Parliament. And the fortunes of the contending forces in the mother country affected profoundly those in the colonies. Echoes of the First Stuart Despotism, the Civil War and Commonwealth, the Restoration, the Second Stuart Despotism, the Glorious Revolution, the laissez-faire period, and the reaction under George III reverberated in the colonies.

But the development of self-government in America was by no means entirely dependent upon events in England. There were forces in the New World which favored democracy. The wide spaces of the frontier made men self-reliant and resourceful and impatient of control by a distant monarch, ever ready to defend old rights, quick to demand new ones. " People remote from the seat of government are always remarkable for their disobedience," wrote Governor Gooch, in 1732.[3] As the historian Foote has pointed out, they and " their children were republicans; in England they would have been styled rebels."

The creating of a vast middle class in the colonies also tended toward democracy. The men who turned their backs on the

[2] R. W. K. Hinton, Government and liberty under James I, *Cambridge Historical Journal* 11 (1).
[3] Gooch to the Lords of Trade, March 30, 1732.

homes of their ancestors to start life over again in the tobacco fields of Virginia were, most of them, desperately poor. Many came under terms of indenture. But they had, prior to the introduction of slaves in large numbers, every opportunity to rise. As a result there emerged a vigorous, intelligent, freedom-loving yeomanry, who had a profound influence in winning self-government.

But the victory at first seemed to be with the King. When James granted a charter to the Virginia Company of London, he took care that it should include no provision for representative government. Instead he kept the control of the proposed colony in his own hands. There was to be a Council resident in England appointed by him and responsible to him. This body was to name another Council which was to reside in Virginia and administer the " Articles, Instructions, and Orders " which the King drew up with his own hand. In practice this body assumed administrative, legislative, and judicial powers, and ruled the infant colony by their own arbitrary will.[4]

Not only was this constitution undemocratic, but it proved inefficient. Had the Council in England made better selections for the Council in Virginia, the colony would have been saved much disorder and suffering. But never was there a more quarrelsome set of men. The fleet had been at sea but a few days when Captain John Smith was accused of plotting to overthrow the government and murder his associates, and was kept in prison below decks. Only some weeks after the landing at Jamestown was he released and permitted to take his seat on the Council.[5]

On the Council with him were Captain Christopher Newport, Edward Wingfield, Bartholomew Gosnold, George Kendall, John Ratcliffe, and John Martin. One would think that this little group, set down in the wilderness and faced with many perils, would have occupied their time better than with plotting against each other. They had enough to do to defend themselves against the Indians, for in a sudden attack four of them were wounded and another had a narrow escape when an arrow passed through his beard.[6]

Kendall was the first to be expelled from the Council. Gos-

---

[4] A. Brown, *Genesis of the United States* 1: 55, 56.
[5] Edward Arber, *Works of Captain John Smith*, 91.
[6] *Ibid.*, lii.

nold died. Wingfield, who was President of the Council, was accused of being an atheist, of plotting to desert the colony, and of misappropriating public funds, and was ousted from his seat. Since Newport had sailed with the fleet for England, Ratcliffe, Smith, and Martin were now the only remaining Councillors. But this did not bring harmony. Kendall was accused of plotting against the other two, tried, and hanged. Smith, too, was in danger of the gallows, when he was held responsible for the death of two men who had been killed by the Indians. Were the " whipping, lawing, beating, and hanging in Virginia known in England, I fear it would drive many well affected minds from this honorable action," Wingfield stated after his return to England. With the drowning of two new Councillors, Captain John Smith alone remained, and for several months was the sole ruler of the colony.[7]

When word of what was going on in Virginia reached the London Company it was obvious to all that the original plan of government had proved a failure. So they secured a new charter empowering them to change it. But for a remedy they turned, not to self-government, but to despotism. They abolished the old Council, and turned the colony over to a Governor who, within the limits of his instructions, was to " rule and govern by his own discretion or by such laws " as he should decree. To assist him he was to choose an advisory Council.

The danger of this system was at first obscured by the wise choice of a Governor. Thomas Lord De la Warr was a man of distinction and ability. He had studied at the Queen's College, Oxford, had served with Essex in Ireland, and had been a member of the Privy Council under both Elizabeth and James.[8]

Upon landing at Jamestown, De la Warr listened to a sermon by the good minister, Mr. Buck. He then addressed the people, " laying some blames on them," and promising, if forced to it, to draw the sword of justice. But there seems to have been no need for this. The people, forgetting former quarrels, were united in their efforts to serve their Governor and bring a degree of prosperity to the colony. The sound of hammering and sawing was heard on all sides as little houses were built, the fort repaired, the church restored. " Every Sunday, when the Lord Governor went to church, he was accompanied by all

---

[7] *Ibid.,* lxxxiv.
[8] A. Brown, *The first republic,* 84.

the Councillors, Captains, and other officers, and all the gentlemen, and with a band of fifty halberdiers in his Lordships
livery, fair red cloaks, on each side and behind him. The Lord
Governor sat in the choir in a green velvet chair, with a velvet
cushion before him on which he knelt." [9]

But that Lord De la Warr proved to be a mild and just
Governor by no means obscures the evils inherent in absolutism.
A good ruler may be succeeded by a bad one. In ancient Rome
the people benefited by the establishing of law and order under
the great Augustus, but they suffered from the cruelty of the
insane Caligula and the dissolute Nero. So it boded no good
for Virginia when De la Warr fell ill. " I was welcomed by a
hot and violent ague," he tells us. This was followed by an
attack of dysentery. " Then the cramp assaulted my weak
body with strong pains, and afterward the gout." Finally
scurvy came to add to his woes, so that he " was upon the point
to leave this world." In desperation he set sail for the West
Indies in the hope of recovering his health.[10]

A few weeks after De la Warr's departure Sir Thomas Gates
assumed command of the colony. In 1614 he, in turn, was
followed by Sir Thomas Dale, Dale by Captain George Yeardley, and Yeardley by Samuel Argall. When Gates was in Virginia in 1610 he had brought with him certain laws, orders,
and instructions which he posted in the church at Jamestown.
As the people crowded into the little building to read them
they must have expressed their resentment and horror, for the
laws were more suited to a penal colony than to a community
of free Englishmen. In 1611 Dale brought additional laws, and
the whole body was revised in England and published. Gates
and Dale had both served with the English army in the Netherlands, and these laws were " chiefly extracted out of the laws for
governing the army " there.

It was ordered that " every man and woman daily twice a day
upon the first tolling of the bell shall upon the working days
repair into the church to hear divine service upon pain of
losing his or her day's allowance for the first omission, for the
second to be whipped, for the third to be condemned to the
galleys for six months." Equally severe was the law that " no
man shall give any disgraceful words or commit any act to the

[9] *Ibid.*, 130.
[10] A. Brown, *Genesis of the United States* 1: 479.

disgrace of any person . . . upon pain of being tied head and feet together upon the guard every night for the space of one month." To kill any cattle, or horse, goat, or pig, or chicken without leave was punishable with death. No doubt conducive to health but not to liberty was the order that no man or woman should wash linen or pots and pans " within twenty foot of the old well . . . upon pain of whipping." [11]

De la Warr was a humane man, who thought that order could be maintained without cruelty. Gates, also, seems not to have enforced the severe laws. But the situation changed when Dale, and after him Argall assumed power. These two men were guilty of reigns of terror that would have shamed an Ivan the Terrible or a Hitler. The Virginia Assembly of 1624 testified that the colony suffered " under most severe and cruel laws sent over in print," contrary to the King's promise. And these laws were " mercilessly executed, often times without trial or judgment." Some who sought relief by fleeing to the Indians were captured and executed, either by hanging, or shooting, or even by being broken on the wheel. One man who had stolen some oatmeal had a knife thrust through his tongue, and then was tied to a tree where he was left to starve. In 1612 several men tried to steal a barge and a shallop in order to risk their lives in a desperate attempt to reach England. For this they were " shot to death, hanged and broken upon the wheel." [12]

But better things were in store. Many of the leading spirits of the London Company, who " stood best affected to religion and liberty " were " distasted with the proceedings of the Court. This group began now to dream of migrating to Virginia to set up a government there which would be sympathetic with their views. " Many worthy patriots, lords, knights, gentlemen, merchants, and others . . . laid hold on . . . Virginia as a providence cast before them." [13] Had not the Pilgrim fathers shown the way to New England a few years later, it might have been in Virginia rather than in Massachusetts that the Bible commonwealth was established.

Prominent among the liberal faction in the Company was Sir Edwin Sandys. In his youth he had studied at Corpus Christi, Oxford, under Richard Hooker, the future founder of Connecticut, and this ardent Puritan influenced profoundly his

[11] Peter Force, *Tracts* 3 (2).
[12] A. Brown, *The first republic*, 148, 172.
[13] *Ibid.*, 85.

views and career. It was from Hooker that he got the theory that the King derived his authority from a contract with the people, and not by divine right. Later, when as a member of the Commons he enunciated this theory, he drew down on his head James' bitter hatred. Sandys, who had long been a member of the Council of the London Company, was elected to the important post of Treasurer in 1617. To prevent his re-election three years later, the King sent the names of four other men to the Company with the demand that they elect one of them. When the Company sent a delegation to him to protest against this interference with their affairs, James blurted out: " Choose the devil if you will, but not Sir Edwin Sandys."

Sandys seems to have planned to secure successive charters, each granting the Company greater powers than its predecessor, under the pretext that this was necessary for the success of the enterprise. The second charter, granted in 1609, is of especial importance because by it the King resigned the immediate control of the colony into the hands of the Company. The charter of 1612 still further strengthened their hands.

But the Sandys faction met strenuous opposition in the Company itself. Many of the stockholders thought it a mistake to involve the Company in the political and religious struggle which was convulsing the nation. At times the Quarter Courts resounded with the angry debates of the contending parties. A momentous struggle it was, since upon the outcome depended the establishing of self-government in America. So there was rejoicing among the liberal party when Sandys was victorious.

It is probable that Sandys drew up with his own hand what has been called the Magna Carta of Virginia in the fall of 1617, granting the colony the right to representative government. Lord De la Warr, who was still the Governor, had expected to leave at that time with this famous document. But his sailing was delayed until April, 1618. Unfortunately De la Warr, who probably had never fully recovered his health, became ill during the voyage and died.

When news of De la Warr's death reached the London Company, they chose Captain George Yeardley to be his successor. In January, 1619, Yeardley sailed from England with several documents, probably duplicates of the Magna Carta, authorizing him to hold an election for a General Assembly.[14] His

---

[14] A. Brown, *The first republic*, 293.

instructions have been preserved, but his commission, or constitution for the colony, has been lost. Yet undoubtedly it was similar to, if not identical with the Magna Carta of 1617, and with the " Ordinance and Constitution " of July 24, 1621, given Sir Francis Wyatt.

This constitution called for a Council to be chosen from time to time by the Company to assist the Governor in maintaining the " people in justice and Christian conversation amongst themselves, and in strength and ability to withstand their enemies." Another body " to be called by the Governor once yearly and no oftener but for very extraordinary and important occasions, shall consist for the present of the said Council of State, and two Burgesses out of every town, hundred, or other particular plantation, to be respectively chosen by the inhabitants." This body, which was called the General Assembly, was to " have free power to treat, consult, and conclude, as well of all emergent occasions concerning the public weal of the said colony . . . as also to make, ordain, and enact such general laws and orders . . . as shall from time to time appear necessary." To the Governor was reserved a negative voice.

The Governor and Assembly were directed " to imitate and follow the form of government, laws, customs, and manner of trial, and other ministration of justice used in the realm of England." And a limit was put to the authority of the Assembly by a provision that no law should " continue in force " unless ratified by the Company. But a degree of independence was granted in the instruction that " after the government of the said colony shall once have been framed . . . no orders of court afterwards shall bind the said colony, unless they be ratified in like manner in the General Assemblies." [15]

There must have been rejoicing in Virginia when Yeardley arrived with orders " for the better establishing a commonwealth." Perhaps there were cheers, perhaps tears of joy in the crowd which assembled in Jamestown to listen to his proclamation. It promised that those cruel laws by which they had so long been governed were now abrogated, and that they were to be governed by those free laws which his Majesty's subjects in England lived under.[16]

On August 9, 1619, the first representative assembly in Ameri-

[15] *Bath papers* I.
[16] A. Brown, *The first republic*, 312.

can history met in the crude little church at Jamestown. When
Governor Yeardley had taken his seat in the choir, the members
of the Council sat beside him, some on one side, some on the
other. "But forasmuch as men's affairs do little prosper when
God's service is neglected, all the Burgesses took their places in
the choir till a prayer was said by Mr. Buck, the minister."
Then the Burgesses were called in order by name, and so every
man took the oath of supremacy. [17]

The Assembly assumed from the first that it was to be the
Parliament of Virginia. But they realized that they must make
no laws which contravened those of England, or the charter, or
the instructions of the London Company. During the first
session, acts were passed concerning the Church, Indian affairs,
land patents, morality, prices, trade, etc. But by far the most
important law was one ordering "that every man and man servant above sixteen years of age shall pay into the hands and
custody of the Burgesses . . . one pound of the best tobacco." [18]

The control of taxation by the representatives of the people
was to play a vital role in the development of self-government
in America. It was based on the fact, universally recognized by
Englishmen, that no power had the right to take a man's property without his own consent. A century after the first session
of the Virginia Assembly the New York Assembly reminded
Governor Robert Hunter that their inherent right "to dispose
of the money of the freemen" did "not proceed from any commission, letters patent, or other grant from the Crown, but from
the free choice and election of the people, who ought not to
be divested of their property (nor justly can) without their
consent." Similarly the Virginia House of Burgesses declared:
"The rights of the subjects are so secured by law that they
cannot be deprived of the least part of their property but by
their own consent."

The Virginia Assembly of 1619, when they assumed the right
to tax the people, probably did not realize that they were laying
the cornerstone of the structure of American liberty. Yet it was
the control of taxation by the representatives of the people in
all the colonies which made it possible to win victory after
victory over the royal Governors. It is an old saying that one
dare not quarrel with one's paymaster. Yet that was just what

[17] L. G. Tyler, *Narratives of early Virginia*, 257.
[18] *Journals of the House of Burgesses*, 1619-1659, 16.

most of the Governors had to do. They needed money, money to cover their own salaries, money with which to pay other government officials, money to raise and equip men to fight the Indians, or the Dutch, or the French. The price they had to pay was a part of the royal prerogative.

It is to be noted that the money raised by the levy of 1619 in Virginia was to be paid, not to the Governor or to a Treasurer appointed by the Governor, but to the Burgesses. The question of who was to receive the revenues and who to decide upon their use was second in importance only to who had the right to levy taxes. It was to give rise to many disputes between Governors and Burgesses.

The people of Virginia in their happiness in the setting up of representative government seem to have overlooked the King's hostility. But they could not have expected him to assent meekly to the duplication in the infant colony of the Parliament, the body which was causing him so much trouble and vexation. They might have been warned of what was coming when James threw Sir Edwin Sandys in the Tower.

This was followed by a frontal assault on the London Company. John Ferrar wrote: " The King, notwithstanding his royal word and honor pledged to the contrary . . . was now determined with all his force to . . . give the death blow. . . ." [19] He began by ordering a certain Nathaniel Butler to write a pamphlet describing conditions in Virginia. In his *Unmasking of Virginia*, as he called it, Butler drew a vivid picture of the suffering of the people from disease, hunger, and the Indians. In reply the Company published *A True Answer*, explaining the misfortunes which had plagued the colony, and denying responsibility for them.[20]

The King now appointed a commission to inquire into " all abuses and grievances " in Virginia. In July, 1623, this body reported that most of the people sent to the colony were now dead, and that the blame must rest on the Company. " If his Majesty's first grant of April 10, 1606, . . . had been pursued, much better effects had been produced than had been by the alteration thereof into so popular a course." [21] The King was elated. He was determined, he said, to " resume the govern-

[19] A. Brown, *The first republic*, 531, 532.
[20] *Ibid.*, 524.
[21] *Ibid.*, 541.

ment, and . . . reduce that popular form so as to make it agree with the monarchical form."

Should the Company agree, he was willing for them to retain their charter. But he told them that he was resolved " by a new charter to appoint a Governor and twelve assistants, resident here in England, unto whom shall be committed the government." These assistants were to appoint a Governor and twelve assistants to reside in Virginia, " whereby all matters of importance may be directed by his Majesty." [22] In essence this was the original plan of 1606. There was " hot debate " in the Company when they met to consider this proposal. Every man present knew that the fate of the Company hung in the balance. Yet when the King's offer was put to the vote, it was rejected by an overwhelming majority.[23]

The Company now appealed to the House of Commons. But before the Commons could act a message came from the King warning them not to meddle in the affair. " Ourselves will make it our work to settle the quiet and welfare of the plantations," he said. So, with some " soft mutterings," they submitted.

The people of Virginia waited impatiently for the outcome of the struggle which concerned them so deeply. When in March, 1624, the *Southampton* arrived with word that James was determined to change the government, they were in despair. Was liberty to be overthrown? Were they to be subjected again to the brutality of a Dale or an Argall? They wrote the Privy Council praying that future Governors should not have absolute authority. " But above all we humbly entreat your Lordships that we may retain the liberty of our General Assembly, than which nothing can more conduce to our satisfaction or the public utility." [24]

If this letter ever reached the Privy Council, it did not stay the King's hand. Attorney General Coventry had already issued a *quo warranto* against the Company. Sandys and others fought the case before the King's Bench, but the outcome was foregone. On June 26, 1624, the charter was overthrown and Virginia became a royal colony.

Certain historians have contended that, in destroying the Company, James was actuated chiefly by economic motives.

[22] *Ibid.*, 542.
[23] *Ibid.*, 554.
[24] William Stith, *History of Virginia*, 313, 315.

They point out that the Company was divided into factions, that the situation in Virginia was desperate, and that the Company was practically bankrupt. Nothing was left to show for the £100,000 which had been expended, and unless this charge was wiped off the books by dissolving the Company, it would remain for decades as a burden on the colony. No doubt this may have influenced James in his decision. But he himself said that it had not been his intention to revoke the charters until the Company drove him to it by refusing to resign the government into his hands. He had resolved, he said, " by altering the charters . . . as to point of government . . . to settle such a course as might cause the said plantation to flourish. . . . But because the said Treasurer and Company did not submit their charters to be reformed, our proceedings therein were stayed for a time until . . . the said charters . . . were . . . avoided."

The future of the colony was now left in doubt. James declared his intention of issuing a new charter. But since this would require " much time and care," he appointed a commission headed by Lord Henry Mandeville, to manage the colony in the meanwhile. This body's first step was to reappoint Governor Francis Wyatt and his Council, and to authorize them to exercise all the powers granted to Yeardley and his Council. But they made no mention of an Assembly.

James, in issuing the new charter, no doubt intended to make it conform to the charter of 1606. Had he done so, he might have delayed the development of self-government in Virginia by decades. But before he could complete the draft, death overtook him. This dissolved the Mandeville commission, and postponed indefinitely a final settlement of Virginia affairs.

Charles I was in sympathy with his father's plans for the colony, but he seems not to have been deeply concerned about carrying them out. His first step was to place the matter before the Privy Council. The Council called on Sir Edwin Sandys for his opinion. Sir Edwin replied in a long document entitled " The Discourse of the Old Company of Virginia," advising the King to restore the Company. This Charles had no intention of doing. On May 23, 1625, he issued a proclamation declaring " that his intention was that the government of Virginia should immediately depend " upon himself. It might be proper to commit matters of trade and commerce to a corporation, but not state affairs. He next outlined a plan of government for the colony which was essentially the same as that under the charter of 1606.

In the meanwhile, the people of Virginia awaited anxiously. Would the King abolish the Assembly? Would another Dale or Argall be sent over for a new reign of terror? They had opposed the dissolution of the Company because they feared it might lead to the abolishing of representative government. Now that the Company no longer existed they pleaded earnestly to be permitted to keep the Assembly. In June, 1625, the Governor and Council wrote the Privy Council asking that the " liberty of General Assembleys " be continued in order " to avoid the oppressions of Governors." This letter they entrusted to Sir George Yeardley, who sailed with it for England and laid it before the Privy Council.[25]

This body hastened to assure the Virginians that the King " doth take all the country and people into his royal protection and government," and that they were to enjoy all their former privileges. Still they made no promise that the people should have a voice in the government. And the King, because of " many other urgent occasions," still delayed making a permanent settlement of Virginia affairs. At last, in March, 1626, he appointed Yeardley to succeed Wyatt, with orders to " continue the same means that was formerly thought fit for the maintenance of the said colony."

Wyatt and Yeardley were men of a different stamp from Dale and Argall. Had they chosen to do so, they could have ruled the colony with no restraint save from the Council. But they preferred to keep alive the spark of representative government. So they called together unofficial gatherings of leading citizens to sit with the Governor and the Council instead of the House of Burgesses. This body they called the " Governor, Council, and the colony of Virginia assembled together." [26]

The Assembly of 1624 was automatically dissolved by the death of James I. So there must have been a new election, since the unofficial House of Burgesses, had they been appointed by the Governor and Council, would not have presumed to tax the people for the funds necessary for carrying on the govern-

[25] A. Brown, *The first republic*, 573.
[26] CO1-3, p. 5. This and similar notations all refer to documents in the British Public Record Office.

ment. As there was no legal authority for the gatherings their acts were translated into proclamations.[27]

Legal authority came in an unexpected way. With the demonstration by John Rolfe, the man who married Pocahontas, that tobacco could be raised in Virginia, the Indian weed had become more and more the staple of the colony. Had it been assured of a monopoly of the English market by the exclusion of foreign tobacco and the prohibition of tobacco planting in England, and not hampered by high custom duties, it would have brought prosperity and rapid growth.[28] But both James and Charles were constantly in need of money, and the revenue from the duty on Spanish tobacco had been important to them. So in excluding all foreign leaf they sought to make good their losses from Virginia tobacco.

In 1627 Charles decided to buy the entire colonial crop in the hope of selling it at a profit. But this he did not venture to do without securing the consent of the planters. That would have violated the principle that a man's property must not be taken without his consent, either directly or through his representative. So he directed the Governor to hold a general election of Burgesses, summon an Assembly, and place his proposition before them. Thus he gave official recognition to the House of Burgesses, and it was upon this recognition that its authority rested.[29] The Virginians rejected the King's proposal, but they kept their Assembly. From this date it became habitual for the Kings to insert in the instructions to a new Governor that he hold an election of Burgesses.

The setting up of representative government in the first English colony in America has a double significance. It may be viewed as a part of the struggle for supremacy between King and Parliament. Sir Edwin Sandys, the champion of liberty in Virginia, was also a champion of liberty in the mother country. Had absolutism won in England, its victory in the colony would have been certain. And had the King succeeded in ruling the colony unrestrained by any representative body there, it would have strengthened his hand in England, would have been a defeat for the liberal group in Parliament.

When the first Assembly met in Jamestown, the year before

[27] W. W. Hening, *Statutes at large* 1: 129, 130.
[28] CO1-4.
[29] CO1-20.

the Pilgrims landed on Cape Cod, they established a precedent which was followed in future English settlements. Had absolutism been firmly rooted in Virginia, the Stuart Kings might have tried to set it up in all the colonies. The Massachusetts Bay charter might have been voided, the charters of Connecticut and Rhode Island might have had no provision for representative government.

On the other hand, as it was the need for money which forced the hand of Charles I and gave legality to the House of Burgesses, so the needs of all the colonial governments made necessary the calling of legislatures which had the right to levy taxes. It is this which forced the Duke of York to call an Assembly in New York in 1684. When the American patriots of 1775 took up arms because Parliament insisted on taxing them, they were not defending some new principle. The principle that one's property could be taken only with one's consent antedated the founding of Jamestown. And upon it American liberty was based from the first.

CHAPTER II

SELF–GOVERNMENT

WITH the calling of the Assembly of 1627 Virginia entered a new epoch. The people no longer looked to a commercial company for instructions and the appointment of the Governor and other officials, but to the King.

On the whole this was a fortunate change. The Company could not finance the enterprise, and it might have bled the colony to make good its own losses. The reactionary group in the Company might in time have won control, and have gone back to the original form of government.

It was this which made the people of Virginia resist all attempts to re-establish the Company. They were greatly alarmed in 1631 when word reached them that some of the former members had " continually importuned his Majesty to renew the charter," and that the King had actually given orders that a new one be drawn up. Someone, no doubt an agent for the colony, protested vigorously. The Governor and Council had " oftentimes petitioned . . . against the renewing of any such corporation," he said, and he pleaded that nothing be done until they were heard from.

But though the Virginians wished to remain under the jurisdiction of the King, and not be " subjects to their fellow subjects," they wanted to place their government upon a firmer basis as a guarantee that there would be no renewal of the " illegal proceedings and barbarous tortures " of former years. On three separate occasions they tried to secure a charter guaranteeing their liberties. In 1639, George Sandys, whom they appointed agent to petition for a charter, seems to have misunderstood his instructions, for instead of doing so he attempted to revive the Company. When this news reached Virginia, the Assembly hastened to disavow his action, and to beg the King to let them remain a royal colony. Their yearly Assemblies, authorized in his instructions, insured their present happiness, they said. So they were much relieved when Charles told them that he had not the least intention of placing any corporation over them.

This satisfied the Virginians for the moment, but during the Restoration period, on learning that the King had made a series of grants in the colony to favorites, they once more petitioned for a charter. And though, after prolonged negotiations, a charter was passed under the Great Seal,[1] it was so unsatisfactory that in 1691 they made still another attempt. When this failed, the colony was forced to remain under its unwritten constitution, based on precedents, royal letters, proclamations, and instructions.

This constitution provided that the Governor be appointed by the King. Consequently he represented the authority of the Crown, and through the Crown the interests of England. If he failed to uphold the royal prerogative against the assaults of the Burgesses and the Council he was sure to incur the frowns of his royal master. If the King were bent on ruling the colony with as little interference from the Assembly as possible, it was the Governor who tried to carry out his orders. In other words, in the century long battle between the King and the representatives of the people, it was the Governor who bore the royal banner.

The Governors varied widely in character and ability. Sir John Harvey and Francis Nicholson were egocentric men, who tried to lash all who surrounded them into obedience to their will. Alexander Spotswood and Robert Dinwiddie, though not friends of representative government, were able administrators. Hugh Drysdale, William Gooch, and Lord Botetourt, because of their amiable dispositions, won lasting popularity. Culpeper and Effingham were hated as instruments in the hands of Charles II and James II in imposing the Second Stuart Despotism on the colony. Dunmore was detested for his role in the opening years of the Revolutionary War.

It is strange that Nicholson, who was in many respects one of the worst of the Governors, should have given an excellent description of the ideal colonial executive. " It is absolutely necessary . . . that the Governor . . . may be esteemed by the people, . . . to be a lover of them and their country . . . and above all distributes equal justice." [2] Had he followed his own advice his second administration would not have ended in failure.

[1] W. W. Hening, *Statutes at large* 2: 531-533.
[2] CO5-1359, p. 344.

The powers of the Governor were great, so great that even the British government at times thought they should be used with caution. " All things are made so entirely dependent on the Governor's single will and pleasure, that whenever there may happen an ill man in that post, it cannot reasonably be expected any person . . . should either oppose such an one in whatever he may attempt or so much as give any advice," wrote the Lords of Trade in 1698.[3]

The Governor's powers differed from time to time, depending upon the situation in England, upon developments in the colony, and upon the character of the Governor. Sir William Berkeley based his power chiefly on the use of the patronage; Effingham's authority was but a reflection of the despotism of the late Stuart Kings. On the whole, the Governors of the seventeenth century exercised more power than those of the eighteenth century.

At all times the Governor was respected because back of him was the awe-inspiring figure of the monarch. If the Councillors or the Burgesses defied him, he might report their " disobedience " to the King with serious consequences. On more than one occasion the King ordered the Governor to rebuke the Burgesses for their " presumption " in disregarding his wishes.

The Burgesses seem not to have hung their heads at these reprimands, and it was only when the King tried to abridge their privileges that they were deeply concerned. But the greatest danger lay, not in overriding the House, but in undermining it by political bribery. The Governor had in his hands many lucrative offices with which to reward those who voted as he wished. " Don't you know there is a sheriff and a clerk in every county, besides other offices of profit in the country? " Benjamin Harrison wrote Philip Ludwell, in 1703. " Is it not the wise man's phrase that a gift will blind the eyes of the wise? . . . Places are now shifted as often as the occasion requires, to put out or in, as men will or will not serve a turn. Sheriffs are turned out in the middle of their collection. Clerks are turned out without ever knowing why and so are other officers. . . . I need not tell you what men too many of our House of Burgesses are, how greedy they are to catch at any little place of profit, without considering the ill consequence that attends it; like the poor harmless fish that eagerly catches

[3] CO5-1359, p. 255.

at the bait without considering the hook of destruction is under it. . . . Add a sheriff, a clerk, or a naval officer's place, and pray who would consider the Queen's service, the interest of the country, or the discharging a Burgess's oath! " [4]

The most tempting plum was a seat in the Council. Though this was in the gift of the King, he almost invariably named the man recommended by the Governor. So the Burgess who aspired to it was a patriot indeed if he set the welfare of the country above his own ambition by opposing the Governor in the House.

It was not necessary for the Governor to make a direct promise; every man of prominence and wealth knew that he was being watched. But in one case at least a bargain was struck. In 1683 Governor Culpeper wrote the Privy Council that Isaac Allerton had assured him " of his utmost services in whatsoever the King should command him by his Governor," and he had promised in return " that he should be of the Council . . . though not to be declared till after the session of the next Assembly." [5] One wonders whether Allerton's conscience hurt him when, several years later, he took the seat which he had gained by betraying the interests of those who had elected him.

In February, 1691, Governor Nicholson wrote the Lords of Trade explaining why he had deferred sending a list of recommendations for appointment to the Council until after a meeting of the Assembly. " I think it a proper time to try men in, especially considering how many of his Majesty's affairs are to be transacted there." [6]

Even when a Carter, or a Byrd, or a Ludwell had taken his seat in the Council, he had to watch his step. If he opposed the Governor too vigorously he might be suspended. In 1677 Deputy Governor Herbert Jeffreys reported that " one Ballard of the Council " was " a fellow of a turbulent, mutinous spirit," and that he had " found very just cause of suspending him at present both from the Council and collectorship . . . and advancing others more loyal, fit, and honest in his place." [7]

The Governor could crack the whip over the head of any Councillor who defied him by threatening to kick him out of certain places of profit and honor. The Councillors " have all along held the places of profit in Virginia by the Governor's

[4] CO5-1314, Doc. 15G.   [6] CO5-1359, p. 320.
[5] CO5-1356, pp. 125, 126.   [7] CO1-40, p. 104.

gift and during his pleasure," Henry Hartwell reported to the Lords of Trade, " which I have always observed has restrained them from due freedom of . . . debate." [8] It was taken for granted that as soon as a man became a Councillor he was to have the next vacancy as colonel of militia, or collector of the export duty, or naval officer. In the Council of 1692 all save three were colonels. And if a Councillor were in high favor with the Governor, he might be in line as Secretary or Auditor.[9]

It was the Governor who appointed sheriffs, justices of the peace, and other local officers. Since the county court had legislative and administrative as well as judicial powers it was the ruling body in the county. It even had the right to tax. That the justices were not elected by the people not only made local government undemocratic, but added greatly to the Governor's power. He could always appoint men who were favorable to his policies or turn out those who opposed him.

Although the Governor was directed by his instructions to secure the advice of the Council before making appointments, he claimed that he did not have to accept it, and he often ignored it. Nicholson was bitterly assailed for appointing sheriffs "without the advice of the Council," and for putting in and turning out " colonels, lieutenant colonels, majors, captains, and other officers of the militia."

On the other hand, as the decades passed it became more and more the custom for the Governor to accept the recommendations of the Councillors in making appointments, until it assumed almost the character of an unwritten law that he must do so. In fact it was a colonial precedent for Senatorial courtesy in the government of the United States.[10]

The Governor had the right to summon, to prorogue, and to dissolve the Assembly. But he was usually instructed to hold an Assembly at least once a year. On the arrival of a new Governor, or the accession of a King or Queen, the Assembly was automatically dissolved. The power of prorogation made it possible for a Governor, when he had a House of Burgesses to his liking, to continue them indefinitely. That Sir William Berkeley refused for at least fourteen years to hold a general election prior to Bacon's Rebellion was bitterly resented by the people.

[8] CO5-1359, pp. 95, 96.
[9] *Ibid.*, 97, 98.
[10] H. J. Ford, *Rise and growth of American politics*, 267.

The Governor's veto over legislation, though absolute, was not frequently used. If he objected to a bill which came up from the House, he could, except on rare occasions, influence the Council to kill it. If the Council insisted on passing it, he might affix his signature but advise the King to disallow it.

The handing out of fat jobs gave the Governor a strangle hold on the courts, if we may believe the testimony of Philip Ludwell and Stephen Fouace. "The influence of a Governor will be great both on judges and witnesses, particularly by the multitude of places and other favors he has to promise in case they favor him in the trial. . . . There is little possibility of having a fair examination." [11] Robert Beverley testified to the bribing of a grand jury by Governor Nicholson. "The foreman was favored with a naval officer's place, . . . others had sheriff's places, etc." [12]

Nicholson was accused, also, of bullying witnesses, lawyers, and juries. "I have heard him at trials, when judges have asked a question or argued or voted contrary to his humor, snap them up and revile them in a very contemptible manner," reported Robert Beverley. In the case of Swan versus Wilson "he did so grosely abuse Mr. Benjamin Harrison, who was counsel for Swan, that everybody cried out shame on it." Finally, James Blair, who was a member of the court, could stand it no longer. So, taking off his hat, he rose and said:

"If Mr. Harrison has done any ill thing . . . I hope your Excellency will find another time to call him to an account for it. . . . I am sorry to see so much of the court's time taken up . . . by reason of your Excellency's prejudice against him."

"Sir, I deny the prejudice, put it down in writing," shouted Nicholson.

"I hope I have liberty to speak my opinion," replied Blair.

"Who hinders you?"

"I am ashamed to sit here and see people so used," retorted Blair.

"Get you gone then. It had been good for the country if they had never seen your face." [13]

The Governor was the legal head of the Church, though his

[11] CO5-1314, Doc. 17.
[12] *Ibid.*, Doc. 10.
[13] CO5-1314, Doc. 23.

authority was disputed after the appointment of a Commissary for the Bishop of London. And both Governor and Commissary exercised very limited powers because of the resistance of the vestries. The Governor had the right to induct ministers after they had been presented by the vestries, but in most cases they refused to do so. The Governor's power of collation to vacant parishes remained throughout the colonial period practically a dead letter.

The Council of State exercised administrative, legislative, and judicial powers. Hartwell, Blair, and Chilton, in their *The Present State of Virginia*, thus describe their functions: " They are the Council of State under the Governor, who always presides; and in the vacancy of a Governor and Lieutenant Governor, the eldest of the Council is President. They are the Upper House of Assembly, answering to the House of Peers in England. They are by custom, but without commission, the supreme judges (together with the Governor who presides) in all causes . . . and there lies no appeal from them but to the King in Council.[14]

As the advisory body to the Governor, the Council wielded great influence. A Governor who had just taken office and was ignorant of conditions in the colony had to turn to them for information and advice. Later, when he was better informed, he still relied upon them for support in upholding the King's authority. If he were confronted with a mutiny, or an invasion by a hostile fleet, or an Indian war, or a decline in the price of tobacco, he was glad to get their views on what he should do.

The members of the Council originally sat with the Burgesses during sessions of the Assembly, and did not constitute a separate house. Though this denied them an equal voice with the Burgesses, since they could always be outvoted, it permitted them to enter into debates with the Burgesses and serve on committees. It was at the suggestion of Governor Culpeper that the King, in 1680, gave orders that the Council should sit as a separate house.

No doubt Culpeper did this so that he could preside at their legislative sessions as he did when they sat as a Privy Council or as a court. In this way he could keep an eye on them, could argue with them, and bring pressure on them to vote as he

[14] P. 34.

wished. It also created a buffer between him and the Burgesses, behind which he could take refuge against popular criticism. The position of the Councillors was not an easy one since as appointees of the King they were supposed to defend the royal authority, and as natives of Virginia they wished to defend her interests. Often they found a way out of this difficulty by voting one way and privately urging the Burgesses to vote the other.

The members of the Council all sat on the General Court. Hartwell, Blair, and Chilton thus describe this body: " It is strange that they never had a commission for holding of this court, nor never took the oath of judges, perhaps it was not designed by the Crown that they should hold it, since besides that they are unskilful in law, it is thought an inconvenient thing in all governments that the justice and policy of the government should be lodged in the same persons, who ought indeed to be a check upon one another." [15] It was as though the United States Senate were also the Supreme Court. In other words, in colonial Virginia the same men who, as members of the Upper House of Assembly, had voted on a law were called upon to interpret it. Prior to 1680 if a man thought himself injured in point of law or equity by a decision of this court he could appeal his case to the Assembly. But after that date, when the judicial powers of the Assembly were voided, his only appeal was to the King and Privy Council, a step seldom taken because of the difficulty " of either prosecuting or defending matters at such a distance."

The judicial function of the Councillors added greatly to their power and prestige. " They are the sole judges of law and property, which makes all depend on them," reported Colonel Quary.[16] The Councillors were well aware of the power and prestige which their judicial position gave them. This is shown by the bitterness with which they resisted when Governor Spotswood tried to weaken it by setting up a court of oyer and terminer with others than Councillors on the bench.

The members of the Council were invariably selected from the wealthiest men in the colony. In their own counties they were respected and feared. To insult a Byrd, or a Custis, or a Carter would land one in jail. But if we may believe Governor Nicholson, the poor man would not cringe before them. " The ordinary sort of planters that have land of their own, though

[15] P. 46.   [16] CO5-1315, Sept. 1, 1706.

not much, look upon themselves to be as good as the best of them, for they know, at least have heard, from whence these mighty dons derive their originals." They know that they or their " ancestors were their equals if not their superiors, and that their getting such estates and places of honor was more by accident than any extraordinary honesty or ability in them." [17]

The Council reached the height of its power during the first thirty or thirty-five years after the Glorious Revolution. Then it was that they defied the Governors, and in three cases were largely responsible for their removal. Nicholson complained that they " set up to have the power and interest of turning out and putting in Governors, and affect the title that the great Earl of Warwick had." Quary said they " had vanity enough to think themselves almost upon equal terms with the House of Lords." " They have by degrees endeavored to lessen the prerogative and render the Governor little better than a cypher, and in truth they have in effect gained their point." [18]

The Burgesses were the representatives of the people. They were expected by all, wealthy landholders and owners of but a few acres, carpenters, coopers, clergymen, to uphold the liberties of all against the assaults of the King or the Governor. The poor turned to them for protection against the rich. Any attempt by the Governor to rule despotically or illegally was sure to arouse their stubborn resistance. They were in effect the House of Commons of Virginia, claimed the same privileges, and observed the same form in their proceedings. Since each county normally sent two Burgesses to the Assembly, the House grew in numbers as new counties were organized.

The Assembly, during its century and a half of existence, was often forced to meet in private houses or taverns because of the burning of the statehouses, now at Green Spring, the residence of Sir William Berkeley, now at William Sherwood's house; now at the ordinary of Thomas Woodhouse. The first statehouse, which occupied a double row of little buildings, went up in flames in 1656, the second, which was also the Governor's residence, burned in 1660. The third statehouse was more pretentious than its predecessors, being two stories high, with a medieval porch in front, the tile-covered roof dominated by chimney stacks probably in the Tudor style. It was burned by Bacon's rebels in 1676. The fourth statehouse, which seems to

[17] CO5-1314, Doc. 43.   [18] CO5-1315, Sept. 1, 1706.

have been built on the foundations of the third, was destroyed by fire in 1698. It was after this last disaster that the seat of government was moved to Williamsburg, where a lovely Capitol, which has been accurately restored by Colonial Williamsburg Inc. in recent years, was completed in 1704.

The sessions of the Burgesses in the hall provided for them in this building presented a picturesque scene. The Speaker, in his gown, sat in a high chair on a raised platform at the semicircular end of the room. Before him, in the center of the hall, was a table covered with green cloth, resting on it the mace, the emblem of the authority of the House. Here sat the clerk, pen in hand, jotting down notes for the journal. Along either side of the room were two rows of benches covered with green serge, where sat the Burgesses. All wore their hats. A strange medley they were, with the " handsome, well dressed, complete " gentlemen from the tidewater contrasting with the roughly clad frontiersmen.

The House was quick to resent any disrespect to themselves as individuals or as a body. It was in October, 1693, that Mr. Matthew Kemp rose to complain of insults offered him and the House by a certain Thomas Rooke. We do not know whether he displayed a bloody nose or a black eye, but he accused Rooke of striking him. Thereupon a committee was appointed to look into the matter, Rooke was arrested and forced on his bended knees to apologize. " Having now a deep sense and abhorrence, and out of a true and unfeigned sorrow and repentence," he repeated, he asked forgiveness.[19] After they had released him he may have cursed them all under his breath, but for the future he kept his resentment to himself.

The qualifications for the right to vote changed from time to time. On the whole they were liberal, for throughout the colonial period most freemen could voice their choice when the candidates for the House of Burgesses were presented. The constitution of 1621 stated that Burgesses were to be chosen by the " inhabitants." If this was interpreted to mean that all men, including indentured workers, enjoyed the franchise, it was later modified by a law restricting the right to vote to those who paid taxes. It is revealing of the high value placed on representative government even by the humblest, that when Governor Berkeley suggested that taxes be assessed, not by the

---

[19] *Journals of the House of Burgesses, 1659-1693:* 477.

poll, but only on landholders, the Burgesses protested that this would disfranchise great numbers of freemen who owned no land at all. " We are so well acquainted with the temper of the people that we have reason to believe they had rather pay their tax than lose their privilege."

Seven years later another attempt to restrict the suffrage was more successful. Probably at Berkeley's suggestion the Assembly passed a law that no man should vote unless he were a landholder or housekeeper. At this time poor men who were apt to " make tumults at the elections " were pouring in, and the Governor thought it the part of wisdom to deny them any participation in the government. In England only property owners could vote, he argued, why have a different practice in Virginia?

Unfortunately this happened at a time when the people were " ripe for rebellion," and it merely added to their resentment against the Governor and his puppet Assembly. It was in an effort to appease them that Berkeley called for a new election, in 1676, and, ignoring the law, took it on himself to extend the franchise to " every free born man." When this Assembly met, and when Bacon's army was marching on Jamestown, they confirmed this ruling by passing a law to give the right to vote to all freemen. But with the repeal of Bacon's Laws in 1677, the franchise was once more restricted to landowners and housekeepers.

When Culpeper was appointed Governor in 1679, he was ordered to make a vigorous assault upon liberty in the colony. Among other repressive measures he was instructed to deprive mere housekeepers of the suffrage and limit it to freeholders. Although this measure was unjust to the large and intelligent artisan class—carpenters, masons, coopers, house painters, shipwrights, saddlers, gunsmiths, etc., it seems to have remained in force throughout the remainder of the colonial period.

The wages of the Burgesses changed from time to time. At one time the pay was ten shillings a day, at another thirteen shillings, at still another 130 pounds of tobacco. In 1718 it was thirty shillings, a sum which Governor Spotswood thought far too much. His criticisms of the politicians of his day show that the species has not changed greatly in the past two and a half centuries. The salary " makes needy men try for the place who are not qualified for a Senate house," he said. " Those upon an approaching election set themselves to inventing most false and malicious stories. . . . The country to be sure is ever represented as if it was to be undone, and none can be judged capable of saving it but some of their own mobbish politicians, who engage to pursue the wild schemes of the electors." [20] But when he tried to cut the ground from under these false patriots by urging a law requiring the Burgesses to serve without salary, and restricting further the qualifications for voters and for candidates for office, it was overwhelmingly voted down.

It was customary for each county to pay the salaries of its two Burgesses. This was unjust, for it made the burden fall much more heavily upon the taxpayer in a small county than one in a large county. It was harmful, also, as implying that the Burgess was concerned with the interests of his county rather than those of the colony as a whole. So the people of the thinly settled counties rejoiced when, in the mid-eighteenth century the Burgesses were paid from the revenue from the duty on the imports of liquors whenever there was a surplus in this fund.

The Burgesses elected their own Speaker. This officer presided over the deliberations of the House, voiced their determinations, and issued warrants to execute their orders. In case of a tie he cast the deciding vote. The office was eagerly sought after, for it carried great influence. In 1699, when Robert Carter was elected, he said in his address of acceptance: " The House of Burgesses, consisting of the better sort of gentlemen from all parts of the country, to be in this fashion the object of their choice I take to be of no small reputation to me." [21]

The prestige of the office grew with the increasing power of the House, until the Speaker became, next to the Governor, the most influential man in the colony. It became a fixed custom for the Burgesses to enhance his pay by making him Treasurer. In 1758, when Governor Fauquier was instructed to separate the two offices, he was greatly perplexed. The Speaker, Mr. John Robinson, is " the most popular man in the country," he wrote the Lords of Trade, " beloved by the gentlemen and the idol of the people." Any slight to him would put a stop to all legislative business.[22]

[20] CO5-1318.
[21] *Journals of the House of Burgesses*, 1695-1702: 133.
[22] June 28, 1758.

With the growth of the House of Burgesses its business more and more was transacted by committees. The most important were the committees on Propositions and Grievances, Elections and Privileges, and on Proportioning the Levy. To the first of these came all manner of complaints. One county asks that ship captains be forbidden to throw ballast into the rivers, another wants a ceiling put on doctors' bills, still another objects to having taverns extend credit to sailors.

The House kept a close watch on elections, and the Committee on Elections and Privileges always went over the writs in search of irregularities. If a sheriff should fail to make a return or should make an imperfect return, the messenger was sent to bring him before the House to explain why. Should he take it upon himself to judge who was eligible or not eligible for election, he was certain to receive a stern reprimand. In 1692 a resolution " that the House of Burgesses are the sole and only judges of the capacity or incapacity of their own members " passed unanimously.[23]

The Committee on Private Causes prior to 1680 was in effect the supreme court of Virginia, to which appeals were made, for the House invariably accepted its findings. But it ceased to function when the Assembly was deprived of its judicial power.

The Burgesses were wary of bills of attainder, the weapon used with such great effect by Parliament. They realized the danger in condemning persons without trial, especially when the colony had so much at stake in preserving liberty and justice. But the Assembly of February, 1677, which had been " hand picked " by Governor Berkeley, did attaint Bacon and fifteen of his followers in defiance of the King's pardon.[24] Since all of the victims were dead, the attaint affected only their property. When Charles II heard what had been done, he promptly nullified the law.[25]

The Burgesses were well aware from the first that the universally accepted principle that no Englishman could be legally taxed without his own consent was the basis of liberty. They alone, as the representatives of the people, could take their property. If a Governor, as the substitute for the King, so far stretched his authority as to attempt to lay a levy, they were

[23] *Journals of the House of Burgesses*, 1659-1693, 381.
[24] W. W. Hening, *Statutes at large* 2: 363, 369.
[25] CO1-41, p. 118.

quick to call him to order. As early as 1624 the Assembly passed a law " that the Governor shall not lay any taxes or impositions upon the colony, their lands or commodities, other way than by the authority of the General Assembly, to be levied and imployed as the said Assembly shall appoint." [26] Similar laws were passed in 1631, 1632, 1642, and 1645.

Several times the Governor and Council requested the Burgesses to authorize them to lay taxes not to exceed a specified sum and for a limited period. In 1661 the House did grant such a power, but thereafter, despite several attempts, the Governor and Council met with emphatic refusals. In 1680, when Charles II was aiming deadly blows at liberty in the colonies, the Burgesses yielded to threats, and surrendered a part of the people's birthright by voting a perpetual revenue to the King.

When the Parliamentary fleet came into the James in 1652 to force the Virginians to recognize the Commonwealth, the Assembly insisted on inserting in the articles of surrender the promise " that Virginia shall be free from all taxes, customs, and impositions whatsoever, and none to be imposed on them without the consent of the General Assembly." [27]

In 1675, when the Virginia Assembly sent agents to England to petition for a charter, they took pains to point out that " neither his Majesty nor any of his ancestors or predecessors had ever offered to impose any tax upon this plantation without the consent of his subjects here." [28] It was so universally accepted that only the Assembly could tax the people, that the agents thought it necessary to explain why they considered it wise to insert an article confirming this right. " Not being taxed but by the General Assembly, as it hath been ever the practice there and the other plantations, so it is a power given them by royal instructions, which we conceive ought to be confirmed under the Great Seal, for though it might be taken for granted that as they never have been, so they never should be otherwise taxed, and that as of right they ought to be; yet the power of the Assembly being only in instructions, we ordered this further confirmation of it." [29]

Certain historians have assumed that the Americans a century later annunciated a new principle in claiming that taxa-

[26] W. W. Hening, *Statutes at large* 1.
[27] W. W. Hening, *Statutes at large* 1: 363-365.
[28] *Bath papers*, IIa, 44.
[29] *Ibid.*, 142.

tion without representation is tyranny. The fact is that the
principle was older than the colonies themselves. All the Revolutionary patriots did was to give it a new and more striking
wording. When Parliament passed the Stamp Act they were
taking an unprecedented step, a step which violated the age-
old rights of Englishmen. And in so doing, they struck a
deadly blow at liberty in America.

The most common and the most hated source of income in
Virginia was the poll tax. It was not entirely unequal since it
was imposed on all male whites over sixteen, all white women
over sixteen who worked in the fields, and all slaves old enough
to work. Thus the poor man paid only for himself and members of his family, while the rich man paid for his servants
and slaves as well. The poll tax provided revenue, not only
for the general government, but for the counties and parishes.

Though the poll tax usually was not excessive, it was a source
of constant irritation. The poor planter who had worked hard
to raise a crop of tobacco just large enough to buy necessities
for his family, thought it hard indeed when the sheriff took
the government's share.

The quit rents paid to the King for all land were an even
greater source of trouble. It was impossible to make men of
large estates pay in full, there were frauds in disposing of the
tobacco in which the rents were paid, at times the people were
so far behind that to enforce payment of arrears would ruin
them. The quit rent fund was drawn upon for war purposes,
building of forts, paying salaries, etc. In 1693 Commissary Blair
received a grant of £1985.14.10 from the quit rent fund to
found the College of William and Mary. When Attorney
General Seymour objected to paying the money, Blair explained that it was the chief purpose of the college to train
young men for the ministry, and begged him to consider that
they in Virginia had souls to be saved as well as those in England. "Souls! Damn your souls! Make tobacco," snapped
Seymour.[30]

Local government was administered by the county courts.
Hartwell, Blair, and Chilton wrote: "There is a county court
in every county, which consists of eight or ten gentlemen . . .
to whom the Governor gives a commission during pleasure to
be justices of the peace for that county. He renews that com-

[30] *The complete works of Benjamin Franklin*, J. Bigelow, ed., 10: 369.

mission commonly every year, for that . . . gives him an opportunity to admit into it new favorites and exclude others that
have not been so zealous in his service. . . . They have court
once a month, . . . and have a power of deciding all sorts of
causes." [31] But they did not have jurisdiction in cases involving
loss of life or limb.

That the people had no voice in selecting the justices was
greatly resented, especially since the courts had the power of
levying taxes. The people of Charles City County complained
in 1677 that the justices had " illegally . . . taken upon them
without our consent from time to time to impose, raise, assess,
and levy what taxes, levies, and impositions upon us . . . they
liked, great part of which they have converted to their own
use." [32] The people of Surry County made a similar complaint:
" It has been the custom of the county courts at the laying of
the levy to withdraw into a private room by which the poor
people not knowing for what they paid their levy did always
admire how their taxes could be so high." [33]

In each county was one or more parishes, presided over by a
vestry of twelve men each. Since the vestry had the right to
lay the parish levy, it was of great importance that they should
be elected by the people. This was the practice until Berkeley's
second administration, when it became the custom for a vestry,
when once chosen at the establishing of a new parish, themselves to fill vacancies in their ranks, and thus to become self-
perpetuating.

Hartwell, Blair, and Chilton thought it deplorable that the
vestries habitually refused to present their ministers for induction, so that they could " keep them in more subjection." This
was such a hardship on the clergy that none who " were informed of it would come into the country." When one did
come, he would have to be wary of preaching against any vices
" that any great man of his vestry was guilty of," for fear of
losing his place.[34] Yet the vestries themselves were supposed
to be the guardians of the morals of the parishioners. In 1648
a vestry in Northampton found the wife of a prominent citizen
guilty of adultery, and ordered the minister and church warden
to present her to the county court for punishment.

[31] *The present state of Virginia,* 44, 45.
[32] *Virginia Magazine,* 3: 142.
[33] *Ibid.* 2: 172.
[34] *The present state of Virginia,* 66, 67.

The most eagerly sought after offices in the colony were those of President of the Council, Secretary of State, Attorney General, Auditor, and Treasurer. It was the custom for the senior member of the Council in point of service to become President when the office of the Governor was temporarily vacant.[35] This was an unsatisfactory arrangement since it might happen that the senior Councillor was too old to take on important and arduous duties. In 1749, when Governor Gooch was about to leave for England, it was decided by the Council that Colonel John Custis, the senior member, was " utterly incapable of managing the business of the government." [36] At their request the Governor suspended him from the Council, so that Thomas Lee, next in order of seniority, could become President.

The Secretary of State was appointed by the King. Until 1723 he held office only " during the pleasure " of the Governor, but thereafter for life. The Secretary claimed the right to appoint the clerks of the county courts, who acted as his deputies, and paid him a percentage of the income from fees arising from lawsuits and other court proceedings. But he seldom made an appointment " without the Governor's knowledge and good liking."

Contemporary writers agree that the Secretary's office was a jungle of court records, surveys, commissions, deeds for land, probates of wills, writs of elections, marriage certificates, etc. If we may believe Benjamin Harrison it was usually in wild confusion. " Nothing hath been more common of late years than to hear people complain that they could not find the records of their patents or other deeds for their lands." [37] Apparently all kinds of documents were piled up together instead of being sorted and filed separately. " It is almost impossible to give a full and perfect account of the Secretary's office, there is such a medley in it that its scarce credible," wrote Hartwell, Blair, and Chilton.

The Auditor for Virginia was appointed by the Auditor of the Plantations, usually upon the recommendation of the Governor. This officer audited the accounts of the quit rents, the export duty, escheats, etc., certified their accuracy, and reported to England. He received $7\frac{1}{2}$ per cent of all the monies passing through his hands. There seems to have been great laxness at

[35] CO5-1359, 344.
[36] *Executive journals of the Council* 5: 299.
[37] CO5-1361, p. 426.

times in the handling of funds. When Auditor William Byrd died in December, 1704, it was found that the account was overdrawn by £7,698.9.10.[38] It is not surprising that Governor Nicholson, while waiting for William Blathwait, the Auditor of the Plantations, to appoint Byrd's successor, decided to "take that trouble" on himself.[39]

Philip Ludwell, who was made Auditor in 1712, seems to have been just as careless as Byrd. In December, 1715, Governor Spotswood called the attention of the Council to the confusion in his office. "Only gross sums are entered in one general account," he said, "and the particular accounts of the receivers . . . only kept in loose papers." [40] When he recommended several reforms, Ludwell told him in effect to mind his own business, and that he would take orders only from the Auditor General. Thereupon Spotswood suspended him from his office. Ludwell came back with a letter "stuffed with virulent invectives," denying the legality of this action.

Prior to 1691 the Treasurer was appointed by the Governor, but that year the Burgesses claimed the right of naming him, and despite the opposition of the Governors, eventually had their way. The Treasurer received the funds from various taxes and made up the accounts. He received six per cent of the money collected.

Outwardly the government of Virginia changed little during the century and a half from the fall of the London Company to the Declaration of Independence. Actually throughout the colonial period vital developments were taking place. Both the Council and the House of Burgesses were tireless in whittling away at the King's prerogative; the Council gradually took out of the Governor's hands the right of naming local officials; the control of the purse by the Burgesses was used to such good effect that by the middle of the eighteenth century their influence was greater than that of either Governor or Council.

We gain glimpses of the changes which were taking place, not by changes in the laws, but by seemingly unimportant incidents, and by the spirit of the times. What would Charles II have thought had Sir William Berkeley written him, boasting of his influence with the Speaker of the House of Burgesses? Yet that is just what Governor Fauquier did in 1758.

[38] *Executive journals of the Council* 2: 406.
[39] *Ibid.*, 407.   [40] *Ibid.* 3: 421.

It was the determined, unflagging, bitter battle for self-government which brought victory to the people. We see them putting Governor John Harvey aboard a vessel and sending him back to England, when he tried to play the despot; we see them rising in wild rebellion against the misgovernment of Sir William Berkeley; we see them defending their liberty against the assaults of Charles II and James II.

The English government was warned repeatedly of what was going on. " I may truly say that now or never is the only time to maintain the Queen's just prerogative and put a stop to these wrong, pernicious notions which are improving daily, not only in Virginia, but in all her Majesty's other governments," wrote Colonel Robert Quary, in 1705. " A frown now from her Majesty will do more than perhaps an army hereafter." [41] In another report he said that the Assembly " conclude themselves entitled to all the rights and privileges of an English Parliament." Nicholson said that the Virginians wished to set up a commonwealth.

But Nicholson was wrong. The Virginians of his day, and their sons and grandsons after them were loyal to the British Kings, wished to remain in the British Empire. But they were determined to govern themselves in all except imperial matters. What they wanted was liberty, not independence. And liberty they attained decades before the Stamp Act, decades before Patrick Henry said: " Give me liberty or give me death."

[41] CO5-1314, Doc. 63I.

CHAPTER III

WE PREFER ANOTHER GOVERNOR

THE people of Jamestown in the years from 1626 to 1640, when they saw a vessel coming up the river, must have crowded around the landing place to ask sailors and passengers for the latest news from England. Was King Charles still raising funds with which to run the government by means of forced loans? Was he still billeting his soldiers on the people? Was martial law in force? They must have been thrilled to hear of the Petition of Rights in which the House of Commons protested against Charles' arbitrary rule.

When the Burgesses came to town for a session of the Assembly, the struggle between King and Parliament must have been the chief topic of conversation around the table in each crude little tavern. Now it was the jailing of nine members of the House of Commons; now the granting of monopolies; now the collecting of ship money; now the suppression of free speech; now the proceedings of the Star Chamber; now the efforts of Archbishop Laud to enforce religious conformity.

The Virginians were fully aware that these events affected them profoundly. They had just won a degree of self-government. If the King succeeded in his efforts to make himself absolute in England, all their gains might be lost. Might he not overthrow their Assembly? If he could imprison men arbitrarily in England, he would not hesitate to do so in Virginia. If he could tax the people of England under the thin veil of loans, or the revival of ancient laws, would he hesitate to tax the colonists without their own consent? Might he not place over them another Dale or Argall to hang men or break them on the wheel?

So when Sir George Yeardley, their liberal Governor, died in November, 1627, they were filled with grief. They remembered that it was he who had brought over the Virginia Magna Carta, and had called the first Assembly. We have lost " a main pillar of this our building and thereby a support to the whole body," wrote the Council.[1]

[1] CO1-4, p. 18.

Their concern must have been all the greater because Yeard-ley's commission of March 14, 1626, named John Harvey as his successor. The Virginians knew this man well. He had been one of the King's commissioners who came to the colony in 1624 to draw up a report on conditions there to be used in overthrowing the charter of the Company. Just why it was thought that he was the right man to act as Governor is not apparent, for he was a mariner by vocation and had served as captain of a ship which went to the East Indies in 1617. In November, 1625, we find him in command of a ship in the expedition against Cadiz. He may have owed his appointment as Governor to Viscount Dorchester, the Secretary of State, whom he thanked for his " wonted nobleness " to him.

But Virginia was to have a breathing space before Harvey's arrival. Yeardley's commission had specified that in the absence of Harvey the Council should elect one of their number to act in his place. They chose Captain Francis West, brother of Lord De la Warr.[2] West was a seasoned Virginian, for he had come to the colony in 1608 with Captain Newport. He had been commander of Jamestown many years, and a member of the Council since 1619. It was during his brief administration that the first legal Assembly since the dissolution of the London Company was called together, the Assembly which rejected the King's proposal for a tobacco contract.

In March, 1629, West was appointed agent for the colony and sent to England. To serve as Governor until his return or the arrival of Harvey, the Council chose Dr. John Pott. This man had been in Virginia since 1621, when he came over as " Physician to the Company " and member of the Council. He was described as " a Master of Arts . . . well practiced in chirurgery and physic, and expert in distilling of waters, besides many other ingenious devices." [3] He seems to have consumed a goodly quantity of " distilled waters " himself, for he was fond of his cups and jovial company. George Sandys wrote of him that " he kept company too much with his inferiors, who hung upon him while his good liquor lasted." [4]

The most notable of Pott's " ingenious devices " was the poisoning of a large number of Indians after the massacre of

[2] *Virginia Magazine* 13: 301.
[3] E. D. Neill, *Virginia Company of London*, 221.
[4] *Ibid.*, 79.

1622. In justification of this act, his friends explained that the
barbarous and perfidious savages knew nothing about the rules
of war, so it was fair play to resort to anything that tended to
their ruin. But this did not save Pott from criticism in England.
The Earl of Warwick was so shocked that at his request Pott
was left out of the Council because " he was the poisoner of the
savages there." But he seems to have been forgiven, for in
1626 we find him once more in his seat.

It was during Pott's administration that Lord Baltimore
visited Virginia. In 1623 he had received a grant of land in
Newfoundland, and had planted a colony of English Catholics
there. But when four years later he visited the place, he found
" the air so intolerable cold as it is hardly to be endured." He
wrote King Charles that he had decided to move with some
forty persons to Virginia, and petitioned for " a precinct of land
there."

On October 1, 1629, he, with his wife and children, arrived
at Jamestown. Here he met with a cool reception. A certain
Thomas Tindall got into an altercation with him, called him a
liar, and threatened to knock him down. The Virginians did
not want in their midst a group of Catholics who were trying
to lop off one of the most fertile parts of their territory. So
to get rid of them the Governor and Council tendered my Lord
the oath of supremacy, knowing that as a Catholic he could not
take it, for to do so was to acknowledge the King as the supreme
authority in ecclesiastical matters. When he refused they asked
him to leave. This he did, but since he left his family in
Virginia, it was obvious that he intended to return. So William
Claiborne was sent after him as agent for the colony to oppose
his designs.

To add to the troubles of the people, in the early spring of
1630 Harvey arrived and took his seat as Governor. He had
lingered in England to make sure that the office would yield a
good return. Only after the King had promised him the fines
imposed by any of the courts did he set sail. His voyage was far
from being pleasant, for his ship was leaky, he was delayed at
the Cape Verde Islands by a Dutch fleet, and he was laid low by
" a great sickness " that attacked him at sea.[5]

After landing it was several weeks before he was able to take
over his duties. But after he had done so, his intentions at once

became apparent. The man was by nature a despot. The despotism of Sir Edmund Andros in New England and of Lord Howard of Effingham in Virginia in the years just preceding the Glorious Revolution stemmed, not so much from the character of these men, as from the deliberate policy of Charles II. There is no evidence that Charles I ordered Harvey to make himself absolute. He had too many troubles at home to give much thought to Virginia.

It may have been Harvey's training as a sea captain which made him impatient of restraint. In Virginia he acted as though he were still on the deck of his ship thundering out commands which no one must question. If the King were in Virginia, would not his orders be obeyed? Then why not the orders of his Governor? He never tired of reminding the members of the Council and others that he was the King's substitute. When to his passion for power are added his rudeness and violence, his avarice and disregard for the rights of others, we have the picture of one utterly unsuited to be the chief executive of a liberty loving people.

Harvey was accused of diverting public funds to his own pocket, but of this we have no direct proof. It is probable that he tried to levy taxes without the consent of the Assembly. Otherwise one wonders why the Assembly should have thought it necessary to order " that the Governor and Council shall not lay any taxes or impositions upon the colony . . . otherwise than by the authority of the Grand Assembly." [6]

But it was chiefly through the courts that he carried out his designs. He himself presided over the quarter court, and it was he who appointed the commissioners or justices who sat on the local courts. Thus it was not difficult for him to secure any verdict he wished. So he had at hand an instrument to satisfy his lust for power by crushing those who resisted him, and his lust for money by imposing heavy fines. It should have been obvious to Charles I when he agreed to give Harvey all fines and amercements, that it was a dangerous thing to permit a judge, or one who appointed judges, to profit from his or their decisions.

The most notorious abuse of the judicial power by Harvey was his prosecution of Dr. Pott. Charging the pleasure-loving physician with pardoning murder and marking other men's

[6] W. W. Hening, *Virginia statutes at large* 1: 171.

cattle for his own, he suspended him from the Council, and confined him to his plantation pending the day of his trial. When Pott defied the Governor's order and came to Elizabeth City, Harvey put him in prison and set a guard around it. In July, 1630, he was put on trial.

We have only one detail of the proceedings, but that like a flash is revealing of Pott's character and of the farcical character of the prosecution. When a certain Richard Kingswell testified against him, Pott declared that he was as great a liar and hypocrite as Gusman of Alfrach. He was referring to the book by Mateo Alemán, of Seville, in which Gusman is shown first as a scullion, then as an errand boy, then as a thief, then as a pretended gentleman who cheated his creditors.[7] But this thrust did not save him. He was convicted, and his entire estate confiscated.[8]

It would seem that in this case Harvey was actuated more by a desire to show his power than by avarice. If he could humble so prominent a man as Pott, one who had been acting Governor, others would stand in awe of him. " It will be a means to bring people to . . . hold a better respect to the Governor than hitherto they have done," he wrote.[9] But having shown his power to ruin, he now sought to show that he could also restore. So he wrote the King suggesting clemency. " For as much as he is the only physician in the colony, and skilled in the epidemical diseases of the planters . . . I am bound to entreat " your Majesty to pardon him.[10]

A more sincere plea came from the doctor's wife, Elizabeth. Getting up from a sick bed, she made the long and dangerous voyage to England to complain to the King " touching the wrong " done her husband. Charles referred the case to the Virginia Commissioners, who listened sympathetically as she poured out the story of injustice and persecution.[11] They concluded that there had been " some hard usage against " Pott, and recommended that the King pardon him. Accordingly, Charles forgave his " offences " and restored his property.[12] But the jovial doctor never regained his seat in the Council.

[7] E. D. Neill, *Virginia Carolorum*, 79.
[8] CO1-5, p. 32.
[9] *Ibid.*
[10] *Ibid.*, 33.
[11] CO1-5, p. 33.
[12] *Ibid.*

The prosecution of Pott set the example for others. " The Governor usurped the whole power in all causes without any respect to the votes of the Council," reported Samuel Mathews, " whereby justice was done but so far as suited his will to the great loss of many men's estates and a general fear in all." If other members of the court opposed him, he would revile them and tell them they were there merely to advise him. He could accept or reject their opinions as he liked, since " the power lay in himself to dispose of all matters as his Majesty's substitute." [13]

With the General Court dominated by the overbearing and avaricious Governor no man was safe. At any moment one might be hauled before the bar, charged with some petty offence, found guilty, and given a ruinous fine. Mathews said that there were an " infinite number of particular men's grievances." [14] William Claiborne thought it strange that Harvey " should so demean himself," for " all men were wronged, and even good and bad had forsaken him." [15] It was in every man's mouth that " no justice was done." When a report of these things reached England, Sir John Wolstenholm, one of the Virginia Commissioners, said that " Sir John Harvey stunk in Court and city." [16]

Harvey's attempts to make himself absolute, his disregard of other men's rights, his perversion of justice did not go unchallenged. Soon the meetings of the Council became stormy. The Governor insisted that he, as the King's substitute, had a right to determine all things. The Councillors were merely his assistants, whose duty it was to advise him, but not to oppose him. But the Councillors dissented vigorously. Look at your commission, they told him, and you will see that it directs that all matters must be determined by the majority of voices. Does it not say that the King grants to the Governor and Council " and the greater number of you respectively full power and authority to execute " the duties of the executive body?

Soon Harvey was filling his letters with complaints of the opposition of the Council. " For instead of giving me assistance, they stand contesting and disputing my authority, averring that I can do nothing but what they shall advise me, and that my power extendeth no further than a bare casting voice." [17] He

[13] *Virginia Magazine* 1: 416.
[14] *Ibid.*, 417.
[15] E. D. Neill, *Virginia Carolorum*, 122.
[16] *Virginia Magazine* 1: 430.
[17] CO1-6, p. 34.

had shown them a letter from the King strengthening his commission, but they refused to budge from their position. He would be grateful if his Majesty would be so explicit " that the place of Governor and the duty of Councillors may be known and distinguished." [18]

The Privy Council answered by warning both sides to put an end to their disputes and cooperate with each other in advancing the good of the colony. So they drew up and signed a formal reconciliation. They promised " to swallow up and bury " all complaints, and to turn their " alienated and distempered " minds to thoughts of love and peace. The Councillors vowed to give the Governor " all the service, honor, and due respect which belongs to him as his Majesty's substitute." [19]

The reconciliation proved a sham. Harvey continued to be overbearing and arbitrary; the Councillors were as bitter as ever. When one of them, Thomas Hinton, in an outburst of anger gave Harvey some " ill words," he ousted him from his seat. Love and peace were far indeed from the Governor's mind when he responded to some " ill language " from Captain Richard Stevens by landing a blow in his face with a cudgel and knocking out some of his teeth.[20]

In 1634 a certain Captain Thomas Young arrived in Virginia with a commission from the King authorizing him to discover and search the unexplored parts of the colony. Needing two shallops, and hearing that one of the planters had an indentured worker who was a skilled shipwright, he seized him and put him to work. In this violation of property rights he was supported by the Governor. But it aroused the anger of the Council, and several of them came to Harvey to demand an explanation.

Harvey may have had in mind the Forced Loans as a precedent for taking the property of the subject, when he replied that his Majesty had given Young " authority to make use of any persons he found there." Young needed the shipwright " to prosecute with speed the King's service," he said. Speaking for the others, Samuel Mathews retorted angrily that if things were done in that fashion it would breed ill blood in Virginia. Turning his back he whirled a truncheon he carried in his hand, and lashed off the heads of some high weeds.[21] The

[18] *Ibid.*, 37.
[19] *Ibid.*

[20] *Virginia Magazine* 8: 405.
[21] CO1-8.

Governor, ignoring this, said: " Come, gentlemen, let us go to supper, and for the night leave this discourse." But they were in no humor to be appeased. With one accord they turned their backs and left " in a very irreverent manner."

The Virginians were further embittered against Harvey for the aid he gave to Lord Baltimore's settlers. It was on February 27, 1634, that the *Ark* and the *Dove*, with Leonard and George Calvert, twenty " gentlemen adventurers," and three-hundred laborers, arrived at Point Comfort. They bore a letter to the Governor from the King requiring him to treat them with courtesy and respect, permit them to buy cattle and other commodities, and do all he could to advance their settlement.

Harvey did his best to comply. He sent them some of his own cows and promised to procure more. But this was not easy. The planters were so outraged at having a part of their territory torn away for a colony of Catholics that they swore they would knock their cattle on the head rather than sell them to the Marylanders. Some of the members of the Council had been informed by letters from England of Lord Baltimore's plans. When Samuel Mathews opened one of them, he threw his hat on the ground in a fury, stamped, and cried: " A pox upon Maryland! " [22] He, with William Claiborne and other members of the Council, held many secret meetings to decide upon a course of action. But they were powerless to prevent the *Ark* and the *Dove* from moving up the Chesapeake Bay with the newcomers, and the founding of a little town near the mouth of the Potomac.

Three years before their arrival Claiborne had made a settlement on Kent Island in the Chesapeake near the site of Annapolis. So now he found himself torn from Virginia and handed over to another government. The result was open warfare. It was prophetic of the battle between the Merrimac and the Monitor in Chesapeake waters more than two centuries later, when two pinnaces full of armed men captured an armed vessel sent out by the Kent Islanders.

When this news reached Jamestown there was great indignation. Harvey tried to justify the Marylanders, but this merely intensified the people's hatred of him. So he not only aids in the dismemberment of Virginia, it was said, but upholds the

[22] CO1-6, p. 46.

intruders in murdering our people. Is it right that one who is Governor of the colony should side with her enemies?

The crisis came in 1635. King Charles, ever pressed for money, tried once more to secure a tobacco contract. So he wrote Harvey directing him to call an Assembly and to ask for " the sole pre-emption of all tobacco," at a lower price and a reduced quantity. The members of the Council, especially Samuel Mathews, John Utie, and William Pierce, opposed the contract " very saucily." [23] As for the Burgesses, they hated all contracts. So they drew up an answer which was in effect a refusal. In order to give the paper the character of a petition they all signed it. This they gave to Harvey to send to the King.

But instead of forwarding it, the Governor detained it. In excuse of this arbitrary action he said he feared the King " would not take well the matter thereof, and that they should make it a popular business by subscribing a multitude of hands thereto, as thinking thereby to give it countenance." [24] The people were outraged. So our Governor takes it on himself to decide what or what not we shall say to our King. Is it not the right of all Englishmen to address their sovereign? " The wrong done by the Governor to the whole colony in detaining the foresaid letters to his Majesty did exceedingly perplex them, whereby they were made sensible of the condition of the present government," wrote Samuel Mathews.[25]

Things had now come to a head. A petition demanding a redress of grievances was drawn up, which Francis Pott, brother of Dr. John Pott, took about the country. Everywhere he found the people tired of Harvey's arbitrary conduct, tired of his injustice to individual persons. So they pressed forward eagerly to sign the petition. Harvey says that only in Accomac did they refuse.[26]

It was in April, 1635, that Pott, Captain Nicholas Martian, and William English, the sheriff of York County, addressed a gathering at the house of William Warren. This meeting has a special significance in the long struggle for American liberty, for Warren's house was on or near the site of the Moore House, at Yorktown, where the British army under Lord Cornwallis surrendered a century and a half later. The speakers were

[23] CO1-8.
[24] CO1-8.
[25] *Virginia Magazine* 1: 416.
[26] *Ibid.*, 427.

denouncing Harvey's despotic government when some friends
of the Governor tried to enter. A servant kept them out, but
they hung around outside and "bended themselves to hearken
to the discourse among them." [27] When the speeches were concluded those present gathered around the petition and affixed
their signatures.

When this was reported to Harvey, he flew into a rage. Calling the Council, he issued warrants for the arrest of Francis
Pott, English, and Martian. They were brought up in irons.
Pott handed over the petition and declared that if he had
offended he appealed to the King. "He was sure of no justice
from Sir John Harvey." When the prisoners asked why they
were arrested, the Governor told them that they would be told
at the gallows. So they were hustled off to prison.[28]

Harvey then called the Council together again and told them
that it was necessary to try the prisoners by martial law. But the
Councillors insisted on a legal trial. In the dispute which followed Harvey became violently angry. Finally, he sat down and
ordered the others to sit. Looking around with a frown, he
said: "I am to propound a question to you. . . . What do you
think they deserve that have gone about to persuade the people
from their obedience to his Majesty's substitute?"

Turning to George Menefie, he said, "I begin with you."
Menefie answered that since he was but a young lawyer he did
not dare give an opinion "upon the sudden." Here Nicholas
Farrar interposed to protest against this method of proceeding.
But Harvey cut him short with the command to hold his
tongue until he was spoken to. Thereupon Samuel Mathews
spoke up to enter his protest. But instantly, in the King's name,
he was told to be silent. Mathews insisted there was no precedent for this attempt to make men incriminate themselves
unless it was that by a tyrant. Here he was alluding to the
passage in Shakespeare's *King Richard* III in which Richard
asked Lord Hastings what should be done to the women who
had bewitched him. Hastings replied that if they had done
so they ought to die. "Talk'st thou to me of ifs," replied
Richard, "thou art a traitor. Off with his head." Harvey
evidently did not relish being compared to Richard, and so
retorted with many "bitter languages." [29]

[27] *Ibid.*, 303.   [29] *Virginia Magazine* 1: 418, 419.
[28] CO1-8, p. 48.

The Councillors were now determined to bring their dispute with the Governor to an issue. The next time he summoned them to meet, they brought with them fifty musketeers and concealed them near the house. Harvey asked them with a stern look what they thought was the reason for the petition against him. " The chief cause was the detaining of the letters to his Majesty," replied Mr. Menefie. This infuriated Harvey. Rising from his chair, he struck Menefie a resounding blow on the shoulder, saying: " I arrest you on suspicion of treason to his Majesty." But now he had gone too far. Utie and Mathews seized him, exclaiming: " And we you upon suspicion of treason to his Majesty." [30]

At this juncture Dr. Pott, who was standing near the door, held up his hand as a signal, and the musketeers came running up " with their pieces presented." " Stay here until there be use of you," Pott commanded. In the meanwhile, Mathews had forced Harvey down into a chair. " Sir, there is no harm intended against you only to acquaint you with the grievances of the inhabitants," he told him. So he poured out the recital of the wrongs done the colony and demanded that they be redressed. But the Governor, who was in no mood for making concessions, denied that any wrong had been done. After an ominous pause Mathews said: " Sir, the people's fury is up against you and to appease it is beyond our power, unless you please to go for England." Harvey replied that the King had sent him to Virginia to be Governor, and he would not leave until he ordered him to do so.

But he soon changed his mind. That night a courier came riding up with a letter to Harvey from Thomas Purifie, who seems to have been one of his few friends in the Council, giving an alarming report of the threatening attitude of the people. At first the Governor said he would defy them to do their worst. Would it not be better to remain, though he be cut in a thousand pieces, than to desert his charge? he asked Secretary Richard Kemp. Kemp replied that for him to remain might " hazard the King's service " by provoking the infuriated people to further acts of violence. So at last he yielded and promised to leave.[31]

The rebellious Councillors now took over the government.

[30] *Virginia Magazine* 8: 304.
[31] *Ibid.*

They released English, Martian, and Francis Pott, forced Harvey to deliver his commission and instructions to Secretary Kemp, set an armed guard around him ostensibly to protect him from violence, posted armed men in " all ways and passages," called a General Assembly, and sent out a proclamation inviting the people to lay their grievances before it, and appointed their senior member, John West, a brother of Lord De la Warr, acting Governor.[32]

In the meanwhile, Harvey had left Jamestown to seek refuge in the house of Mr. William Brocas, " whose wife was generally suspected to have more familiarity with him than befitted a modest woman." Here he thought himself secure enough to dismiss his guard. And from here he wrote a threatening letter to the members of the Assembly, commanding them in the King's name to disperse. He also wrote Secretary Kemp demanding the return of his commission and instructions. The Councillors seized the first letter, refused to read it to the Burgesses, and the Assembly went on with the consideration of the grievances, " which were innumerable." As for the commission and the instructions, they had taken them from Kemp and turned them over to Menefie for safe keeping.[33]

The Assembly now passed resolutions accusing Harvey of misgovernment and injustice, and explaining why the people had been driven to the extreme expedient of sending him back to England. As their agent to deliver these papers to the King they appointed one of the Burgesses, Thomas Harwood. With him went Francis Pott to plead his case before the King. Since it would be several months before the tobacco ships sailed for England, there seems to have been only one vessel leaving at the time. So Harvey, as well as Pott and Harwood, had to embark on it.

As events turned out this was unfortunate. Not that Harvey's frowns and threats frightened Pott and Harwood, but that it gave him a chance to frustrate their plans when they landed at Plymouth. Hardly had the ship touched dock when he hastened to see the mayor of the city to tell him of the " late mutiny and rebellion " in Virginia. So the mayor put Pott under arrest " as a principal author and agent thereof," and seized the trunk containing the papers entrusted to Harwood.

[32] *Virginia Magazine* 1: 421.
[33] *Ibid.*, 422; CO1-8.

Pott was dragged off to London and locked up in the old debtors' prison called the Fleet.[34]

In the meanwhile, Harwood had set off post haste to get to London ahead of Harvey so as to make friends and tell of his misgovernment. He got a ride with the postman who was carrying the mail. At Exeter he stopped at the Sign of the Valiant Soldier, and drank a pint of wine with the proprietor. This seems to have loosened his tongue, for he poured out the story of Harvey's misdeeds to this stranger, told him of his mission, and added that if Harvey ever returned to Virginia " he would be pistolled or shot." [35]

We do not know whether Harwood or Harvey won the race to London. But it was the Governor who succeeded in gaining the support of the King and the Privy Council. It is possible that his accusation that Harwood " was one of the chief of the mutineer Burgesses that opposed his Majesty's service in the tobacco contract and in stirring up the country to this mutiny," may have landed him in prison. At all events, when the Privy Council met, the Governor had things his own way.

The King was greatly surprised that the Virginians had dared defy him by ousting their duly appointed Governor. He was determined to send Harvey back if but for one day, he said. And should he clear himself of the charges against him, he would keep him there longer than he had intended. As a further vindication of his authority, he gave orders that West, Mathews, Utie, and Pierce, the leaders of the mutiny, be brought to England " to answer their misdemeanors." He also directed the Attorney General to draw up a new commission for Harvey with an enlargement of his powers.[36]

Though Harvey may have been a bit nervous over the threat of " pistoling," he was too anxious to regain his confiscated property and get revenge on his enemies to hesitate to return to Virginia. He made no secret of his intention to confiscate the property of those who had so humiliated him. As for Samuel Mathews, whose estate consisted largely of cattle, he vowed he would leave him not worth a cow's tail.[37] Yet he thought it prudent to ask for one of the King's ships, explaining that this would " much abate the boldness of the offenders." So on October 2, 1636, he set forth proudly in the *Black George*.

[34] CO1-8, p. 61.
[35] *Ibid.*, 403.
[36] CO1-8, p. 61.
[37] CO1-10, p. 64.

But he did not get very far. The *Black George* proved so leaky that for a while it seemed that it might prove a Godsend to Virginia by taking Sir John to the bottom. But it turned back and succeeded in reaching port. The Governor set sail again, this time on a merchant vessel.

When he reached Virginia, in January, 1637, Harvey could not wait for the ship to wend its way up to Jamestown before asserting his authority, but landed at Point Comfort and established a temporary capital at Elizabeth City. Here he began immediately to turn sheriffs and justices out of office and replace them with men more to his liking.[38] Messengers were sent to summon the Council to meet in the Elizabeth City church. It must have been with an air of triumph that he greeted the Councillors, for now the day of retribution had come.

One would think that Harvey's expulsion would have taught him a lesson. Instead, his desire for revenge drove him into new excesses. With the enlarged powers of his new commission, with the Council submissive to his will, with the courts manned by his favorites, with the prestige of the King's backing, he went to great extremes. The Reverend Anthony Panton accused him of " many arbitrary and illegal proceedings in judgment, tyranny, extortion." The " unjust whippings, cutting of ears, fining and confiscation of honest men's goods," must have brought back memories of Dale and Argall. The converting of fines to his " own profit and use," or to reward his henchmen, convinced the people that men were accused and sentenced, not because they were guilty of any crime, but merely to have an excuse for taking their property.[39]

In the meanwhile, West, Mathews, Utie, and Pierce had been sent as prisoners to England to answer the charge of mutiny, where a bill was exhibited against them in the Star Chamber. But here the matter hung fire. George Donne, Muster General of Virginia and a member of the Council, who had come to England to prosecute them, became ill. Harvey neglected to put up the money for necessary fees. The great cost of the voyage across the Atlantic prevented the sending over of witnesses.

[38] *Virginia Magazine* 10: 265.
[39] E. D. Neill, *Virginia Carolorum*, 150; *Report of Commission on Historical Manuscripts*, 3.

But in the absence of the accused men, Sir John took ample revenge on them. They were informed by letters from Virginia that "divers of their goods, cattle, and servants" had been confiscated. So they complained to the Privy Council. Mathews assured them that Harvey was bent on ruining him, and that he had been heard to say that if one "stood, tother should fall, and if he swum, the other should sink." He seems to have convinced the Privy Council, for on May 25, 1637, they wrote Harvey ordering him to restore Mathews' property.[40]

But so reluctant was Harvey to be cheated out of his revenge that he postponed compliance in the hope that something might occur to give him an excuse for not obeying. This excuse he found in a letter from the Privy Council expressing satisfaction with his administration. It was his excuse, also, for further severities against Mathews. Kemp and others entered his house, broke open the doors of several rooms, ransacked his trunks, examined his papers, and carried off a part of his goods and eight of his servants.[41]

When word of this reached the Privy Council, the sub-committee to whom the case was referred gave it as their opinion that Mathews had been "very hardly dealt with." "We cannot but clearly discern somewhat of passion in the said proceedings," they reported. So the Privy Council wrote again to Harvey, commanding him once more to restore Mathews' property. This time the Governor complied, writing the Privy Council a long, but lame excuse for what he had done.[42]

Another victim of Harvey's malice was the Reverend Anthony Panton, minister of the parishes of York and Chiskiack. Panton had quarreled with the Governor's warm friend, Secretary Kemp, and had incurred his lasting enmity by calling him a "jackanapes," who was "unfit for the place of secretary," adding that "his hair-lock was tied up with ribbon as old as St. Paul's." So he was now brought to trial, charged with mutinous speeches and disobedience to the Governor, and with disrespect to the Archbishop of Canterbury. The farcical character of justice as administered by Harvey is shown by the fact that in the trial Kemp acted not only as prosecutor but as one of the judges. Panton's conviction was a matter of course. He was

[40] *Virginia Magazine* 9: 179, 180.
[41] CO1-9, p. 121.
[42] CO1-10, p. 14.

fined £500, forced to make public submission, and was banished from Virginia and forbidden ever to return on pain of death, and authority was given " to any man whatsoever to execute him." [43]

Throughout Virginia colonial history the parties to any dispute who were in London to urge their side had a great advantage. So Mathews, Utie, Pierce, and Francis Pott, after they secured their liberty under bail, devoted their time to undermining Sir John at Court. The Governor charged that they planted spies in all parts of the city to invite persons who had just arrived from Virginia into taverns, treated them to wine to make them talkative, and got them to state their grievances. So they poured out the stories of Harvey's confiscations, extortions, whippings, and pressure on the courts of justice. [44]

As the evidence against Harvey piled up the exiles gained the support of the subcommittee of the Privy Council to whom colonial affairs were usually referred. Sir John wrote at length to refute what he called " the malicious untruths of such who by all means do go about and study to traduce us." But in vain, for the Privy Council decided to remove him. [45]

The shoe was now on the other foot. On January 11, 1639, Sir Francis Wyatt received a commission as Governor of Virginia. When this news reached the colony there was rejoicing, for Wyatt had shown himself a staunch defender of liberty during his previous administration. The people could be sure that he would redress their wrongs and see to it that justice was done all men. Nor were they disappointed. No sooner had Wyatt arrived than he summoned the General Court and brought Harvey before it to answer for his misdeeds. [46]

Kemp, who was retained as Secretary and Councillor by order of the Privy Council, was helpless to prevent his fellow judges from passing sentence on the deposed Governor. " They of the old commission have been persecuted with much malice," he wrote in March, 1640, " the weight whereof hath hitherto principally fallen on Sir John Harvey, whose estate is wholly sequestered at present, and at the next court now approaching will assuredly be swept away." [47] Harvey wrote that he groaned

[43] CO1-10, p. 32.
[44] Ibid., 15.
[45] Ibid., 3.
[46] CO1-10, p. 61.
[47] Ibid.

under the oppression of his enemies, and that he was so closely
watched that he hardly had privacy enough to write a letter.
His enemies had now been advanced to be his judges, and were
tearing his estate from him by inviting his creditors to clamor
against him. Both Harvey and Kemp asked permission to go to
England, but this was refused. Not only were they held to
answer charges, but because the new administration had no
desire to have them clamoring against them at Court.

" Sir John being . . . laid flat," Wyatt next took up the case
of Anthony Panton against Kemp.[48] This matter had been
sifted out by the Privy Council, who reported that they could
find no proof of the charges against the minister. It seemed
strange to them that he should be accused of mutinous behavior
throughout six or seven years, in view of the fact that ten
months previously Harvey had presented him to a benefice. So
they suspended the harsh sentence, and referred the matter to
Governor Wyatt. The Virginia court promptly reversed the
previous action, declared Panton guiltless, and restored his
estate. So he returned in triumph and resumed his duties in
his two parishes. To Kemp this was the crowning humiliation.
" I am exceedingly injured, and shall suffer without guilt unless
my friends now assist me," he wrote. " The Governor and
Council aim at my ruin." [49]

The men employed to watch Harvey and Kemp must have
relaxed their vigilance, for both escaped and made their way
back to England. Thomas Stegg, who aided Kemp in getting
away, had to pay dearly, for the Governor and Council fined
him £50 and imprisoned him. In London, Harvey and Kemp
sought influential friends, poured out their complaints to them,
and tried to undermine Wyatt at Court. Kemp later returned
to Virginia, where he resumed his place as Secretary, and his
seat in the Council. Harvey seems to have given up politics as
a bad business and returned to the sea as what he probably
considered a less dangerous vocation. He died in 1650.

The thrusting out of Sir John Harvey is a landmark in the
long struggle for self-government in Virginia. It showed that
there was a point beyond which no Governor dared go in
trampling upon the rights of the people. It was a daring thing
for the Virginians to defy the King by deposing the man he had

[48] *Ibid.*, 64, I.
[49] CO1-10, 64.

sent as their Governor, and notifying him in effect that they wanted him to make a better selection. That Charles sent Harvey back and that he was as tyrannical after his return as he had been before, does not obscure the meaning of this uprising as a clash between the royal assertion of despotic right and the American devotion to liberty.

Harvey based his claims to supreme power on the theory that he was the King's substitute, and as such should have the unquestioning obedience of the people. The Virginians contended that his power was limited by law. Even had his rule been marked by justice and moderation, they would have denied his pretensions. But when he made them the basis for an odious tyranny, they took a step unique in American colonial history, by laying violent hands on him, and sending him back to his royal master.

CHAPTER IV

ROYALTY OVERTHROWN

IT was in August, 1641, that Charles I appointed Sir William Berkeley Governor of Virginia to succeed Sir Francis Wyatt. The King knew this young man well, for he had been a gentleman usher of the Privy Chamber under the Lord Chamberlain, and as such had attended various ceremonies at Court. He was the fourth son of Maurice Berkeley, of the ancient Berkeley family of Bruton, Somerset, had studied at Oxford and the Middle Temple, and in 1630 had made the " grand tour " on the continent. He seems to have had thoughts of following in the footsteps of the great Shakespeare, for in 1638 he published a tragedy which he named *The Lost Lady*. He was knighted in 1639.

No doubt Charles thought he was doing the Virginians a great favor in sending them this accomplished young man. But he probably was actuated also by less unselfish motives. Berkeley was warmly attached to him, considered his person sacred, defended his claim to rule by divine right, and considered the Parliamentary leaders who were defying him enemies of their country. It would be good policy to place such a man in a post of authority in Virginia, to hold the colony in line for the royal cause. Sir William too must have had this in mind when he consented to lay aside his pen and the pleasures of the Court, to face the difficulties and perils of life in the forests of America.

But even as he was preparing to leave, the clouds were gathering for the storm which broke over England. The long quarrel of King and Parliament was nearing a crisis; high churchmen and Puritans were locked in bitter battle. In December, 1640, a petition signed by 15,000 persons for the abolition of Episcopacy " with all its roots and branches " was presented to the Commons. A few months later a bill of attainder against the Earl of Strafford was passed, and this able statesman and friend of the King was led to the block. The Puritans demanded that the Book of Common Prayer be cast aside. Charles threatened his foes in London by bringing in soldiers, and men went about their daily tasks under the shadow of an English Saint Bartholomew's Day massacre. In January, 1642, the King fled from London and both sides made ready for war.

Berkeley arrived in Virginia early in 1642. When the Councillors assembled and took the oath of allegiance and supremacy, they must have viewed their polished and courtly new Governor with keen interest mixed with apprehension. Would he follow the example of Harvey in trying to rule like an Eastern despot? Would he try to set himself above the law? Would he take sides in the quarrels which had divided the colony and resume the persecution of one group or the other?

Berkeley soon made it evident that he wished to do justice to all men. It mattered not whether they had been friends of Harvey or his enemies so long as they were loyal to the King. So Kemp, Mathews, Menefie, West, Pierce, and others who sat around him at the Council table, had to stifle old resentments and unite in support of the new administration.

Harvey had assumed that since the King was absolute and so could do no wrong, he, as his substitute, could trample on the rights of the people at will. Berkeley, in contrast, acted on the theory that at a time when the Throne itself was in peril, it was his duty to show that under the royal authority there could be justice, security, and even freedom. Virginia had had ten years of experience of his policies when he asked what they could expect from a change of government. " Is it liberty? The sun looks not on a people more free than we are from oppression. Is it wealth? Hundreds of examples show us that industry and thrift in a short time may bring us to as high of it as the country and our conditions are capable of. Is it security to enjoy this wealth when gotten? Without blushing I will speak it, I am confident there lives not that person can accuse me of attempting the least act against any man's property." [1]

There is every reason to believe that this boast was justified. The first Assembly that sat after Berkeley's arrival spoke of the " good and wholesome laws " that they had passed under his leadership. They were especially proud of " the near approach we have made to the laws and customs of England in proceedings of the court and trials of causes." [2] So we hear no more of the prosecution of men on trivial charges, of the over-

[1] *Virginia Magazine* 1: 77.
[2] W. W. Hening, *Statutes at large* 1: 237.

awing of judges, and of ruinous confiscations. Thomas Ludwell, after the surrender of the colony to the Commonwealth, when Berkeley's enemies might easily have hounded him in the courts, declared that there was not one man that either publicly or privately charged him with injustice.[3]

It must have produced a general sense of security when Sir William affixed his signature to a bill giving either the plaintiff or the defendant in any court the right to demand trial by jury. No more could a body of justices, appointed by the Governor, and perhaps looking to him for further favors, deprive a man of his property without the judgment of his peers.[4] And should one be brought before the General Court to plead for life or limb, one need not submit to their decision if unjust, for now, apparently for the first time, appeals were permitted to the Assembly.[5]

One of the chief grievances of former times had been the conscripting of men for public service or the service of the Governor. So now when Berkeley "in preferring the public freedom before his particular profit" gave up any claim to forced labor, he won the gratitude of the people. He has restored to us the birthright of our mother nation, men said. No longer need the poor planter fear that the sheriff would lead him off to work in the Governor's garden while his tobacco field went to weeds, or the carpenter curse the day when he was forced to give his time for the construction of a fort.[6]

The Assembly admitted that before the arrival of the new Governor they had not done their full duty in passing wholesome laws and redressing grievances. But they now proudly submitted to the public judgment the many benefits to the colony from "their late consultations." Among these was the relief given the poor by the revising of the tax law, so as to make the levy "in some measure" proportionate to "men's abilities and estates."

The Assembly thought it wise to assert once more that the Governor and Council had no authority to lay taxes.[7] There would seem to have been no need for this since, though Harvey may have tried to levy taxes on his own responsibility, there is

[3] CO1-20.
[4] W. W. Hening, *Statutes at large* 1: 273.
[5] *Ibid.*, 272.
[6] *Ibid.*, 237.
[7] *Ibid.*, 244.

no evidence that Berkeley made such an attempt. It seems
likely that the Assembly had no more in mind in re-enacting
this law than the emphasizing of a vital principle.

Berkeley's liberal policies won something more tangible than
the gratitude of the people, for the Assembly made him a
present of two houses and an orchard.[8] When the Civil War
in England cut off the Governor's pension and the allowance
granted him by the King, they levied a tax of two shillings a
tithable to raise a fund for his support. It is true that they did
this with grave misgivings. To excuse themselves to the people
they pointed out that such a thing had never occurred before
from the infancy of the colony, and they prayed God it would
never happen again. The Assembly promised that when the
present crisis had passed they would never again consent to
place the burden of maintaining the Governor upon the people.

They seem not to have considered that to do so would be
well worth the cost, since it would make him less dependent
on the King and more amenable to their wishes. In the struggle
for self-government in the American colonies nothing tended
more to bring victory than the fact the Assemblies usually were
paymasters for the Governors.

But now Berkeley had to decide whether it was his duty to
remain at his post in Virginia or whether he should hasten
back to England to offer his sword to his King. Every vessel
which came in brought news of the bitter conflict which was
convulsing the mother country—the battle of Edgehill, the victory of the Londoners at Turnham Green, the murderous
struggle in the lanes and ditches of Newbury. Though it
seemed that final victory for the royal forces was certain, Berkeley decided that he was needed more in England than in Virginia. Turning the government over to Richard Kemp, he set
sail for England early in 1644. We next hear of him in the
following summer in Cornwall with the King when he was
bearing down on the Parliamentary forces under Essex.

It is eloquent of the work done by Berkeley in reconciling
the bitter factions left by Harvey, that Mathews, Pierce, Menefie, and West seem to have accepted Kemp's appointment in
good grace. But one wonders whether Kemp, with this dignity,
got a new ribbon for his hair lock, and whether he patched up
his quarrel with the Reverend Anthony Panton. But he was

[8] *Ibid.*, 267.

left little time for personal matters, for a few weeks after Berkeley's departure the Indians, under the leadership of the aged Opechancanough, fell on the outer settlements and massacred no less than five hundred persons.[9]

Even when this terrible news reached Berkeley he seems to have delayed his return, for it was only on June 7, 1645, over a year after the massacre, that he arrived at Jamestown.[10] In the meanwhile, the whites had taken ample revenge on their treacherous enemies. Expeditions had gone out to bring fire and destruction to the Indian villages, and to cut down the ripening corn. No sooner had the Governor set foot on Virginia soil than he took personal charge of the war, leading out the forces, exposing himself to danger " night and day on the water and on the land," " visiting the remoter parts and with his presence encouraging the people." So indefatigable was he that " he scarce ate or slept to the hazard of his health." [11] At last, when he had captured Opechancanough, the disheartened savages sued for peace.[12]

Having removed the Indian menace, Sir William was faced with the task of saving Virginia for the King. The news from England was alarming—Parliament was everywhere victorious; the use of the Book of Common Prayer was forbidden; hundreds of Anglican clergymen had been expelled from their livings; the King had fled to the Isle of Wight.

The Governor knew that there was a powerful faction in the colony, composed chiefly of merchants and Puritans, who favored Parliament. Some of the merchants had bought plantations in Virginia, entered actively into public life, and perhaps held high offices. Thomas Stegg, one of the most prominent of them, in 1643 had been Speaker of the House of Burgesses. Richard Lee, who traded to London, was " faithful and useful to the interest of the Commonwealth." Richard Bennett adhered to Parliament not only because of his mercantile interests, but because he was an ardent Puritan.

But the people as a whole were linked by self-interest to whatever government was in power in England. Virginia's prosperity depended upon trade. It was vital to the planters to ship their tobacco abroad and to get manufactured goods in

[9] Robert Beverley, *History and present state of Virginia*, ed. L. B. Wright, 60.
[10] *Virginia Magazine* 8: 73.
[11] CO1-30, p. 71.
[12] W. W. Hening, *Statutes at large* 1: 323.

exchange—cloth, clothing, household utensils, tools, farm imple-
ments, etc. London, the great trading center of England, was
held by the enemies of the King. Even though the Dutch took
off part of the tobacco crop, if Parliament should prohibit trade
with the colony the effect might be disastrous. This helps to
explain why such a prominent man as Samuel Mathews, who
made a good income by selling beef to victual the English ships,
became " a most deserving Commonwealth man."

Fortunately, Parliament realized that an embargo was a sword
that cut both ways. At first they tried to bring pressure on the
colony by freezing their goods in England, but, no doubt at
the solicitation of the London merchants, in October, 1644,
the Commons wrote the Virginia Assembly that this action had
been reversed. Traders hesitated even then to load their vessels and sail for Virginia, fearing that Berkeley, in his rage
against Parliament, might have persuaded the Assembly to
exclude them. But they were soon reassured. In February,
1645, the Assembly passed an act declaring that since " the
great wants and extremities of the colony " made it necessary to
encourage commerce, free trade would be allowed " to all his
Majesty's subjects of England." [13] They went still further the
next year when they thanked the House of Commons " for all
its favors " to them.[14]

Yet the planters, not knowing what would come out of the
clash of religions, political forces, and armies which was convulsing England, did all they could to encourage trade with the
Dutch. The merchants of Amsterdam paid well for their
tobacco, and sold their wares at figures well below those charged
by the English. In January, 1649, whereas there were only
seven vessels from London and two from Bristol trading in the
James River, there were twelve from the Netherlands.

Though Berkeley had to yield to the Virginia merchants in
their demand that trade be kept open with the mother country,
he was determined to stamp out Puritanism in the colony.
Most Virginians were attached to the Church of England; the
use of the Book of Common Prayer was almost universal; the
ministers adhered to Anglican canonical law. But here and
there, especially where there were many new arrivals who had

[13] *Ibid.,* 296.
[14] Report of Royal Commission on Historical Manuscripts, Part 1: 158.

been under the influence of Calvinist ministers in England, there were pockets of Puritans.

Most of the nonconformists were concentrated in south-eastern Virginia in the counties bordering on Hampton Roads. In May, 1640, the people of the Lower Norfolk County parish elected the Reverend Thomas Harrison their minister, " to instruct them concerning their souls' health." Apparently Mr. Harrison did not think that the use of the Book of Common Prayer or catechising on Sunday afternoons was necessary for the health of their souls, for he neglected both.[15]

Two years later a group in Upper Norfolk, headed by Richard Bennett, John Hill, and Daniel Gookin, wrote letters to the Elders of Boston, Massachusetts, bewailing " their sad condition for the want of the means of salvation." They would be grateful if the Elders would send them several ministers to instruct them in the truth as it is in Jesus. These letters they intrusted to Mr. Philip Bennett, brother of Richard Bennett, and sent him in a small pinnace on the dangerous voyage to Boston.[16]

The Elders listened with sympathy to this appeal, for they regarded it as an opportunity " for enlarging the Kingdom of Christ." After much deliberation, they selected John Knowles, of Watertown; William Thompson, of Braintree; and Thomas James, of New Haven, and sent them off. But they had a rough time even before they reached Virginia. No doubt they thought it was Satan's effort to thwart them that threw their pinnace on the rocks at the appropriately named Hell Gate. But the ministers, accustomed as they were to getting the better of the Evil One, secured another vessel and proceeded on their way.[17]

Upon their arrival in Virginia they were welcomed by the Puritans. Going from house to house they preached " openly to the people," and " the harvest they had was plentiful for the little space of time they were there." " It fared with them as it had done before with the Apostles in the primitive times that the people magnified them, and their hearts seemed to be much inflamed with an earnest desire after the Gospel." [18]

But when Governor Berkeley heard of this invasion of New

[15] *Lower Norfolk County Antiquary* 1: 83, 84.
[16] E. D. Neill, *Virginia Carolorum*, 166.
[17] *Ibid.*, 167.
[18] *Ibid.*, 172.

England divines to woo the people from the established Church, his heart too was inflamed. At the Assembly of March, 1643, he secured a law against heresy prohibiting ministers to teach or preach publicly or privately unless they conformed to the orders and constitutions of the Anglican Church, and directing the Governor and Council to expel nonconformist clergymen.[19]

The Puritan missionaries to Virginia were less determined than were the Quakers who sought to convert the people of Massachusetts to their way of belief and after being expelled returned to face whippings, mutilation, and the gallows. Upon hearing the order of banishment, they left Virginia and did not return.

But both Governor Winthrop and Edward Johnson were certain that the Indian massacre of 1644 was God's punishment of the Virginians for expelling his servants. " Oh! poor Virginia, dost thou send away the ministers of Christ with threatening speeches? " wrote Johnson in his *Wonder Working Providence.* " No sooner is this done but the barbarous, inhuman, insolent, and bloody Indians are let loose upon them." Certainly a terrible and indiscriminate revenge for a loving Heavenly Father.

Though the New Englanders left, Harrison for the time being defied the law by remaining in his parish. Knowing that Cromwell was winning victories, he looked to Parliament to protect him. He was elated when he received word that the Commissioners for Plantations had issued a proclamation in November, 1645, granting freedom of worship in all the colonies. " That golden apple, the ordinance of toleration is now fairly fallen into the lap of the saints," he wrote Winthrop. " We have received letters full of life and love from the Earl of Warwick." [20]

This seems to have given pause to Berkeley, and for two more years Harrison continued to preach. But by the autumn of 1647 the Governor seems to have decided to root out Puritanism in defiance of Parliament, and at his urging the Assembly again ordered all ministers to conform to the canons of the Church of England.[21] Under this act Harrison was banished. After leaving Virginia he went to Massachusetts, where he remained two years before going to England.

[19] W. W. Hening, *Statutes at large* 1: 277.   [21] *Ibid.,* 206.
[20] E. D. Neill, *Virginia Carolorum,* 200.

His congregation, which had now grown to 118 persons, appealed to the Commons, and on October 11, 1649, the Commissioners wrote Governor Berkeley, ordering him to permit Harrison to return. They had heard that he had been banished because he would not use the Book of Common Prayer. " You cannot be ignorant that the use of the Common Prayerbook is prohibited by the Parliament." By this time Berkeley was so embittered against the Commons that if this letter ever reached him he treated it with scorn. After the surrender of the colony to the Commonwealth in 1652, Harrison could have returned had he so desired, but he chose to remain in England.

In the meanwhile Berkeley prosecuted the remaining Puritans. A certain William Durand who took it upon himself to preach in the Elizabeth River chapel was arrested, imprisoned, and fined, and severe action was taken against the members of his congregation. Thereupon Durand, Richard Bennett, and many others left the colony and settled in Anne Arundel County, Maryland.[22]

When the news reached Virginia that King Charles had been tried before a Commission of the Commons, that he had been condemned to death, and that the sentence had been carried out at Whitehall and the bleeding head held up for the awe-stricken crowds to view, Berkeley was horrified. He at once proclaimed Charles II King, and so won for Virginia the title of the Old Dominion. There was no thought on the Governor's part of submitting to Parliament. The Assembly passed a law making it treason to question the " undoubted and inherent right of his Majesty . . . to the Colony of Virginia." To defend the proceedings against the late King was to become accessory after the act; to asperse his memory was punishable at the discretion of the Governor and Council; to propose a change of government was high treason.[23] You should be thankful above all else, Berkeley said, " that God has separated you from the guilt of the crying blood of our pious sovereign of ever blessed memory. But mistake not, gentlemen, part of it will yet stain your garments if you willingly submit to those murderers' hands that shed it." [24]

Parliament countered by declaring the Virginians rebels and

[22] *Lower Norfolk County Antiquary* 2: 14, 61.
[23] W. W. Hening, *Statutes at large* 1: 361.
[24] *Virginia Magazine* 1: 77.

by trying to bring them to terms by economic pressure. In
October, 1650, they passed an act prohibiting all persons
" foreigners and others " from having commerce or traffic with
them. English warships were to be used to enforce the act,
and all commanders were ordered to seize any foreign vessels
found trading with the colony. English ships were not to sail
for Virginia without a special license from the Council of
State.[25]

The planters realized fully that if they were cut off from all
overseas commerce it meant ruin. Their loyalty to the monarchy would be dearly purchased if their tobacco were left on
their hands, and all supplies of cloth, clothing, and other manufactured goods denied them. Yet under the passionate urging
of Governor Berkeley they remained firm.

Calling an Assembly for March, 1651, Sir William delivered
an address ringing with defiance. You see by the declaration of
the men of Westminster how they mean to deal with you, he
said. Surely they could have proposed something which might
have strengthened us to bear the heavy chains they are making
ready for us, though it were no more than the assurance that
we shall eat the bread for which our own oxen plow, and
which we reap with our own sweat. " Surely, gentlemen, we
are more slaves by nature than their power can make us if we
suffer ourselves to be shaken with these paper bullets. . . .
Gentlemen, by the grace of God we will not so tamely part
with our King and all those blessings we enjoy under him; and
if they oppose us do but follow me, I will either lead you to
victory or lose a life which I cannot more gloriously sacrifice
than for my loyalty and your security." [26]

We do not know to what extent the act of 1650 was effective
in stopping trade to Virginia. It is probable that Dutch merchants continued to come in, eluding English warships, and
taking off a part of the tobacco crop. Had it not been for this
it is probable that the colony would have been forced to surrender, and it would have been unnecessary for Parliament
to send a force to subdue it.

During the turmoil of the early months of the Commonwealth there was little opportunity for the Council of State
to consider what should be done about Virginia. But in

[25] Scobell, *Collection of acts* 2: 132.
[26] *Virginia Magazine* 1: 77.

October, 1649, they directed the Committee of the Admiralty
to recommend steps " to reduce them to the interest " of Parliament. This committee called in several merchants interested
in the tobacco trade—Maurice Thompson, Benjamin Worsley,
and others—to ask their advice. These men were deeply concerned lest the defection of the colonies might ruin them by
diverting trade to the Dutch. After long debate, it was decided
that Parliament should be asked to name commissioners " in
whom the government be immediately placed, with power to
settle the same under the government of the Commonwealth." [27]

But this plan could not be put into effect so long as the
Governor and Assembly were holding out for the King. So
when news reached England that the blockade had not been
successful in bringing them to terms, it was decided to send
over a naval and military expedition. Thomas Stegg, who was
in London, no doubt told the Council of State that there were
many in Virginia who favored the Commonwealth, and that by
cooperating with them they might take over the colony without
firing a shot. So in naming a commission to offer terms they
included not only Stegg himself, but Richard Bennett and
William Claiborne, both of whom were in Virginia. The
commission was headed by Captain Robert Dennis. In the
event of his death, his place was to be filled by Captain Edmund
Curtis.

They were ordered to " use their best endeavors " to bring
the Virginians " to their due obedience," and were authorized
to grant pardon to all who would submit. In case this did not
prove effective they were to use " all acts of hostility . . . to
enforce them." They were directed, also, to augment their
force by making recruits in the colony, appointing captains and
other officers, and promising freedom to all indentured workers
who would take up arms for the Commonwealth.[28]

So now a fleet of two warships, the *John* and the *Guinea
Frigate*, and a number of armed merchant vessels was assembled,
a force of six hundred men embarked, and arms and stores
brought aboard. Captain Dennis sailed in the *John*, Captain
Curtis in the *Guinea Frigate*. Arriving at Barbados, and finding
a large royalist force ready to resist them, they landed their
soldiers, and defeated them in a pitched battle. This caused

[27] *Calendar of state papers, Colonial* 1: 332.
[28] CO1-11.

a delay of several weeks before they could proceed on their way to the Chesapeake Bay. But now disaster struck, for off the coast of Carolina they ran into a storm which sent the *John* to the bottom, taking Captain Dennis and Stegg with her. Unaware of this, the rest of the fleet proceeded on their way and arrived safely in Hampton Roads.

Even without the *John* the fleet must have seemed formidable to the planters who paused in their work to view it. It must have seemed formidable, also, to Governor Berkeley. But he was determined to resist to the end. For months he had done all in his power to create hatred of the Commonwealth leaders, calling them bloody tyrants, and accusing them of planning to restore the old London Company. The Anglican ministers, hurling invectives from the pulpit, " stirred up the people in all places." At the gatherings for the sessions of the county courts, in taverns, in churchyards after services, everywhere when two or more men came together " little else was spoken of." [29]

With the enemy in Virginia waters and with messengers riding through the counties to summon men to the colors, the planter dropped the hoe to fasten on the helmet and the breastplate, and take up the fusil, the sword, the halberd, and the pistol. Embarking on shallops, or trudging through the woods and fields the trained bands converged on Jamestown until there were between a thousand and twelve hundred men there ready to defend the little capital.[30]

But there was no battle. With the loss of Dennis and Stegg, Curtis, Bennett, and Claiborne alone were left of the Parliamentary commissioners. Since Curtis could be outvoted by the other two, the final settlement was left to all intents and purposes in the hands of the two Virginians. We do not know how Curtis got in touch with them, but they seem to have come aboard the *Guinea Frigate* to receive their instructions. When they opened them and realized how great was their responsibility, they made up their minds to use every effort to spare the colony the horrors of civil war.[31]

Their first step was to distribute papers among the people refuting Berkeley's charges that Parliament meant to enslave them, which they substantiated by copies of private letters.

[29] *Virginia Magazine* 11: 33.   [31] *Ibid.*, 33.
[30] *Virginia Magazine* 11: 24.

Then, hearing that a council of war was in session at James-town, they sent up a summons to the Governor and Council to surrender. At the same time, although they thought their force inadequate to defeat the Virginians, they set sail up the James River.

In the meanwhile the Governor and Council had been considering their summons. One wishes a record had been kept of that stormy debate, with Berkeley pleading for resistance to the end, and others pointing out that this meant ruin. In the end they sent a reply which reached the fleet on its way up the river, promising to yield if the government were left in their hands for one more year. The commissioners replied with a conciliatory message, which though refusing this compromise, "produced the calling of an Assembly." [32]

The Burgesses fully realized the folly of defying the might of England. Should they succeed in driving off the forces facing them, other and more powerful armies would follow. So they sat " in contemplation of the great miseries and certain destruction which were so nearly hovering over this whole country." When they heard the remarkably liberal terms offered by the commissioners, they yielded.

It was agreed that Virginia should " be in due obedience and subjection to the Commonwealth of England." But following this one vital provision came a series of concessions to the colony. The surrender was to be considered voluntary and not forced by conquest, the Assembly was to be continued, pardon was granted for words and writings denouncing Parliament, Virginia was to be " free from all taxes, customs, and impositions whatsoever," a provision which Parliament might with profit have remembered over a century later when they were debating the Stamp Act. The recognized principle that within the colony the Assembly alone had the right to tax was now for the first time guaranteed. [33]

Then followed two provisions in which the commissioners stretched their instructions to the limit. There can be no doubt that it was Claiborne who was largely responsible for the promise that " Virginia shall have and enjoy the ancient bounds and limits granted by the charters of the former Kings," for this meant that Maryland would once more become a part of Virginia. But it remained to be seen whether Parliament would

---

[32] *Ibid.*, 23.   [33] W. W. Hening, *Statutes at large* 1: 363-365.

ratify so drastic a measure. And when it was stipulated that the colony should have " free trade as the people of England do to all places and with all nations according to the laws of that Commonwealth," it was obvious that there would be strenuous opposition from the merchants of London and Bristol.

Having affixed their signatures to these articles, the commissioners hastened on to Maryland to demand the surrender of that colony. But before sailing they called for election for a new House of Burgesses. With Berkeley no longer in power to urge the return of staunch loyalists, and with Virginia submissive to the Commonwealth, the personnel of the House was greatly changed. When they met at Jamestown on April 30, 1652, one recognized only six familiar faces.[34] In the meanwhile, Bennett and Claiborne, who had returned from Maryland, sat with them in what was in reality a constitutional convention.

Their first act was to elect Bennett Governor for one year. Thus, by one of those strange turns of the wheel of fortune, this ardent Puritan who a few years before had been driven into exile because of his religious beliefs, was placed at the head of the government. Had he been a man of Sir John Harvey's disposition, he might now have taken his revenge. But there is no evidence that he bore malice against Berkeley and the former members of the Council.

The Burgesses next elected Claiborne Secretary of State " to be next in place to the Governor." Then followed the election of a new Council. It is proof of the spirit of reconciliation which prevailed that most of the former members were chosen. But the Burgesses made it clear that the Assembly was to be the ruling power in the colony. They were to appoint the Governor and Council, who were to exercise only such powers as the Assembly delegated to them. And they immediately took from them the control of local government by themselves selecting the county justices.[35]

Thus was self-government established in the colony. In England the clash of arms and the struggle of class and religious groups resulted, not in establishing a republic, but only in exchanging one despot for another. But though Virginia had played but an insignificant role in the great drama, she reaped

[34] *Journals of the House of Burgesses*, 1619-1659, xx.
[35] W. W. Hening, *Statutes at large* 1: 371, 372.

a full reward. For the next eight years it was the people who ruled through their representatives in the House of Burgesses.

And the people, most of them at heart still loyal to the monarchy, would tolerate no persecution of the King's friends. Berkeley and some of the Councillors, thinking that life under the new government would be unendurable, had stipulated in the articles that they be permitted to leave the colony and take their property with them. In July, 1653, Berkeley was still planning to leave. Yet neither he nor any of the others seem to have done so, contenting themselves with sending Colonel Francis Lovelace to Europe to attest to the exiled Prince Charles their continued loyalty. Only when some ardent royalist could not bridle his tongue were severe penalties inflicted. We have an example of this in Northumberland County when a Mr. Calvert had to pay one thousand pounds of tobacco to save his wife from thirty lashes on her shoulders for stigmatizing " the keepers of the liberty of England as rogues, traitors, and rebels." [36]

Nor was there any persecution of Church of England men in retaliation for the expulsion of Puritans under Berkeley. There seems to have been no thought of prohibiting the use of the Book of Common Prayer, no thought of turning Anglican ministers out of their cures. In fact the Burgesses were so deeply concerned at the many complaints of vacant pulpits that they offered a reward of £20 to anyone bringing over a clergyman.[37]

Though Puritans and Anglicans, Commonwealth men and royalists lived together in peace, there was friction between the English merchants and the planters. The former argued that the act of 1650, which prohibited foreign ships from trading with the colonies, was still in force. The latter claimed that the law had been temporary in character and was now invalid. And they pointed out that the articles of surrender had promised them free trade with all nations. So when a Dutch merchant vessel came into the James or the York, they gladly loaded her with tobacco and accepted the cheap goods of Amsterdam in exchange.

But the situation changed when England became involved in war with the Netherlands. In the summer of 1653, when the

[36] *William and Mary Quarterly* 1: 154.
[37] W. W. Hening, *Statutes at large* 1: 418.

Leopolus, a merchantman of Dunkirk, came into the Elizabeth River, the captains of two English ships came on board to demand her special license. Apparently the master had no license, for the vessel was seized by the Virginia authorities and sold for £400.[38]

After this there seem to have been no further seizures by the Virginians. But the English masters took it upon themselves to try to break up the Dutch trade, and the planters looked on helplessly as they intercepted sloops taking their tobacco to the Dutch vessels, or seized the vessels themselves and took them off as prizes. In 1660 the Assembly plucked up courage to declare that " the Dutch and all strangers of what Christian nation soever in amity with the people of England shall have free liberty to trade with us." And they required the masters of all incoming English ships to give bond not to molest any vessels whatsoever in Virginia waters.[39]

It is obvious that during the entire Commonwealth period the trade with Holland was kept open. In 1655 certain English shipowners complained that " there are usually found intruding upon the plantation divers ships, surreptitiously carrying away the growth thereof to foreign parts." [40] It was this which widened the market for tobacco, kept up the price, and brought a degree of prosperity to the colony.

With the articles of surrender stipulating that Virginia should have its original bounds, it seemed a golden opportunity for the colony to regain the territory granted to Lord Baltimore. Surely the Puritan government of England would be eager to root out the group of Roman Catholics in Maryland. So when the Assembly sent Samuel Mathews to have the articles ratified they instructed him to plead for the annulling of Baltimore's patent. But Baltimore had cut the ground from under their feet by recognizing the Commonwealth as early as 1648, appointing a Puritan Governor of Maryland, and proclaiming religious freedom. Though Richard Bennett came over to join Mathews in defending Virginia's claim, the final settlement left Maryland a separate colony.[41]

The people of Virginia watched with intense interest the dramatic events in England in the years from 1652 to the

---

[38] *Virginia Magazine* 3: 310, 311; W. W. Hening, *Statutes at large* 1: 382.
[39] W. W. Hening, *Statutes at large* 1: 535, 536.
[40] G. L. Beer, *Origins of the British colonial system,* 396.
[41] N. C. Hale, *Virginia venturer,* 282-285.

restoration of the monarchy in 1660—the dissolution of the
Rump Parliament, the election of the Praise-God Barebone
Parliament, the naming of Cromwell Protector, the foreign
wars, the death of Cromwell, the brief rule of Richard Cromwell. But they were less affected by them than by happenings
in the mother country at any other time during the colonial
period. Virginia was left to her own devices because the men
in power in London were too greatly occupied with other matters to bother with her. One wonders whether they knew what
was going on, for the correspondence with persons in the colony
dwindled to a trickle.

On August 31, 1658, a group of merchants trading to Virginia wrote the Council of State complaining of " the loose and
distracted condition of that colony." It seems that Cromwell
had already been considering certain proposals " for supplying
that defect," but before he could come to any decision he died.

Thus the people of Virginia were left to make a most interesting experiment in self-government. The House of Burgesses
were elected on a broad franchise. Under the law of 1655 all
housekeepers were given the right to vote.[42] Since it would
seem that everyone must have a place in which to live, this
was a near approach to manhood suffrage. Yet three years later
these liberty loving people made certain that no one should
be excluded, when the Assembly enacted that " all persons in-
habiting in this colony that are freemen " were " to have their
votes in the election of Burgesses." [43] One wonders whether
Edmund Pendleton, George Mason, Patrick Henry, James
Madison, and other members of the Virginia Convention of
1776, who voted that only freeholders should vote, realized
that they were less advanced on the road to democracy than
their ancestors over a century before.

The convention of 1652 gave the right to elect " all the
officers of this colony " to " the Burgesses, the representatives of
the people." However, it seems to have been Cromwell's intention to assume the power of appointing the Governor, for
in December, 1653, his Highness " thought fit to continue
Colonel Bennett " in that office until he should " further signify
his pleasure." [44] But when he did nothing more about it, in

[42] W. W. Hening, *Statutes at large* 1: 412.
[43] *Ibid.*, 475.
[44] W. W. Hening, *Statutes at large* 1: 408.

March, 1655, the Burgesses elected Edward Digges Governor. Three years later, they chose Samuel Mathews, who continued in office until his death in January, 1660.

The Governor and Council for some years accepted with good grace the subordinate position accorded them. But in 1658 they made an effort to regain some of the powers they had held prior to the surrender to the Commonwealth. When the Assembly of that year were concluding their proceedings, they voted not to be dissolved, but merely to adjourn. But the Governor and Council " for many important causes " took it on themselves to override this decision and declare the Assembly dissolved.

When this message was received by the House, some of the members started for the door. But they probably sat down hastily when a resolution was passed that if any Burgess showed his acceptance of the dissolution by leaving, he was to be censured " as a person betraying the trust reposed in him by the country." They then sent a message to the Governor and Council declaring their action illegal and demanding that they revoke the dissolution. To this the Governor and Council replied that they were willing for the Assembly to continue provided they bring their work to a speedy conclusion. As for the " dispute of the power of dissolving and the legality thereof " they suggested that it be referred to the Lord Protector.[45]

But the House was now thoroughly aroused, and was determined to bring the matter to an issue. So they appointed a committee to draw up a report for the " manifestation and vindication of the Assembly's power." This committee proposed resolutions declaring the " power of government to reside in such persons as shall be impowered by the Burgesses (the representatives of the people) who are not dissolvable by any power now extant in Virginia but the House of Burgesses." They also recommended the immediate dismissal of the Councillors. Accordingly the House proceded to recall both Governor and Council. Apparently the Burgesses did not blame Governor Mathews for the crisis for they at once re-elected him, and then asked him to make recommendations for the new Council. It is probable that they thought Nathaniel Bacon and Francis Willis responsible for the attempted dissolution, for they were

[45] *Ibid.*, 499.

the only Councillors who had signed the offensive order who were not re-elected.[46]

When the Assembly met again, in March, 1659, a letter was laid before them from Henry Lawrence, President of the Council of State in England, announcing the death of Cromwell and the accession of Richard Cromwell as Lord Protector. The government of Virginia was being studied by the Council, he reported, and they soon would have some positive orders. In the meanwhile, they directed the Governor and Council to apply themselves to the "management of the affairs of that colony." [47]

When this letter was read to the Burgesses, they must have looked at each other in dismay. Did this mean that the Governor and Council thereafter were to derive their powers, not from the House, but from England? They at once acknowledged the new Lord Protector, but they requested the Governor to join with them in petitioning him to confirm their privileges.

While waiting to hear from England they decided to make important concessions. Mathews was to be Governor for two years, at the expiration of which time the Assembly would choose one of the Councillors to succeed him. Members of the Council were to serve for life, "except in case of high misdemeanors." The Governor was to nominate Councillors, but the Burgesses were to have the privilege of confirming or rejecting. The Council at first assented to these changes until further directions from England, but later " they expressly declined the said act," and declared the Assembly dissolved.[48] It would seem that from March, 1659, to March, 1660, the Governor and Council claimed that they derived their authority, not from the Burgesses, but from the Council of State.

In the meanwhile, the people waited anxiously for news from England. Would the weak Richard Cromwell, Thumbledown Dick as he was called in contempt, gain a firm grasp on the reins of state? Or would there be anarchy? Or would Prince Charles be summoned from exile and placed on the throne of his fathers? When the tobacco fleet drifted in, the word they brought was alarming. Richard Cromwell had been forced to resign; England was subjected to the weak but violent rule of soldiers; a new civil war threatened. " Swordsmen bear the rule of the nation," a London merchant wrote his father in Vir-

[46] *Ibid.*, 499, 505.   [47] *Ibid.*, 509, 510.   [48] *Ibid.*, 537.

ginia in December, 1659. " The soldiers they are divided one
against another, and the people they are divided, some for one
government some for another, and how long thus a kingdom
divided against itself can stand, I know not." [49]

To make matters still more uncertain for the Virginians, in
January, 1660, Governor Mathews died. When the summons
was sent out for the Assembly to meet, the Burgesses straggled
in to the little capital, some on horseback, some by boat. Little
knots must have gathered on the green to discuss the distractions in the mother country, and their meaning for the future
of Virginia.

When they had crowded into the house where they were to
meet, and had taken seats, their first step was to reassert their
authority " as the supreme power in this country." [50] Then they
took a step which for three centuries has puzzled historians—
they elected Sir William Berkeley Governor. That this decision
was made at the opening of the session would lead us to believe
that it reflected the general sentiment of the people. They had
had experience of Berkeley's energy, concern for the welfare of
the colony, refusal to use the courts for personal gain. Certainly this is the view he himself took of his election. " In
consideration of the service I had done the country in defending
them and destroying great numbers of Indians . . . and in view
of the equal justice I had distributed to all men, not only the
Assembly but the unanimous votes of all the country made me
Governor." [51]

It is possible, also, that the Assembly had in mind the possibility that the monarchy might be restored. Their action came
just nine weeks before Charles II set foot on English soil at
Dover amid the cheers of the crowds on the beach. The word
may have gone from plantation to plantation that it would
please Charles and recommend the colony to his favor to know
that they had made choice of the former royal Governor, a man
noted for his devotion to his father and himself.

Yet the Assembly made it clear that Sir William would hold
office from them as the supreme power in the colony. They
stipulated that he must call an Assembly at least once in every
two years, that he should not dissolve the Assembly without

[49] *Tyler's Magazine* 1: 244, 245.
[50] W. W. Hening, *Statutes at large* 1: 530.
[51] *Bath papers* I, " The Declaration and Remonstrance of William Berkeley."

permission from the House, and that in appointing members of the Council he must have their approbation.

Berkeley hesitated. Appearing before the Assembly he expressed his gratitude for the honor done him, and protested that there were many among them who were " more sufficient for it " than he. When he first came to Virginia, he said, he had a commission from his " most gracious master King Charles of ever blessed memory." When the King was put to death, his son sent him another commission to govern Virginia, but Parliament sent a force against him, and finding him defenceless, took over the colony. But Parliament continued not long, and now his intelligence was not enough to tell him who or what ruled England. " But, Mr. Speaker, it is one duty to live obedient to a government, and another of a very different nature to command under it." Yet when he had asked the Council for their advice, and they had concurred unanimously in his election, he consented.[52]

Thus this professed enemy of republican principles became the head of a semi-independent little republic. To Governor Stuyvesant, of New Netherlands, he wrote: " I am but a servant of the Assembly, neither do they arrogate any power to themselves further than the miserable distractions of England force them to. For when God shall be pleased in his mercy to take away and dissipate the unnatural division of their native country, they will immediately return to their own professed obedience." [53]

Though Charles was proclaimed King in England on May 8, 1660, it was only in September that the slow moving vessels of the day brought the news to Virginia. It was with elation that Berkeley wrote to the sheriffs in every county that God had invested " our most gracious sovereign, Charles II," with the " just rights of his royal father," and charged them to proclaim him King forthwith. In Jamestown there was rejoicing, marked by the firing of cannon, and the blare of trumpets. The country people for miles around must have flocked in to aid in making way with six cases of drams and a hundred and seventy-six gallons of cider.[54]

Berkeley's joy was tempered with the fear that the King

---

[52] *Southern Literary Messenger,* Jan. 1845.
[53] Charles Campbell, *History of Virginia,* 246.
[54] *William and Mary Quarterly* 1: 158.

might be angry with him for having accepted office from the
" rebel " Assembly. But Charles reassured him, and sent him
a new commission. Overjoyed, Berkeley replied: " I . . . do
most humbly throw myself at your Majesty's feet . . . that you
yet think me worthy of your royal commands. It is true . . .
I did something, which if misrepresented to your Majesty, may
cause your Majesty to think me guilty of a weakness I should
ever abhor myself for. But it was no more . . . than to leap over
the fold to save your Majesty's flock, when your Majesty's
enemies of that fold had barred up the lawful entrance to it,
and enclosed the wolves of schism and rebellion ready to devour
all within." [55]

Thus the Commonwealth period in Virginia came to an end.
No longer was the Assembly to be the supreme power, selecting
the Governor and Council, and controlling local government.
The old struggle for self-government had to be resumed; the
representatives of the people again had to steel themselves
against the encroachments of arbitrary Kings and arbitrary
Governors. More than a century was to elapse before the rights
surrendered when Charles II was proclaimed were regained.

But the training in self-government received during the eight
years that the people were their own masters stood them in
good stead in the conflicts ahead. Having tasted the sweets of
freedom, they were ready to resist when Governors vetoed their
bills, or corrupted the Burgesses, or swayed the courts, or bullied the Council. The Commonwealth period foreshadowed
Bacon's Rebellion and the American Revolution; the constitutional Assembly of 1652 foreshadowed Bacon's Assembly of
June, 1676, and the Virginia Convention of 1776.

[55] *Southern Literary Messenger*, Jan. 1845.

CHAPTER V

A BACON! A BACON!

SIR WILLIAM BERKELEY was one of the best Governors in the history of colonial Virginia during his first administration; during his second he was one of the worst. The man who had won the gratitude of the people by his respect for their rights, his refusal to use the courts to further his own interests, his efforts to bring prosperity, was followed by their bitter curses when he left Virginia in 1677. The courtly young gentleman who had exchanged the Court of Charles I for the forests and tobacco fields of the colony, had become the crabbed, dictatorial old man. In 1672 the Quaker preacher, William Edmundson, visited him to intercede for the Society of Friends. The next day Richard Bennett asked Edmundson whether the Governor had called him dog, rogue, etc. "No," he replied. "Then you took him in his best humor." [1]

One of Sir William's worst traits, his greed, grew on him with the years. "Though ambition commonly leaves old age, covetousness does not," he wrote Lord Arlington. It may have been this which made him marry Frances Culpeper, the widow of Captain Samuel Stephens, who brought him a large estate. Though there was nothing wrong in this, it was whispered through the colony that it was the marrying of a young wife which was responsible for Berkeley's "old follyage." Frances seems to have been loyal to him amid the troubles which soon followed, even though she may have cast tender eyes on Philip Ludwell, whom she married after Sir William's death.

Whatever is the explanation of the change in Berkeley's character, it obviously was the Civil War in England, the execution of Charles I, and the turmoil of the Commonwealth period which intensified his distrust of republican institutions. They had been tried and the experiment had ended in disastrous failure. True, he had been a witness of the success of self-government in Virginia, but this did not change his views. Monarchy was the form of government ordained by God. In Virginia it was he, as the King's representative, who should rule.

[1] William Edmundson, *Journal*, 71, 72.

So he was determined that there should be no more republican-
ism in the colony than his instructions required.

Berkeley did not attempt the barefaced disregard of law
practiced by Harvey. His methods were more subtle. He
sought to make men obedient to his will by holding out to them
offices of profit or honor. The people of Charles City County
complained that Sir William, "aspiring to a sole and absolute
power over us . . . greatly neglecting the Council . . . did take
upon him the sole naming and appointing of other persons in
their room and place such as himself best liked and thought
fittest for his purposes." [2] The men who sat around the Council
table with him might perhaps venture an opinion now and
then, but they dared not arouse his brittle temper by opposing
him when once he had made up his mind. To do so might lose
one a collector's place, or a colonelship in the militia, or even
one's seat on the Council.

The situation in the House of Burgesses was similar. Berkeley was shameless in corrupting the representatives of the
people by handing out jobs. It was testified that he took on
himself the sole appointment of all officers, military as well as
civil. Offices were created merely " to increase the number of
his party . . . all which offices he bestowed on such persons, how
unfit or unskilful soever, he conceived would be most for his
designs." Thus, by a skilful use of the patronage, he so gained
upon and obliged all or the greatest number of men of parts
and estates " as to . . . do whatsoever he pleased." [3]

If a Burgess voted as Sir William wished, he could count on
perhaps a sheriff's place, perhaps a collector's place, almost
certainly a commission in the militia. If the Burgesses of 1666
wore their uniforms when they took their seats, the session
must have assumed a military aspect, for, of the thirty who
attended, six were colonels, two lieutenant colonels, one major,
and fourteen captains.

Having in this way made a majority of the Burgesses subservient to his will, Berkeley used his right of prorogation to
retain them indefinitely. In this bit of political strategy he
could justify himself with the thought that he had the example
of his royal master. The Long Assembly of Virginia was the
counterpart of the Long Parliament of England. For sixteen

years he refused to hold a general election, and he probably congratulated himself that in the colony there was but a mockery of self-government. The Burgesses might betray the interests of the people with impunity; they could not be made to answer at the polls. So it was with bitterness that the people paid their taxes for the salaries of men over whom they had no control. The people of Charles City County complained that their representatives had been " overswayed by the power and prevalency " of Berkeley and his Council, and had neglected their grievances.[4]

As Sir William was supreme in the Assembly, so he was supreme in local government. The justices of the county courts were his appointees. The well-paid sheriffs' office, which he made the stepping stone to the House of Burgesses, was his to fill. So the county courts, in exercising their judicial, legislative, and executive powers, dared not act contrary to his will.

Berkeley had prided himself on having won the affection of the people in his first administration. One wonders whether he realized that this affection was turning to hatred. Nathaniel Bacon accused him of enriching a few favorites at the expense of the people, and of glaring injustice to individual men. " All the power and sway is got into the hands of the rich, who by extortious advantages . . . have curbed and oppressed them in all manner of ways," Bacon wrote in a fiery manifesto.[5] The constant breach of laws, unjust prosecutions, excuses, and evasions, showed that the men in power were running the government " as if it were but to play a booty, game, or divide a spoil." Nor was there any hope of redress, for to lay the people's grievances before the House of Burgesses was to appeal " to the very persons our complaints do accuse." [6]

Some of the Burgesses, as well as the members of the Council, could expect large grants of land if they were in the Governor's good graces. " Some take up 2,000 acres, some 3,000, and others 10,000, and many more have taken up 30,000," it was said. Unable to cultivate such vast tracts, they merely built little shacks, or perhaps " hog houses " on them so as not to forfeit the deed. When the soil of the little farms of the poor began to wear out, or when new settlers arrived, the only available

---

[4] *Virginia Magazine* 3: 141, 142.
[5] CO5-1371, p. 241.
[6] *Bath papers*, " Virginia's Deplored Condition."

land was on the frontier. Here they made a precarious living on " barren lands " where they were in constant danger from the Indians.[7]

But the most urgent complaint was of the heavy load of taxes. When the sheriff came to the poor planter to demand a part of his little crop of tobacco, he wanted to know to what use it would be put. He knew that a goodly share went to Governor Berkeley, some to the Councillors, some to pay the salaries of the Burgesses, but much was not accounted for. When the members of the county courts retired into a private room to lay the local levy, there were angry murmurs of fraud. Of course they will not tell us what the taxes are for, because part of the money they put in their own pockets, it was said.

Bacon echoed these charges. " See what sponges have sucked up the public wealth, and whether it hath not been privately contrived away by unworthy favorites, by vile juggling parasites whose tottering fortunes have been repaired and supported." [8] And the small farmer cursed as Lady Berkeley drove by in her coach, or when they viewed the Governor's wide acres, his six houses, his four hundred cattle, his great flock of sheep, his sixty horses, his well-filled barns. Few had ever seen his costly plate, but its fame must have been spread abroad.[9]

Berkeley was accused of using the courts to punish his enemies and reward his favorites. A manifesto entitled " Declaration of the People,'" said that he had " rendered contemptible the magistrates of justice by advancing to places of judicature scandalous and ignorant favorites." Colonel Henry Norwood wrote Secretary Williamson in 1667 that great injury had been done in the courts " by the insinuation of some that make advantages of the Governor's passion, age, and weakness." It was a grievance, he said, that in the Assembly the chairman of the committee to consider appeals from the county courts was usually a member of the Council.[10]

Berkeley vowed that he knew of nothing in which he had not distributed equal justice to all men, but there is reason to think that he did use the courts to further his own interests. Thomas Mathew states that he cheated Thomas Lawrence out of " a considerable estate on behalf of a corrupt favorite," and

[7] *Ibid.* 1: 173.
[8] *Bath papers*, " Bacon's Manifesto."
[9] *Ibid.*, Berkeley to Right Honorable, Feb. 9, 1677.
[10] CO1-21, Norwood to Williamson, 17, 1667.

we know that Lawrence never forgave him. William Drum-mond was another who had a personal grievance and it was his efforts to gain revenge which drove the Governor to such acts of savage cruelty when he had him in his power.

Though Berkeley may have been indifferent to the rights of others, he was quick to complain when his own interests were concerned. He had been eloquent in denouncing the restrictions on the trade of Virginia under the Commonwealth, and now he was greatly concerned when his adored Charles II gave his assent to even more stringent acts. All goods sent to the colonies, even though of foreign growth or manufacture, must come by way of England; all tobacco, sugar, wool, etc., produced in the colonies must be shipped to England or her dominions.[11]

The results for Virginia were disastrous. The Dutch traders had paid three pence a pound for tobacco; the English merchants now offered a half penny or in some cases only a farthing. The mass of the people were reduced to poverty and rags. Secretary Ludwell reported that when the small planter had paid his taxes, very little remained for him for the support of his family. "So much too little that I can attribute it to nothing but the mercy of God that he has not fallen into mutiny and confusion."[12] Nine years later Ludwell had occasion to remember these words when the poor did fall into mutiny and confusion.

Berkeley sailed for England in May, 1661, where no doubt he talked with his brother Lord John Berkeley in an effort to have the Navigation Acts repealed. But he had no success. The fault is your own, he was told. Stop planting so much tobacco and produce the more useful commodities needed by England. Send us masts for our ships, flax for our linen, hemp for our ropewalks, potash for our woolens.[13]

Berkeley made a sincere effort to turn the colony to the production of commodities other than tobacco, but all his experiments ended in failure. Ten years later, when the Lords of Trade asked him what impediments there existed to trade, he blurted out: "Mighty and destructive by that severe act of Parliament which excludes us from having any commerce with any nation in Europe but our own . . . If this were for his

---

[11] G. L. Beer, *The old colonial system.*
[12] CO1-21.   [13] CO1-16.

Majesty's service or the good of his subjects we should not re-
pine, whatever our sufferings are for it. But on my soul it is
contrary to both." [14]

Not only did the Navigation Acts impoverish Virginia, but
they brought additional disaster to the people by provoking
the Dutch to war. In 1667 a fleet of five Dutch warships entered the Chesapeake Bay. The crew of the English frigate
Elizabeth, not suspecting danger, had careened her to clean her
bottom. So they had to stand by helpless as the enemy moved
up and captured her. The Dutch then turned on the tobacco
fleet and took twenty vessels. [15] In a second Dutch war a desperate engagement was fought off Lynhaven Bay. Nine or ten
of the tobacco ships, in their haste to get away, ran aground
and were taken. [16]

Had Edward Johnson been in Virginia in the year 1667, he
would have been sure that the series of misfortunes which befell
the colony came as a sign of God's anger. "This poor, poor
country . . . is now reduced to a very miserable condition,"
Thomas Ludwell wrote Lord John Berkeley. "In April . . .
we had a most prodigious storm of hail, many of them as big as
turkey eggs, which destroyed most of our young mast and
cattle. . . . But on the 27th of August followed the most dreadful
hurricane that ever the colony groaned under. . . . The night of
it was the most dismal time that ever I knew or heard of, for
the wind and rain raised so confused a noise, mixed with the
continual cracks of falling houses. . . . But when the morning
came and the sun risen it would have comforted us after such
a night, had it not lighted us to the ruins of our plantations,
of which I think not one escaped. The nearest computation is
at least 10,000 houses blown down, all the Indian grain laid
flat on the ground, all the tobacco in the fields torn to pieces
and most of that which was in the houses perished with
them." [17] Even then the misfortunes of the planters were not
ended, for in 1673 an epidemic occurred among their cattle,
which carried off fifty thousand animals. [18]

In the midst of their suffering the people looked back on
the Commonwealth period as a golden era. Then they had
enjoyed self-government; now their representatives had be-

[14] CO1-26, p. 77.
[15] CO1-21, pp. 61, 62.
[16] CO1-30, pp. 51, 53.

[17] CO1-21.
[18] CO1-30, pp. 17, 51.

trayed them. Then the trade with the Dutch had brought prosperity; now the Navigation Acts had made their tobacco almost
worthless and reduced them to rags. Then men were advanced
to places of trust and honor because of their ability; now the
chief offices were reserved for those who toadied to the
Governor. Then taxes had been moderate; now they were
crushing.

The legend built up by Berkeley that Charles I had been
the loving father of the people received a crushing blow when
it became known that he had granted all the vast region between the Potomac and the Rappahannock to Lord Hopton
and several other noblemen. Charles II so far responded to
the plea of the Virginians for relief as to recall the patent and
issue another in its place containing promises to protect their
rights and property. But when they noted that the new patent
required them to duplicate the quit rents of the past eleven
years to pay off the patentees, they were in despair. This would
amount to so vast a sum that it would wipe out many estates.[19]
So they appointed Major General Robert Smith, Colonel Francis
Moryson, and Thomas Ludwell to plead their cause in England.

In the meanwhile, the patent had been assigned to the Earl
of St. Albans and three others. The agents began negotiations
with these men and apparently purchased it for a large sum to
be raised in the colony. Several years later Berkeley wrote that
the two great taxes of sixty pounds of tobacco per poll to buy
in the Northern patent had so aroused the people that many
were " ripe for mutiny."

Negotiations with St. Albans were still under way when the
agents were amazed to find that the King had issued a patent to
the Earl of Arlington and Lord Culpeper to all Virginia, with
such rights and powers as to make them practically masters of
the colony. To them were to go all escheats, quit rents, and
duties formerly belonging to the Crown; they could create new
counties and parishes, issue patents to land, appoint civil
officers.

This not only revokes former grants and privileges, but leaves
us at the mercy of these lords who may look after their own
interests " without regard to the liberty of the people," complained the Assembly. The common people were so wrought
up " by being left to the oppression of their fellow subjects "

---

[19] *Bath papers*, " The Assembly to the King." Sept., 1674.

that they might mutiny or desert the colony.[20] Fortunately, Arlington and Culpeper agreed to give up their patent in exchange for a grant of the Northern Neck, with the quit rents and escheats.

To protect the colony from such grants in the future, the agents now pleaded for a charter guaranteeing that the people should have their immediate dependence upon the Crown. They sought a promise, also, that they should be taxed only by the Assembly. Had it not been for the outbreak of Bacon's Rebellion the charter might have gone through, for twice it reached the great seal. As it was, when it was granted it contained little more than the promise that Virginia should be directly dependent on the Crown.

Never in American history were a people more greatly wronged than the Virginians in the Restoration period. With Charles II repaying their loyalty by sacrificing them to the greed of favorites, with the Governor they had trusted making a mockery of self-government by corrupting the Burgesses, with their economic interests ignored to build up English commerce and shipping, they reflected bitterly that they had been betrayed. It was Berkeley himself who thought that if they saw an opportunity, the poor planters might go over to the Dutch in " hopes of bettering their condition by sharing the plunder of the country with them." [21] They " speak openly there that they are in the nature of slaves, so that the hearts of the greatest part of them are taken away from his Majesty," reported a certain John Knight.[22]

In 1674, when the sheriffs began to collect the heavy taxes, there was a wild burst of anger. The money is not to be used for the benefit of the colony, it was whispered, but merely " the enriching of some few people." [23] In two separate places the people rushed to arms, determined to resist. Berkeley at once issued a proclamation, requiring them to disperse. But had they had a leader, some " person of quality," they would probably have anticipated Bacon's Rebellion by flying in the face of the government. As it was, by " the advice of some discreet persons that have an influence upon them," they refrained from violence.[24] But in many an humble cottage there were

---

[20] *Ibid.*, July 1, 1776.
[21] CO1-30, p. 51.
[22] CO1-30, p. 78.

[23] CO1-36, p. 37.
[24] CO1-36, p. 55.

prayers that God would send a leader to direct them in righting their many wrongs.

This leader they found two years later in Nathaniel Bacon. The son of a wealthy English squire, Thomas Bacon of Friston Hall, Suffolk; fellow-commoner in St. Catherine's Hall, Cambridge; a pupil of the great scientist John Ray and his companion in his celebrated tour of the continent, he seemed as much out of place in the forests of Virginia as Berkeley had been when he arrived three decades earlier. Bacon had been in Virginia but a few months when the Governor made him a member of the Council. " Gentlemen of your quality come very rarely into this country, and therefore when they do come are used by me with all respect," [25] he explained.

It was with Sir William's friendly approbation that Bacon purchased a plantation at Curles Neck, on the James, forty miles above Jamestown. He bought also, a " quarter," or farm to be managed by an overseer, on the frontier at the site of Richmond. " I chose to seat myself so remote, I having always delighted in solitude," he said.[26]

Bacon soon found himself at odds with the dictatorial Governor. It seems probable that prowling Indians made off with some of his livestock and that he, without consulting Berkeley, had retaliated. When Sir William reproved him, he lost his temper and was guilty of " unbecoming deportment." [27] At the meetings of the Council he obviously did not like the way things were conducted, for he absented himself as much as possible.

When he was in Jamestown it is certain that he knew both Lawrence and Drummond. In fact it is probable that he boarded with Mrs. Lawrence, who took in paying guests, and no doubt was one of several persons accused of keeping ordinaries " at extraordinary prices." When the Assembly or the General Court was in session, her house was crowded. To her clients Lawrence, in so subtle a manner as not to cause suspicion, suggested the possibility of curbing " the forwardness, avarice, and French despotic methods of the Governor." [28] That he poured out the story of his own and the people's wrongs in Bacon's ears, and that Bacon proved a sympathetic listener,

[25] *Bath papers*, Berkeley to Bacon, Sept. 21, 1675.
[26] *Ibid.*, July 18, 1675.
[27] *Ibid.*   [28] Thomas Mathew, *Bacon's rebellion.*

hardly admits of a doubt. Otherwise he would not have risked his neck to seek him and Drummond out for a midnight conference after Berkeley had proclaimed him a rebel.

With Virginia a mass of explosives, the match which set them off was an Indian war. The Susquehannocks, a tribe friendly with the whites, had been attacked by the Senecas and driven from their towns at the head of the Chesapeake Bay to the north bank of the Potomac near the site of Fort Washington. Here they began a series of raids on the plantations on both sides of the river in search of food. When a band of Indians of another tribe crossed over to Virginia, killed several people, and escaped into Maryland, an enraged party of whites pursued them. Unfortunately, they made the mistake of attacking the Susquehannocks and killing fourteen of them. The Susquehannocks retaliated with a series of murders, and the Indian war was on.[29]

While the Virginians and Marylanders were gathering their forces, the Indians busied themselves building a fort with high embankments, moat, and corner bastions. It presented so formidable an appearance that before attacking it the white commanders summoned the Indian " great men " to a parley. But when they came out, Major Trueman, of the Maryland forces, charging them with the recent murders, had them knocked on the head. Infuriated at this breach of faith, the Indians in the fort made a successful resistance, and at last broke through the besieging forces, made their way up the left bank of the river, and crossed over to Virginia.[30]

Falling upon the frontier plantations, they took ample revenge for the murder of their " great men." In a few days they had wiped out a number of families. Dragging off their miserable captives to secluded spots in the forest, they staged scenes of horror that would have staggered the imagination of a Dante. Some they roasted alive and cut off pieces of their flesh, which they offered to their other victims. Others they bound to stakes, pulled their nails off, stuck feathers in their flesh, ripped them open and wound their entrails around the trunks of trees.[31]

Memories of the days when he led his men to victory over Opechancanoe must have come to Sir William, but he was now

[29] T. J. Wertenbaker, *Virginia under the Stuarts*, 146, 147.
[30] CO1-36, p. 78. 605-1381, p. 367.
[31] *Bath papers*. May 23, 1676.

too old to take the field. But he collected a strong force to go out against the Indians, and gave the command to Sir Henry Chicheley. Then, to everyone's amazement, he changed his mind and disbanded the soldiers.[32] This he seems to have done for fear Chicheley might not be able to discriminate between friendly and unfriendly Indians. He stated that he planned to use the Pamunkeys and Appomatox to be his "spies and intelligence to find out the more bloody enemies."

Unfortunately, these tribes were no longer friendly. The gradual encroaching on their lands by the frontier families had forced them to "live remote in the woods," and caused them to harbor a deep sense of injustice. But even after Berkeley finally came to realize this, and admitted that the neighboring tribes were aiding the Susquehannocks, he kept reverting to this policy.

So, when the savages renewed their raids, he called the Assembly together and pushed through legislation for a defensive war. It called for the erection of forts on the frontier, the enlistment of five hundred men, and the use of friendly Indians.[33]

To the exposed families this seemed mere folly. Is it not easy for the Indians to sneak in between forts to fall upon us and commit their devilish murders? they asked. We are already burdened enough with taxes without having more piled on for works which give us no protection. What is needed is a large mobile force to seek out the enemy and destroy them. When petition after petition reached Berkeley, asking him to send a leader, it merely aroused his brittle temper. As one group stood humbly before him, they spoke of themselves as " Your Honor's subjects." " Why you are a set of fools and loggerheads. You are the King's subjects, and so am I. A pox take you." [34]

In this Berkeley made his greatest mistake. Since he would not send the frontiersmen a leader of his own selection, they picked a leader for themselves. When the dread news spread in Charles City County that large bodies of Indians were on the upper James ready to descend on them, hundreds of angry men assembled in arms to resist them. Bacon, whose outer plantation had been plundered by the Indians and his overseer

[32] CO5-1371, pp. 373, 411.   [34] CO1-40, p. 106.
[33] CO5-1371, pp. 373, 411.

murdered, was easily persuaded to join them. When he appeared a shout went up, " A Bacon! A Bacon! A Bacon! A Bacon! " From that moment they were ready to follow wherever he would lead.

From the first Bacon made it clear that he would try to redress the people's grievances as well as save them from the Indians. As the frontiersmen gathered around him he addressed them, denouncing " the government as negligent and wicked," calling the ruling clique " treacherous and incapable," the " laws and taxes unjust and oppressive," and dwelling on " the absolute necessity of redress." [35] Amid the shouts of approval he made them sign a large paper, " writing their names circularwise that the ringleaders might not be found out." He then sent out " emissaries " to all parts of the colony to denounce the Governor, complain of the restrictions on the franchise, and demand the dismissal of the Long Assembly and a new election of Burgesses.[36] Instantly he became the hero of the people, " the only patron of the country and the preserver of their lives and fortunes."

He hoped to gain his ends by peaceful means, and wrote the Governor asking for a commission to fight the Indians. When Berkeley, enraged at the accusations of misgovernment, proclaimed him a rebel, he wrote that he had taken up arms only to defend the country against the Indians. He then marched into New Kent, a county " ripe for rebellion " to attack the Pamunkeys, whom he had reason to believe had participated in some of the murderous raids. But when they fled, he turned south in pursuit of a band of Susquehannocks. When he arrived at the Roanoke River, the Occaneechees, a friendly tribe living on an island in the river, volunteered to go out and give battle to the Susquehannocks. But after they had defeated them and returned to the island they became involved in a quarrel with Bacon. A desperate battle ensued in which the Indians were defeated and forced to flee. After gathering up the spoils, Bacon turned his face homeward.

In the meanwhile, Berkeley had raised a force of three hundred men to intercept Bacon at the falls of the James. But he hastened back when he received word that the people everywhere were rising against him. Astonished, he asked the Council

[35] *Ibid.* p. 377.
[36] *Bath papers,* " The Council to Most Honorable."

what the people wanted. They replied that they were crying out against his refusal to hold an election for so many years, and the denial to many of the right to vote. Since Berkeley's whole structure of political control was based on these two points, to waive them must have seemed to him like complete surrender. But he yielded, and called for an election of Burgesses in which all freemen had the right to vote.

Berkeley watched anxiously as the returns came in, and his henchmen, one after the other, were defeated. When on June 5, 1676, the Burgesses assembled in the little statehouse in Jamestown, all but eight were of "Bacon's faction." Bacon, himself was elected as one of the representatives of Henrico County. Had he been permitted to take his seat, with an overwhelming majority behind him, he undoubtedly would have dominated the proceedings and pushed through the reforms he had demanded.

But he was not destined to take his seat. Instead of coming to Jamestown on horse with a strong force, and posting the men in or near the town, he set out in his sloop with only forty armed men. When they attempted to land they were fired on. That night Bacon slipped into town and held a long conference with Lawrence and Drummond.[37] We can only surmise what passed between these two embittered men and the daring young leader. But it is safe to say that they discussed, not only Berkeley's "French despotism," but what reforms Bacon should propose in the Assembly. It is probable that Lawrence and Drummond had already talked with some of the pro-Bacon leaders, for the Governor warned the Burgesses not to be misled by these "two rogues."

As Bacon was returning to his sloop he was discovered and captured and brought before the Governor.

"Now I behold the greatest rebel that ever was in Virginia," Sir William said.

Then, after a pause, he asked: "Mr. Bacon, have you forgot to be a gentleman?"

"No, may it please your honor."

"Then, I'll take your parole."

A few days later, when the Council and Burgesses were assembled in the Statehouse, Berkeley rose and said:

"If there be joy in the presence of the angels over one sinner

[37] CO5-1371, p. 380.

that repenteth, there is joy now, for we have a penitent sinner come before us. Call Mr. Bacon."

Bacon then stepped forward and handed in his written submission. The Governor resumed:

" God forgive you! I forgive you! "

" And all that were with him? " asked one of the Councillors.

" Yea, and all that were with him. Mr. Bacon, if you will live civilly but till next quarter court I will promise to restore you again to your place there," resumed the Governor, pointing to Bacon's vacant seat.[38] In fact it was the very next day that he reappointed him to the Council.

Philip Ludwell explained this great leniency by pointing out that there were hundreds of armed men within a day's march of Jamestown ready to revenge any harm done to their leader. But Berkeley had an additional motive. Bacon in the Council was far less dangerous than Bacon in the House of Burgesses. In the Council he would be under his watchful eye; in the House he would put himself at the head of the majority in pushing through reform measures.

So Bacon had to sit as a helpless and dissatisfied spectator, as Berkeley once more dominated the Assembly. Thomas Mathew, who was present, tells us that " some gentlemen took this opportunity to endeavor the redressing several grievances the country then labored under," when they were interrupted by pressing messages from the Governor to meddle with nothing until the Indian business was dispatched.

With the matter of reform sidetracked, there followed a debate as to whether two Councillors should be asked to sit on the committee on Indian affairs. " The great sway that those of the Council bear over the rest of the Assembly in matters of laws and also in orders upon appeals, being commonly appointed chairman in all committees," [39] had been a long-standing grievance. So now one member rose and pointed out that if they had bad customs they had come together to correct them. In the end the matter " was huddled off without coming to a vote, and so the committee must submit to be overawed, and have every carped at expression carried straight to the Governor." [40]

[38] Thomas Mathew, *Bacon's rebellion*, 12, 13.
[39] CO1-21. Henry Norwood to Sec. Williamson, July 17, 1667.
[40] Thomas Mathew, *Bacon's rebellion*.

Bacon grew more and more restive as he saw the way things were going. The Assembly did not prove " answerable to our expectation," for which they should be censured, he said later. When a motion was presented to request Berkeley not to resign, he must have looked on with disgust as enough pro-Bacon men assented for it to pass.

So under the pretext that his wife was ill, he got permission to leave town. Then, instead of visiting Curles Neck, he headed for Henrico. Here his veterans gathered around him. When they heard that he had suffered humiliation, that he had been denied a commission, and that their grievances had not been redressed, they " set their throats in one common key of oaths and curses." We will have a commission or " pull down the town," they said. " Thus the raging torrent came down to town." [41]

Berkeley made hasty preparations to resist them. But it was too late. In Jamestown all was confusion. The cry was: " To arms! To arms! Bacon is within two miles of the town." When the Governor realized that resistance would be useless, he ordered the guns to be dismantled, and returned to the statehouse. So the motley army streamed into the village— weatherbeaten frontiersmen, demanding to be led out against the Indians; poor planters, seeking relief from heavy taxes; freedmen made desperate by hunger and nakedness. The common cry was, " No levies! No levies! " [42]

The Burgesses, hearing the hubub, rushed to the windows of their hall on the second story of the statehouse to witness the exciting scenes below. Bacon had asked them to grant him his commission, and now he called up to them, " You Burgesses, I expect your speedy result." Whereupon his men cocked their fusils and aimed them at the windows. " For God's sake hold your hands, forbear a little and you shall have what you please," cried the Burgesses.[43]

And have it they did. It was now Berkeley's turn to be humiliated. He was forced to make Bacon General of all the forces in Virginia. When this was followed with a demand that he write the King a letter testifying to Bacon's loyalty and the legality of all he had done, he could no longer contain himself. Rushing out he threw back his coat and cried out; " Here, shoot me, fore God fair mark." Bacon replied that he would

[41] CO5-1371, pp. 381, 382.   [42] CO1-37, p. 17.   [43] CO5-1371, p. 382.

not hurt a hair of his head. And in the end he got the letter he wanted.[44]

He also got "the redress of the people's grievances," he told Berkeley he had come for. He mounted the stairs to the long room where the Burgesses sat and "pressed hard, nigh an hour's harangue," not only on preserving the colony from the Indians, but on "inspecting the revenues, the exorbitant taxes, and redressing the grievances of that deplorable country." Then, to his surprise, he learned that a series of reform laws had already been put through.

Bacon's escape from Jamestown had confronted the Assembly with a completely changed situation. No longer was he a virtual prisoner under the Governor's eye and his veterans without a leader. Now he was at their head once more to march on the town and revenge their wrongs with arms in their hands. "We have all the reason in the world to suspect that their designs are ruinous," said Philip Ludwell. So the pro-Bacon majority in the Assembly took advantage of the general alarm to rush through a remarkable series of reform laws that struck at the very basis of Berkeley's power. Sir William certainly would not have affixed his signature had he not considered his situation desperate. Some months later, after the rebellion had been suppressed, all the laws of this session were repealed on the ground that they had been secured by violence.

These bills may have been outlined by Bacon, Lawrence, and Drummond during their famous midnight conference and introduced by some friend in the House. They may have been drawn up by the committee on grievances. Thomas Blayton was later accused of being "Bacon's great engine" in the Assembly, and James Minge, the clerk, of being "another Bacon's great friends in forming the laws." Virginia historians have long called them Bacon's Laws and rightly, since they struck at the abuses he had denounced, were passed in an Assembly dominated by his friends, and under the pressure of his armed forces.

The very enactment of Bacon's Laws throws a flood of light on the abuses they were intended to rectify. They broadened the franchise by giving all freemen the right to vote; they restored a degree of democracy in local government by giving the people a voice in assessing county taxes and in naming

[44] It is in the British Public Record Office.

vestrymen and by barring Councillors from sitting on the county courts; they fixed fees for sheriffs and other officials; they struck at the Governor's appointive power by making it illegal for sheriffs to serve more than one year at a time, or for anyone to hold more than one of the offices of sheriff, clerk of the court, surveyor, or escheator at the same time.[45] Far-reaching though they were, Bacon's Laws did not include an act to prohibit officeholders from sitting in the Assembly. Such a law, if permitted to stand, would have put an end forever to the Berkeley system of rule by placemen.

After Bacon left Jamestown to battle with the Indians the colony might have enjoyed internal peace had Berkeley remained quiet, contenting himself with placing the whole matter before the King. But he tried to raise forces to take the rebels in the rear, and civil war resulted.

In this war Bacon at first seemed to sweep all before him. As he led his men back from the frontier he was everywhere hailed as the people's friend and savior. On the other hand, none but a handful remained loyal to the Governor, so that he was forced to take refuge across the Chesapeake Bay on the Eastern Shore.

When Bacon found himself master of all Virginia except Northampton and Accomac Counties, he set up his headquarters at Middle Plantation, the site of Williamsburg. Here he was joined by Lawrence and Drummond, who seem to have helped him in drawing up a manifesto against Berkeley, and in holding a conference with a number of leading planters and binding them by oath to be faithful to him.[46]

Soon after this Bacon held a conversation with a certain John Goode which shows that he had thoughts of extending his rebellion to neighboring colonies and setting up an independent state.

"There is a report that Sir William Berkeley hath sent to the King for 2,000 redcoats, and I do believe it may be true," said Bacon. "Tell me your opinion, may not 500 Virginians beat them, we having the same advantages against them the Indians have against us?"

"I rather conceive 500 redcoats may either subject or ruin Virginia," Goode replied.

[45] W. W. Hening, *Statutes at large* 2: 353, 357, 359.
[46] CO1-37, p. 42.

"You talk strangely. Are we not acquainted with the country, can lay ambushes, and take to trees and put them by the use of their discipline, and are doubtless as good or better shots than they?"

"But they can accomplish what I have said without hazard . . . by . . . landing where there shall be no opposition, firing our houses and fences, . . . preventing all trade."

Bacon replied that he knew how to prevent this.

Goode then pointed out that all the principal men in the country would join the redcoats.

"Sir," he added, "you speak as though you designed a total defection from his Majesty and our country."

"Why, have not many princes lost their dominions so?" asked Bacon.

Goode replied that his followers did not think themselves engaged against the King's authority, but against the Indians.

"But I think otherwise, and I am confident of it that it is the mind of this country, and of Maryland and Carolina also to cast off their Governors, . . . and if we cannot prevail by arms to make our conditions for peace, or obtain the privilege to elect our own Governor, we may retire to Roanoke." [47]

Whether Bacon could have enlisted the peoples of Carolina and Maryland in his cause, secured naval and military aid from the Dutch, and anticipated the American Revolution by a century, must remain in the realm of speculation. But before he could proceed far with his plans he suffered an irreparable disaster—he lost command of the water.

In Bacon's Rebellion, as in the Revolution and the War between the States, the great Virginia rivers made it possible for the side which had superior naval forces to penetrate into the heart of the country, while they proved a barrier to the movement of troops by land. So when several merchant vessels, which Bacon had seized and armed, fell into Berkeley's hands, leaving him the undisputed master in Virginia waters, the rebel cause became almost hopeless. [48]

Yet it is remarkable that when the Governor had assembled a formidable force, brought them up the James, and occupied Jamestown, Bacon succeeded in driving him out. The place seemed impregnable, since the only approach was over a narrow

[47] CO5-1371, pp. 232-240.
[48] *Ibid.*, p. 394.

isthmus, protected by barricades and guarded by the cannon of
the ships in the river. Berkeley himself supplies the explanation when he reported that his men refused to fight, but in
spite of his urgent pleas, hurried him on shipboard and away.[49]

So Bacon's men entered the little capital unopposed. But
they realized that they could not hold it, for Berkeley's fleet
was still nearby, while other loyalist forces were threatening
from the north. After a consultation, the leaders decided to
burn the town. Lawrence applied the torch to his own house.
Drummond to his, Bacon to the little church, others to Berkeley's five houses, and the statehouse.[50] As Berkeley saw the
flames rising above the rooftops and reflected on the waters
of the James he cursed the cowardice of the men who had
forced him to desert the place.

But now the end was at hand for Bacon. While at the house
of Major Thomas Pate, in Gloucester County, he became ill
of dysentery. As he lay on his deathbed, he kept inquiring
whether the redcoats had arrived, and whether there was a
strong guard around the house. We do not know whether
his wife was there to comfort him in his last hours, but it is
probable that she was far away at Curles Neck. He died October
26, 1676. Knowing that Berkeley would want to expose the
body on a gibbet, Lawrence is said to have disposed of it in
secret, probably with a night service somewhere in the Virginia woods, and then to have had a public funeral with a
casket weighted with stones.[51]

Bacon was mourned in many a humble cottage throughout
the colony. Who now would lead the people in their struggle
to gain their rights? One of his followers wrote in touching
verse that death had ended " our hopes of safety, liberty, our
all." [52] There was no one else who had won the confidence and
affection of the people to take his place.

The struggle continued for three more months, the rebels
won more victories, but something like anarchy ensued. There
was no central government, some of the county courts were
closed, crops were rotting in the fields, servants and slaves left
their masters to join the rebel forces, there was indiscriminate

[49] *Bath papers* 1: 350-355.
[50] *Ibid.*, 355; CO5-1371, p. 405.
[51] *Virginia Historical Register* 3: 133, 134.
[52] T. J. Wertenbaker, *Torchbearer of the revolution*, 179, 180.

plundering, the masters of the incoming merchant vessels refused to sell their goods to the rebels or buy what tobacco they had on hand.

As soon as Berkeley got his hands on some of Bacon's followers, he began a series of executions unparalleled in American history. Thomas Hansford pleaded that he might be shot like a soldier, but Sir William told him he was condemned, not as a soldier, but as a rebel. As he stood on the scaffold he addressed the assembled crowd, declaring that he died a loyal subject and lover of his country.[53] When Major Cheeseman was brought before the Governor, his wife rushed in to plead that she be hanged and her husband spared. Berkeley spurned her with a vile insult. Cheeseman cheated the hangman by dying in prison.[54] But Captain Wilford, George Farloe, Thomas Young, and others soon followed Hansford to the gallows.

The end came before the arrival of the English troops. Group after group surrendered, and their leaders took the oath of loyalty, kissed the Governor's hand, and were pardoned. But there was no pardon for Bacon's two chief advisers. "I so much hate Drummond and Lawrence that though they could put the country in peace into my hands, I would not accept it from such villains," Berkeley declared.[55]

Lawrence escaped. He was last seen with four others on the extreme frontier, riding through the snow and disappearing into the forest. Their fate is unknown. Drummond was found hiding in Chickahominy Swamp and brought before the Governor. He was greeted with a mocking bow. "Mr. Drummond, you are very welcome. I am more glad to see you than any man in Virginia. Mr. Drummond, you shall be hanged in half an hour." He was treated with savage brutality, and then, after the pretence of a trial, hurried off to the scaffold.[56]

Bacon and Drummond did not die in vain. Though they and thousands of others were stigmatized as rebels and traitors, though the cause they contended for ended in disastrous failure, Bacon's Rebellion had a lasting influence on American history. It served as a warning that Americans would not submit to misgovernment and despotism under whatever form. Had not the

[53] *Ingram's proceedings*, 33.
[54] *Ibid.*, 35.
[55] *Bath papers* 3: 170.
[56] *Virginia Historical Register* 3: 135; *Ingram's proceedings*, 49.

British Government under George III forgotten that warning there might have been no American Revolution.

To contend, as some have done, that Bacon's Rebellion was no more than a quarrel between a rash young man and an old fool, is to make the most shallow interpretation. Men do not rush to arms, and risk their lives and property in a wild uprising because of a dispute between individuals. As Professor Charles M. Andrews has pointed out, revolutions " are the detonations of explosive materials, long accumulating and often dormant. They are the resultant of a vast complex of economic, political, social, and legal forces, which taken collectively are the masters, not the servants, of statesmen and political agitators. They are never sudden in their origin, but look back to influences long in the making."

CHAPTER VI

RECONSTRUCTION AND DESPOTISM

WHEN the news of Bacon's Rebellion reached Charles II he thought it past belief that " so considerable a body of men, without the least grievance or oppression, should rise up in arms and overturn the government." He did not stop to consider that he himself, by giving away huge areas in the colony to favorites, was in part responsible, or that the passage of the Navigation Acts and the consequent precipitous break in the price of tobacco could be called a grievance. As for Berkeley's policy of rule by placemen, if he knew anything about it, he could but reflect that he himself had set the example.

But he realized that something had to be done, not only to restore order, but to remove at least some of the causes of discontent. So he appointed Colonel Herbert Jeffreys, Sir John Berry, and Colonel Francis Moryson a committee to go to Virginia to enquire into all grievances and report back to him. As for Berkeley, though he was to retain the title of Governor, he was ordered to return to England " with all possible speed." During his absence Jeffreys was to be Lieutenant Governor, with all the powers of Governor.[1]

The King then drew up a proclamation, which he directed Jeffreys to publish in the colony, stating that he was willing to extend his royal compassion to all except Bacon who would return to their duty and obedience, and authorizing the Governor in his name to pardon all he thought " fit and convenient for our service." [2] But he mingled force with leniency by placing a thousand well-equipped men under Jeffrey's command. For the second time within twenty-five years an English expedition set sail to bring the Virginians to " obedience." Berry and Moryson, with part of the army, arrived in the James River in January, 1677, and Jeffreys soon followed with the rest.[3]

[1] CO389.6, pp. 113, 137.
[2] H. W. Hening, *Statutes at large* 2: 423, 424.
[3] CO389.6, p. 116.

They found the colony in a deplorable condition. With the
people bitter and sullen, with neighbor arrayed against neighbor, with hundreds of houses and barns in ashes, with trade
disrupted, there was need for unselfish and statesmanlike guidance. There should have been an immediate restoration of the
rule of law, so that no man could be made to suffer without a
trial before his peers. There should have been an election of
Burgesses, in which the people could make their choices without
pressure from the Governor and the Council. There should
have been an honest effort to assuage flaming resentments, to
give heed to the people's grievances, to unite all classes in
binding up the wounds of war and bringing peace and some
measure of prosperity to the distracted colony.

The situation was not unlike that in the South at the close
of the War between the States. And as the South, after the
assassination of President Lincoln, was left a prey to vultures—
the so-called Carpetbaggers and Scaliwags—Virginia after the
collapse of Bacon's Rebellion, was sacrificed to the vindictive-
ness and greed of Berkeley and his supporters.

"Two wrongs do not make a right." Though a loyalist may
have suffered severely by the plundering of rebel bands, he
was not justified in trying to make good his losses by robbing a
neighbor, even though that neighbor had sided with Bacon.
But the Governor, instead of insisting that his friends seek
restitution only through the courts, himself was foremost in
making illegal seizures. When he returned to Green Spring,
the sight of his plundered house and barns, and the empty
meadows where once hundreds of cattle and sheep had grazed
drove him to fury. He showed "a greedy determination thoroughly to heal himself before he cared to staunch the bleeding
gashes of the woefully lacerated country," by seizing men's
"estates, cattle, servants, and carrying off their tobacco." [4] Some
of the wretched men who were dragged before him he threatened with hanging unless they gave him most or all that they
owned. A certain James Barrow was imprisoned at Green
Spring, where "by reason of the extremity of cold, hunger,
loathsomeness of vermin," he was forced to agree to the payment
of a ruinous composition. [5]

The King's commissioners received a cool reception from
Berkeley. He wanted no investigation of the causes of the

[4] CO1-40, p. 23.   [5] CO1-40, p. 23.

rebellion, he wanted no interference with his hangings and seizures. He pointed out that he had suppressed the rebellion before the arrival of the troops, and pretended to be surprised that the King had thought it necessary to send them.[6] When the commissioners told him that illegal seizures must stop, he flew into such a rage that they decided that future communication with him should be by writing. This would avoid the " loud and fierce speaking " necessitated by his deafness.[7]

But there must have been " loud and fierce speaking " indeed when the commissioners went to Green Spring and showed Berkeley the King's proclamation of pardon, and the order that he return immediately to England. All his life Berkeley had regarded the King's command as sacred. To resist his will was as wicked as it was illegal. But now, on flimsy pretexts, he deliberately disobeyed him. He postponed his departure for three months, declaring that the word " conveniency " gave him the right to remain as long as he wished. He did publish the proclamation, but here again he found an excuse to balk the King's obvious intent to pardon all save Bacon. Issuing a proclamation of his own he " saw fit " to exempt from pardon not only a long list by name, but all persons then in prison charged with rebellion. Since the jails were overflowing, this left scores of miserable men trembling for their lives.

So the trials and executions continued. Gyles Bland, despite the pleading of influential friends in England, was hastened off to the gallows. When Robert Jones showed the wounds he had received fighting for the King in the Civil War, Moryson pleaded with Lady Berkeley to intercede for him. " I would with more easiness of mind have worn the canvas linen the rebels said they would make me glad of," replied this proud lady.[8] Yet she weakened, and the Governor did pardon him. Others were not so fortunate. Not until the Assembly requested him " to hold his hand from all other sanguinary punishment," after a score or more had paid the extreme penalty, did he put an end to the executions.[9]

Yet the Assembly was overwhelmingly loyalist. If we may believe William Sherwood most of the Burgesses were Berkeley's " own creatures and chose by his appointments before the arrival of the commissioners." [10] In the elections intimidation

[6] CO5-1371, pp. 27, 33.   [7] CO5-1371, pp. 55, 60.
[8] *Ibid.*, p. 152.   [9] CO5-1371, p. 152.   [10] CO1-40, p. 43.

and even fraud were used freely. Jeffreys wrote that the Assembly "by reason of the unsettled condition of the country
was not so legally nor freely elected." [11] In Charles City County
a petition was posted on the courthouse door demanding a new
election on the grounds that there had been illegal voting.[12]

As was to be expected, this Assembly backed Berkeley in all
he had done and was doing. They praised his wisdom, bravery,
justice, and integrity. They did their best to block the commissioners in their inquiry into the causes of the rebellion.
When the people presented their grievances they were denounced as "libellous, scandalous, and rebellious." [13] Many
former rebels were forced to make humble submission on their
knees before the Governor and Council, with ropes around
their necks.[14] Some were attainted, some were banished. To
speak ill of the Governor and Council was made a high crime
punishable by whipping.

The people were deeply angered by the brutality of the
Governor and his puppet Assembly. Governor Notley, of Maryland, thought that, should a leader appear who was bold enough
to risk his neck, "the commons of Virginia would enmire
themselves as deep in rebellion as ever they did in Bacon's
time." [15] Many a sullen planter eyed his fusil longingly, in the
hope that Lawrence might emerge from the forests to head a
new mutiny.[16] "The putrid humor of our unruly inhabitants
are not so allayed, but that they do frequently vent themselves
. . . and were they not awed by the overruling hand of his
Majesty would soon express themselves by violent acts," wrote
Secretary Nicholas Spencer.[17] That the Assembly was not unconcerned at the danger is shown by their re-enacting in much
the original form of several of Bacon's reform laws.

Berkeley and his friends treated Jeffreys with contempt. "A
pitiful little fellow with a periwig," Philip Ludwell called him.[18]
But it took a woman's spite to give him the greatest insult.
When the commissioners heard that at last Berkeley was about
to leave for England, they called on him at Green Spring. On
leaving they found the Governor's coach waiting for them at
the door. They did not realize that Lady Berkeley was peeping

[11] *Bath papers* 3: 155.
[12] CO1-40, pp. 73, 106.
[13] CO1-39, p. 38.
[14] W. W. Hening, *Virginia statutes at large* 2: 366, 386.
[15] CO1-40, p. 88.
[16] CO5-1371, p. 132.
[17] CO1-40, p. 89.
[18] *Virginia Magazine* 18: 12.

through "a broken quarrel of glass to observe how the show looked." But they were horrified to learn on reaching their destination that the coachman was the "common hangman." "The whole country rings of . . . the public odium and disgrace cast on us, as the Exchange itself shortly may," they wrote.[19]

It was on May 5, 1677, that Berkeley sailed for England on the *Rebecca*. The passage, though quick, was a terrible one for him. As he paced the deck, he could but reflect that the time was at hand when he must account to his royal master, not only for the failure of his administration, but for his flagrant disobedience. By the time he reached England the "tedious passage and grief of mind" had reduced him to great weakness. But he pleaded for an opportunity to "clear his innocency." If it is true, as was whispered about, that word reached his ears that the King had said that that old fool had hanged more men in that naked country than he for the murder of his father, it must have broken his heart. He died on July 13, 1677, and was interred at Twickenham.

Berkeley's departure did not bring peace to the distracted colony. The loyalist faction had spread the report that Jeffreys was merely Sir William's deputy, that he could not exercise the full powers of Governor, and would retire upon his return. To refute these rumors Jeffreys issued a proclamation a few days before Berkeley left, formally taking over the government. In it he declared that he had as much power as any other Governor, and warned all men against belittling his office. And he put his finger on the very foundation of the Berkelean system when he declared that he would strive to reform, regulate, and redress "all apparent abuses, oppressions, excesses, and defects in the power, practice, and proceedings of all county courts."[20]

But reform was just what the loyalists did not want. They wanted the grievances of the people suppressed, the county courts to be packed with their friends; they wished to continue their illegal seizures. The leader of this group was the colorful and vigorous Lady Berkeley. She held such frequent meetings at her home that the loyalists became known as the Green Spring Faction. Here came Colonel Edward Hill, "a great oppressor, of unparalleled impudence"; Philip Ludwell, Lady Berkeley's future husband; Robert Beverley, who Jeffreys de-

[19] CO5-1371, pp. 220-231.
[20] CO1-40, Doc. 53.

clared had risen from a "mean condition" by toadying to Berkeley; and others.[21]

As they sat in the spacious hall where the Assembly had met after the burning of the statehouse in Jamestown, they denounced Jeffreys as a nincompoop, who was not worth a groat in England, as a liar, as a "worse rebel than Bacon." They would secure compensation for their losses despite all he could do. So they planned their strategy. Lady Berkeley was to strike terror into the people by threatening dire things when Sir William returned. Nor did they relax their efforts when word of Berkeley's death reached the colony. It was known that Lord Culpeper was his successor, so Lady Berkeley gave it out that he was her close friend, and promised great favors upon his arrival. To plead their cause in England they engaged Captain Alexander Culpeper, Lady Berkeley's brother.[22]

After Berkeley's departure Jeffreys had called for the election of a new Assembly to meet October 10, 1677. Unfortunately, at this moment, when he was most needed, he became ill. Early in September a letter from the Privy Council to the Governor and Council had been received, making void Berkeley's proclamation of February 10, which had excepted so many persons from the royal pardon. Had Jeffreys been a well man he would certainly have published this letter immediately and relieved the people from their fear. But the Council urged him to conceal it for the present, and being weak and in bed, he yielded. This daring defiance of the King's orders had an important effect on the election, for the people were still trembling for their lives and property, and so were bullied by the sheriffs into returning loyalist Burgesses. Daniel Parke reported that there had been illegal elections in James City County, Kent, and elsewhere.[23]

It was in October that Parke arrived from England and delivered to Jeffreys a letter from Secretary Coventry, telling him that Berkeley had died and that Culpeper had kissed the King's hand as Governor. Even then the Council was opposed to the publication of the King's order to void Berkeley's proclamation, protesting that it had been procured by misinformation. But the contents leaked out, and there was bitter resentment at the delay. Most of the Assembly demanded its publication. At last,

[21] *Bath papers* 3: 187-198.   [23] CO1-42, p. 17.
[22] *Ibid.*

when Jeffreys and Parke had won over a majority of the Council to the view that it would be unwise to trifle further with the royal command, the two Ludwells flung themselves away in " a seeming passion." But there was great relief and widespread rejoicing among the people.[24]

The Assembly met at Middle Plantation, the site of Williamsburg, in the house of Captain Otho Thorp. Despite the irregularity of the elections it showed a far greater spirit of independence than its predecessor. It passed a law against making unreasonable compositions for injuries done during the rebellion; it imposed a penalty for the use of such terms as traitor, rebel, or rogue; it forbade the impressing of cattle, boats, or provisions without compensation; it regulated fees.[25] But it placed a crushing burden on the prostrate colony by levying a tax of 100 pounds of tobacco per tithable. " This, with the county and parish tax is in some counties 250 pounds, in some 300, and in some 400, which falls very heavily on the poorer people," Parke reported.[26]

The Thorp house rang with protests when Robert Beverley, who was clerk of the Assembly, reported that the King's commissioners had taken their journals, orders, and acts from him by force. In a vigorous protest to Jeffreys, they declared this a great violation of their privileges. This seizure we " humbly suppose his Majesty would not . . . command, for that they find not the same to have been practiced by any of the Kings of England." So they asked Jeffreys to give assurance that such a thing would not happen again.[27]

When this was reported to Charles II he was surprised at the presumption of the Assembly in calling in question his authority. Referring the matter to the Lords of Trade, he asked them what he should do to bring the Assembly to a sense " of their duty and submission." The Lords thought that the protest tended to rebellion, and that the Governor should rebuke the Assembly and punish the " authors and abettors." [28] Charles issued the order, but later, on the earnest plea of the Virginia Council, rescinded it. But he insisted that the protest be " razed out of the books of Virginia." [29] It was a strange twist of fate which caused an attempt by the King to investigate the griev-

[24] *Bath papers* **3**: 206.
[25] W. W. Hening, *Statutes at large* **2**: 407-432.
[26] CO1-42, Doc. 1.
[27] CO1-41, Doc. 87.
[28] CO1-42, Doc. 11.
[29] Sainsbury, **18**: 129.

ances of the people to result in what may be considered the opening act of the Second Stuart Despotism in Virginia.

In the meanwhile, during Jeffreys' illness, Thomas Ludwell presided over the meetings of the Council. So the King's commands were ignored, and the plundering, confiscations, and banishing continued. "Great numbers of poor men, having wives and children to maintain," faced utter ruin.[30] The lengths to which the Green Spring Faction was prepared to go is illustrated by a statement of Colonel Edward Hill at one of their gatherings. One of those present remarked that William Byrd would certainly win a case pending in which he was involved because he was in England and could secure the King's backing. "That will not do," said Hill, "for if the King should send in his letter, in that case we are not to take notice of it."[31]

This is just what they did when Charles wrote in behalf of Sarah Drummond, widow of William Drummond. This poor woman made the long voyage across the ocean to lay her case before the King. So great was Governor Berkeley's hatred of her husband, she said, that he had not only taken his life, but had seized his small plantation for his own use and forced her to flee with her five small children into the woods, where they might have starved had not the commissioners befriended them.[32] Moved by her misfortunes, the King sent an especial command that her property be returned. But when she brought an action in the General Court against Lady Berkeley, and the King's letter was read, one of the Councillors, turning to the crowd in the courtroom, declared in a loud voice that it was based on nothing but lies. "So they dismissed the case."[33]

In the meanwhile, Jeffreys had sufficiently recovered his health to strike back at his enemies. He had tried to win them over by appointing them to collectors' places and doing them other favors, but without success. So at last he retaliated upon Beverley by ousting him from his civil and military offices and "silenced him from pleading in the courts."[34] When Philip Ludwell's many insults were reported to Jeffreys he had him arrested and charged him with "scandalizing the Governor and abusing the authority of his Majesty." This was a serious matter indeed, for the penalty was whipping or the payment of a

[30] CO1-42, Doc. 23.
[31] Ibid., Doc. 107.
[32] Virginia Magazine 18: 2-5.
[33] Bath papers, 3: 168, 169.
[34] Virginia Magazine, XVIII, p. 20.

fine of 500 pounds of tobacco. The jury pronounced Ludwell guilty, and asked the Council to fix the punishment. Since most of the Council were Ludwell's warm friends, Jeffreys appealed the case to the King. Ludwell countered by appealing to the Assembly. In the end it was decided that the whole case, including the matter of appeal, should be left to his Majesty.[35]

But in the summer of 1678 Jeffreys again became ill, and the Green Spring Faction renewed the "old exactions and abuses." William Sherwood reported: "The colony would be as peaceful as could be wished except for the malice of some discontented persons of the late Governor's party, who endeavor by all the cunning contrivances that by their artifice can be brought about, to bring a contempt of Colonel Jeffreys, our present good Governor. . . . It is to be feared unless these fiery spirits are allayed or removed home, there will not be that settled, happy peace and unity which otherwise might be, for they are entered into a faction which is upheld by the expectation of my Lord Culpeper's doing mighty things for them."[36]

Jeffreys died on December 17, 1678. A well-meaning man, who tried to rule justly, he lacked the strength of character needed to bring peace to the colony. With an army at his command, he should have put Governor Berkeley on board ship and sent him to England when he refused to obey the King's commands. This would have prevented many hangings, relieved the fears of the people, and given pause to the Green Spring Faction. But Jeffreys knew that Berkeley's brother, Lord John Berkeley, was in high favor with the King, and he dared not offend him.

Jeffreys' wife came from England to join him, but she was just in time to say a farewell, for he was seized with a violent sickness four hours after her arrival and died soon after.[37] So bitter were the Green Spring Faction against him that they tried to prevent the payment to his widow of £1,200 due him for nine months' salary, and to charge her with all the perquisites he had received. When, as a consequence, she could not meet all his obligations, they imprisoned her for debt. It was only by appealing to Secretary Coventry that she received the arrears due her and was able to free herself from the power of her enemies.[38]

[35] *Bath papers* 3: 214.
[36] CO1-42, Doc. 117.
[37] *Bath papers* 3: 295.
[38] CO5-1355, Docs. 304, 305, 309, 370.

Upon the death of Jeffreys, Sir Henry Chicheley produced a commission as Deputy Governor given him in 1674. Chicheley was a "most loyal, worthy person, and deservedly beloved by the whole country." [39] He had been a Burgess, a member of the Council, had commanded the Virginia forces in the Indian war, had remained loyal to Berkeley during the rebellion, and had been imprisoned by Bacon. But he was now "old, sickly, and crazy," and lacked the vigor to force obedience and restore order. During the eighteen months of his administration the old factions were not reconciled to one another.[40]

Yet Chicheley, to the extent of his ability, ruled impartially and well. At the election of 1679 he insisted that the people be protected from intimidation at the polls. As a result the Assembly showed a spirit of independence and a desire to rectify the people's grievances. A degree of democracy was introduced into local government by an act empowering the voters of each parish to elect two men to sit in the county courts in the making of by-laws. A limit was put to fees demanded by the collectors of customs and the clerks of the courts. The claim of the Green Spring Faction for compensation for their losses was referred to the next session.[41]

In May, 1680, Lord Culpeper arrived in Virginia after a tedious passage of two and a half months, in which scurvy and other diseases took a heavy toll. Chicheley handed over the government to him and the reconstruction period came to an end.

The patriotic Virginian, as he looked back over the years from the collapse of Bacon's Rebellion to the arrival of Culpeper must have seen in them nothing but confusion and disaster. The colony was divided against itself, the most pressing of the people's grievances had not been redressed, many families had been reduced to poverty, the right to vote was denied to hundreds, taxes were higher than ever, and tobacco was still a drug on the market.

Yet important changes were taking place which gave reason for hope. During Berkeley's administration the newly created aristocracy, the men of wealth, the leaders in their own counties —the Ludwells, the Parkes, the Custises, the Coles—had worked in close alliance with the Governor. The common people, on the other hand, lacked leaders to guide them in their struggle

---

[39] CO1-41, Doc. 121.   [40] Sainsbury, 14: 230.
[41] W. W. Hening, *Statutes at large* 2: 441, 443, 456.

for their rights. But with Berkeley's departure the aristocrats, so far from allying themselves with his successor, came into violent conflict with him. And the Governor now assumed the role of the people's friend and protector.

So engrossed were the Virginians in their own disputes that their attention was diverted from events in England, events that were to affect them profoundly. For many years Charles II had lived in comparative peace with his Cavalier Parliament, maintaining his mistresses in luxury despite the meagerness of his revenue. But the rise of the Whig Party under the leadership of the able Earl of Shaftesbury was now threatening to undermine his power. All London was in terror when Titus Oates came forward with a wild story that the Catholics were plotting to bring in Irish and French troops, massacre the Protestants, and murder the King. The Whigs were demanding the exclusion from the succession of Charles' Roman Catholic brother James, and some actually proposed that the King divorce his Catholic wife and marry a Protestant.

Faced with the loss of his prerogatives, the indolent King struck back. His father had tried to free himself from dependence on Parliament by illegal taxation; he by sacrificing England's foreign interests for French gold. In March, 1678, Charles negotiated a secret treaty with Louis XIV in return for £300,000. Now he was in a position to thumb his nose at the Commons when they tried to control and thwart him. It was the beginning of the Second Stuart Despotism.[42]

The change was immediately reflected in colonial policies. The old Council of Plantations, and its successor the Council of Trade and Plantations had done little to supervise and control the conduct of affairs in America. But in December, 1674, after the fall of the Cabal Ministry, the direction of colonial matters was turned over to a committee of the Privy Council, presided over by the Secretary of State. In this way the King's most trusted ministers were brought into close touch with the colonies. Sir Joseph Williamson, Secretary from 1674 to 1678, was a most obedient servant of the King; his fellow Secretary, Sir Henry Coventry, had defended Charles I on the field of battle, and now defended his son before the public; Sir Leoline Jenkins was called " the most faithful drudge of a Secretary that ever the Court had."

[42] G. M. Trevelyan, *England under the Stuarts*, 396.

We have no way of knowing whether these men, in their assault on liberty in the colonies, were merely carrying out the commands of Charles II and James II, or whether on their own initiative they shaped colonial policy in accord with domestic policy. In either case it was the Second Stuart Despotism in England which was responsible for the Andros despotism in New England, and for the equally dangerous attack on liberty in Virginia.

It was prophetic of what was to come that Secretary Coventry, in January, 1678, read to the Committee on Foreign Affairs a series of proposals concerning Virginia. Three companies of soldiers were to be left in the colony, a fort was to be erected "whereby the King may be safe from rebellions," all laws were to be sent to England for revision. The last proposal was an innovation of serious import.[43] The Virginians had never questioned the right of the King to veto the acts of Assembly, but never before had he demanded the right to revise laws already on the statute books.

Of even greater significance was the initiation of bills by the King. Charles wrote Culpeper that whereas certain laws had been recommended to him in Council of which he approved, "these bills we have caused to be under the Great Seal of England, and our will is that the same bills . . . you shall cause to be considered . . . in our Assembly of Virginia . . . and to these bills you do give and declare our royal assent." One was an act of general pardon, one an act for naturalization, and the other an act for raising a public revenue.[44]

This was accompanied by an attempt to deprive the Assembly of the right to initiate legislation. Culpeper was commanded to send to the King a draft of such bills as he and the Council should think fit to be passed, so that he could go over them and return them in the form he thought they should be enacted in. "Upon receipt of our commands you shall summon an Assembly and propose the said laws for their consent."[45]

As though this were not enough, Charles demanded the sole power, heretofore exercised by the Governor, of calling sessions of the Assembly. "It is our will and pleasure that for the future no General Assembly be called without our special directions, but that, upon occasion, you do acquaint us by letter with the

[43] CO1-42, Doc. 152.
[44] CO1-43, Doc. 165.
[45] *Ibid.*, p. 313.

necessity of calling such an Assembly, and pray our consent and directions for their meeting." [46]

The King struck a fatal blow at the control of justice in Virginia by the people, by depriving the Assembly of its privilege of acting as the supreme court of appeals. " Our pleasure also is that for the better and more equitable administration of justice in our said colony, appeals be allowed in cases of error from the courts . . . to our Governor and our Council there, and to no other court or jurisdiction whatsoever." [47]

Although Thomas Culpeper had been too young to fight in the Civil War, he donned a suit of armor with breastplate, shoulderpieces, and brassarts, to have his portrait painted. But the face is not that of a warrior. It is draped by the flowing hair of the Cavalier, has a prominent nose and a weak mouth with the trace of a sneer. Culpeper had followed Charles into exile, and with the Restoration had expected compensation for his losses. But since there was not enough to go round among all the hungry Cavaliers, the King repaid him at the expense of his subjects in Virginia, first with the Arlington-Culpeper grant, and then by making him Governor of Virginia.

The outlook for the colony was gloomy. The King was determined to override the people's rights and make himself absolute. Culpeper was interested in filling his pockets. The Green Spring Faction were still seeking to make good their losses at the expense of the rebels. The common people were suffering from the high taxes and the low price of tobacco.

The King had as much trouble in getting Culpeper to sail for Virginia as he had had in making Berkeley come back to England. My Lord had no desire to exchange London for the forests of Virginia; he had little interest in carrying out his instructions. All he wanted was his salary and anything he could make out of the Northern Neck. At last, after two years of dillydallying, the King told him that unless he sailed at once he would remove him as Governor. So in February, 1680, he left the Downs with the tobacco fleet.[48]

On his arrival at Jamestown, the members of the Council and other leading planters flocked around him, eager to give their version of the troubles in the colony and to secure his support. When the Council met, Culpeper was assured that the King had been misinformed on many points by Moryson and Berry.

[46] *Ibid.*, p. 334.   [47] *Ibid.*, p. 349.   [48] CO5-1355, p. 378.

Philip Ludwell was a loyal, honest servant of the King, and should be restored to his place in the Council. Injustice had been done to Colonel Hill, and they begged the new Governor to intercede for him.[49]

As for the King's rebuke to the Assembly for questioning his right to seize their records, the Council advised Culpeper not to present it. To do so would " unravel and disturb the good and cheerful settlement we are now in by your Excellency's great prudence and conduct." [50] So they induced him to suspend the rebuke until the King should order to the contrary.

Culpeper seems to have brought a degree of peace to the contending factions. The act of pardon ended the plundering of the estates of the former rebels, and the aggrieved loyalists were encouraged to seek redress through the Assembly. Colonel Spencer wrote that the " late different interests " had been " perfectly united to the general satisfaction of all."

United the people had to be to defend their liberties. When the wealthy landholder and the humble owner of but fifty acres, the loyalist and the former rebel alike realized that Charles was bent on reducing both Council and Assembly to impotence, their domestic quarrels seemed unimportant compared to the public danger.

Since the statehouse at Jamestown was still in ashes, the Assembly of June, 1680, crowded into the house of Mrs. Susanne Fisher. Some of the Burgesses had come on horseback from their James City or Charles City plantations, others by shallops from the Upper James, still others from the far-off Eastern Shore. A sturdy, stubborn group they were, like other Burgesses before and after them, determined to uphold the rights of the people.

They were dismayed, then, when Governor Culpeper placed before them the three bills prepared and signed by the King. What right has he or the Privy Council to introduce bills in this Assembly? they asked. And they were especially concerned over the King's demand for a perpetual revenue.

There had existed since 1661 a law for laying a duty of two shillings for every hogshead of tobacco exported from the colony. But the revenue was to be disposed of by the Assembly. It was they who decided whether it should be used to pay the Governor's salary, or to defend the colony against the Indians,

[49] CO5-1376, p. 265.　　　　　[50] CO5-1355, p. 384.

or for repairing the statehouse, or for paying the salaries of the
Burgesses. Now the Privy Council took it upon themselves to
draw up a similar act, but differing from the old one in one all-
important respect—it specified that the returns should go, not
to the Assembly, but " to the King's most excellent Majesty,
his heirs and successors forever."

The debate which followed was long and bitter. Every man
in the Assembly, whether Burgess or Councillor, knew that the
King was demanding the surrender of their birthright.[51] So
they replied to the Governor: " The House do most humbly
desire to be excused if they do not give their approbation to
his Majesty's bill." [52] And when the matter was brought again
before them by the Governor, they refused even to resume the
debate.

But Culpeper knew that he would be severely blamed by
Charles if he did not succeed in forcing this bill through. Returning to the attack he pointed out that the King claimed
the right of disposing of all revenues. Moreover, they were in
no position to defy him, for he had it in his power to ruin most
of them by demanding all arrears of quit rents. We do not
know how many lucrative jobs Culpeper handed out to bring
the reluctant Burgesses around, but he himself tells us that he
won over one influential member by the promise of a seat in
the Council.[53]

In the end the King had his way. The Burgesses made two
minor amendments, and then passed the bill. When it came
before Charles again, he vetoed one of these amendments, and
allowed the other. A quarter of a century later, when the
Board of Trade asked Attorney General Simon Harcourt and
Solicitor General James Montague to pass on the validity of the
act, they reported that it had been put through irregularly. " It
would be wise," they said, " if any part of her Majesty's revenue
depends on this act, to have another in its place." [54]

Yet the act was permitted to stand, and the cause of self-
government in colonial Virginia suffered its greatest reverse.
No longer could the Assembly force the Governor to sign this
bill or that by refusing to vote his salary. No longer did they
hold a sword over the heads of the Council. It is true that they

[51] *Journals of the House of Burgesses*, 1659-1693: 126.
[52] *Ibid.*   [54] CO5-1315, Dec. 23, 1707.
[53] CO5-1356, pp. 125, 126.

still retained in part their grip upon the purse, since the export duty together with the quit rents seldom met even the ordinary needs of the government, and were entirely inadequate in times of emergency. It is this which explains why such notable gains for liberty were made during the colonial wars. Yet from this time until the Declaration of Independence the Virginia Assembly had to fight the royal prerogative with one hand tied behind its back.[55]

Having secured the passage of the King's three laws, Culpeper rested on his laurels. He seems to have yielded to the plea of the Council not to deliver the King's rebuke to the Assembly. If he ever told the Council of his instruction to initiate bills with their advice and secure the King's approval before sending them to the House, they must have argued that it was impractical. They had no desire to have representative government in the colony made a mockery. Were the Burgesses to have the right of amending bills? they must have asked. If so, would the amended bills have to go back to England for the King's approval? Under such conditions, it might take years to enact the simplest laws. So this instruction was ignored.

Equally impractical was it to secure the King's permission before calling an Assembly. In case of a sudden emergency it might be fatal to wait until the Governor had written to Secretary Coventry, until he had taken the matter up with his Majesty, until some vessel sailed and had made the tedious voyage to Virginia. If the need were the outbreak of war with the Indians, half the colony might be scalped before the Assembly could meet to raise men and money for arms and forts. So Culpeper ignored this instruction also.

As for the instruction to forbid appeals from the General Court to the Assembly, the Governor kept it to himself. Three years later, at an inquiry held on his neglect of his office, he explained: " Having some thoughts of getting a revenue bill to pass, I was unwilling actually to repeal the laws relating thereunto till the next session of Assembly should be over, well knowing how infinitely it would trouble them." [56]

As soon as the Assembly had been dismissed Culpeper made ready to return to England, after having been in Virginia only a few weeks. Yet for his supposed services he had been receiving

[55] *Journals of the House of Burgesses*, 1659-1693: 134.
[56] CO5-1356, p. 142.

£2,000 a year from the revenues of the colony ever since the death of Berkeley.[57] Not content with this, he contrived to rob the English soldiers who had remained in Virginia after Bacon's Rebellion of more than £1,000. These men had received no pay for many months, and were discontented and mutinous.[58] So the Privy Council gave Culpeper money to satisfy them and the families on whom they had been quartered. On his arrival he bought up all the worn Spanish pieces of eight he could find, arbitrarily proclaimed them legal tender at six shillings, which was a shilling more than they were worth, and then paid the soldiers and landlords. But before his salary became due, he restored the ratio to five to one.[59]

In 1682 news reached England of a series of tobacco-cutting riots in Virginia. The glut of tobacco in the English warehouses and its consequent low price had convinced the people that a restriction on the output was necessary. It was to be a kind of soil bank, though without the subsidy. When this failed because Maryland refused to join in, angry mobs went from plantation to plantation, cutting down the tender plants. Fearing that this might be the beginning of a new rebellion, the Privy Council ordered the reluctant Culpeper to go back at once to suppress the riots and punish the ringleaders.[60]

Culpeper arrived in December, 1682. Finding that the riots were over, he contented himself with hanging two of the most notorious of the plant cutters, and then hastened back to England. By this time Charles had lost patience with him for his neglect of his government, the Attorney General was ordered to take action against him, and his commission as Governor of Virginia was declared void. In September, 1683, Lord Howard of Effingham was made Governor in his place.

Effingham was well fitted to carry out the King's attack on liberty in Virginia. Deceitful, persistent, unscrupulous, he would have ridden roughshod over the people's rights had he not encountered the determined resistance of the House of Burgesses. No sooner had he arrived than the struggle began.

When the Assembly met in April, 1684, he put on his peer's coronet and velvet and ermine robes, and told the Burgesses that he intended to enforce the King's order to prohibit appeals

[57] *Ibid.*, p. 56.
[58] CO1-42, p. 152.
[59] Robert Beverley, *The present state of Virginia*, ed. L. B. Wright, 89, 90.
[60] CO5-1356, p. 76.

to the Assembly. This was received with dismay. They appealed to Effingham and the Council to join them in an address to the King imploring him to restore a privilege enjoyed from the earliest times. But in vain. " It is what I can in no part admit of," was Effingham's curt reply. Since this made the General Court the last court of appeals in Virginia, the structure of justice became aristocratic rather than democratic.

Future Governors had reason to regret this change, for it added greatly to the influence of the Council, and the day was not distant when the Council was to become so powerful as to threaten to make the Governor a mere figurehead. It was the Council which was to be responsible for the dismissal of Andros and Nicholson. Governor Spotswood, in his bitter quarrels with the Councillors tried to undermine their power by striking at their judicial privileges, but he failed, and he too was forced out of office by their influence.

Even more alarming to the people than the ending of appeals to the Assembly was an order from the King that certain causes arising in the courts be referred to England for decision. The Burgesses protested. Such a thing would be "grievous and ruinous," they said, and would involve delays and great expense. Moreover, they could not find that appeals to England had been allowed " from the first settling of the colony." When Effingham and the Council refused to join them, they sent their petition to the King as the protest of the Lower House alone.[61]

But James II, who had succeeded to the throne on the death of Charles in February, received their appeal with contempt. In the new instructions to Effingham drawn up in October, 1685, he wrote: " Whereas . . . our Committee of Trade and Plantations . . . have received from some unknown persons a paper entitled An Address and Supplication of the General Assembly of Virginia to the late King . . . which you have refused to recommend as being unfit . . . we cannot but approve of your proceedings. . . . And we do further direct you to discountenance such undue practices for the future, as also the contrivers and promoters thereof." [62]

At this dark hour, when American liberty hung in the balance, the Burgesses were quick to repel any attempt to tax the people without their consent. In May, 1688, they stated

[61] *Journals of the House of Burgesses*, 1659-1693: 228.
[62] CO5-1357, p. 58.

that they had received " many grievous complaints " that unlawful fees had " under color of his Majesty's royal authority "
been unjustly imposed upon the people. They protested especially against a fee of 200 pounds of tobacco for affixing the great
seal of the colony, a fee of 30 pounds of tobacco for recording
surveys of land, and a fee of £5 for escheats.[63]

And they were adamant in refusing repeated demands for
permission for the Governor and Council by themselves to levy
a tax even though a very small one. " Your Lordships will . . .
find their total denial that the Governor and Council should
have any power to lay the least levy to ease the necessity for so
frequent Assemblys," Effingham wrote the Committee of Trade
and Plantations in February, 1686. " This was propounded by
me to them before his Majesty's instructions came to hand . . .
but nothing would prevail, nor I believe will, unless his Majesty's special command therein." [64]

There was consternation in the Assembly when they learned
that the King was attempting to build up a revenue independent of the Burgesses by increasing the returns from the quit
rents. This tax on land, for such it really was, had always been
paid in tobacco. In 1662 the Assembly had fixed the rate of
payment at twopence a pound, which at that time approximated
the current price. But the decline in the value of the leaf had
greatly lessened the value of the returns. So in 1684 the King
ordered Effingham to accept only specie, " that is to say in
money and not in tobacco or in any other commodity." [65] Since
tobacco was then selling at a halfpenny a pound, this would
have quadrupled the value of the quit rents, imposed a heavy
burden on the impoverished country, and strengthened the
authority of the Governor.

The controversy over this matter led to another and a more
serious encroachment on the rights of the people, for when the
Assembly refused to repeal the law of 1662, the King voided
it by proclamation. Having heard that " persons go about. . .
imposing bad tobacco upon our collectors at the rate of 2d per
pound, under pretence of an act of Assembly . . . we have
thought fit to repeal the said act." [66] Upon receipt of this order
Effingham sent for the Burgesses to meet him in the Council
Chamber. When they filed in he soon found that they were

[63] *Journals of the House of Burgesses*, 1659-1693: 316, 317.
[64] CO5-1357, p. 95.   [65] CO5-1356, p. 282.   [66] CO5-1357, p. 113.

in no mood to yield. Not only did they again refuse to repeal the law of 1662, but they "rudely and boldly disputed the King's authority in repealing laws by proclamation." [67] Moreover, they pointed out, it was impossible to pay in pounds or shillings since there were not enough in the entire colony. This argument was unanswerable, and in the end the Governor was forced to assent to a compromise by which the tax was to be paid in tobacco, but at the rate of one penny per pound instead of two.

The difference in the theories of government held by Charles and James on the one hand, and the people of the colony on the other was brought into focus by a dispute over the King's right to revive a law by repealing a law which had repealed it. When James revived a law of 1680 concerning attorneys by annulling the repealing law of 1682, the Burgesses rose as one man in angry protest. "A law may as well receive its beginning by proclamation as such a revival," they said. "Some Governor may be sent to govern us who under the pretence of the liberty he hath to construe prerogative and stretch it as far as he pleaseth, may by proclamation revive all the laws that for their great inconveniences to the country have been repealed through forty years since." [68]

The Councillors as well as the Burgesses must have been startled when Effingham in reply told them that the King had the right to nullify or revive what laws he pleased, since the only authority the Assembly had to legislate at all rested on a grant from the Throne. They had been under the impression that the right of the people to make laws through their representatives was inherent in all Englishmen. If it were a grant from the King, which the King might at will withdraw, liberty in America rested on a shaky basis indeed. In an address to Effingham they stated that they did not dare "to say what is prerogative and what is not," [69] but they made it clear that when prerogative was stretched so far that it threatened to enslave them, they would resist by every means within their power.

Despots throughout the years have feared a free press, and have either prohibited printing or controlled it for their own purposes. So it was in keeping with the spirit of the Second

[67] *Ibid.*, p. 126.
[68] *Journals of the House of Burgesses*, 1659-1693: 305.
[69] *Ibid.*, 308.

Stuart Despotism that Charles and James would allow no press in Virginia. It was in 1682 that John Buckner, a prominent merchant and landowner of Gloucester County, and a member of the House of Burgesses, employed William Nuthead to set up a printing establishment at Jamestown. But they had picked an inauspicious time for their venture. Nuthead was ordered to appear before the Council " to answer for his presumption in printing the acts of Assembly . . . and several other papers without licence." The Council ordered that " for prevention of all troubles and inconveniences that may be occasioned through the liberty of a press . . . Mr. John Buckner and William Nuthead the printer enter into bond for one hundred pounds sterling . . . that from and after the date hereof nothing be printed by either of them . . . in this colony until the signification of his Majesty's pleasure shall be known." [70]

His Majesty's pleasure therein was a foregone conclusion. " Whereas we have taken notice of the inconvenience that may arise by the liberty of printing in Virginia," stated Charles in his instructions to Effingham, " no person is to be permitted to use any press for printing upon any occasion whatsoever." [71] So Nuthead took the press to Maryland and for nearly half a century Virginia was without a printer. [72]

The quartering of troops upon the people has been a serious grievance wherever it has been practiced. People object to having rough soldiers thrust into their homes, to disrupt their daily life, or perhaps to create disorders. When the British troops sent over to suppress Bacon's Rebellion were quartered on the people, there were bitter complaints. " Instead of being a guard and safety " to us as was intended, " they have by their long stay and ill behavior not only been totally useless, but dangerous," and the greatest of our terrors. [73] To make matters worse, complaints came in to the Assembly from Isle of Wight, York, James City, and Nansemond Counties that payments for quarters were in arrears by six months or more. So it was with thanksgiving that the people received the announcement that the money to pay for the quarters had arrived from England together with orders to disband the troops. [74]

[70] *Executive journals of the Council* 1: 493.
[71] CO5-1356, p. 271.
[72] D. C. McMurtrie, *A history of printing in the United States*, 276-279.
[73] CO5-1376, p. 285.
[74] CO5-1356.

Effingham was even more brazen than Berkeley in using the patronage openly to force obedience to the King. Berkeley ruled chiefly by rewarding those who did as he told them; Effingham by punishing all who opposed him. To acquiesce in everything he proposed was the only way for one to retain one's job. William Sherwood and Colonel Thomas Milner, for forwarding an address of the Burgesses to the Privy Council, were dismissed from office. Mr. Arthur Allen was " turned out of all employment, civil and military " to his great loss, " he being a surveyor of land at that time." [75] Effingham himself explains why. He was " a great promoter of those differences between me and the Assembly concerning the King's negative voice . . . as not thinking it fit that those who are peevishly opposite to his Majesty's interest should have any advantage by his favor." [76]

Another prominent member of the House of Burgesses, Mr. Charles Scarburgh, was " turned out of all employment, and as a mark of his Lordship's displeasure, a command was sent to the clerk of the county to raze his name out of the records as a justice of peace." [77] Mr. William Anderson, Scarburgh's colleague from Accomac County, must have been even more active in opposing the Governor, for when the session of 1688 was over he had him " put in the common jail," where he was " detained seven months without trial, though often prayed for. . . . Nor could he obtain the benefit of habeas corpus." [78]

" From whence the people conclude these severities are inflicted rather as a terror to others than for any personal crimes of their own," it was said, " and is of such ruinous consequence that either the public or particular interests must fall, for if none oppose, the country must languish under the severity of the government, or fly into mutiny to save themselves from starving. If any do appear more zealous in prosecuting the country's complaints they know what to expect. It being observable that none has been thus punished but those who were forward in the Assembly to oppose the encroachments on the people, and promote the complaint to England, being out of hope of relief on the place." [79]

[75] *McDonald papers* 7: 26.
[76] CO5-1357, p. 129.
[77] *McDonald papers* 7: 437-441.
[78] *Ibid.*
[79] *Ibid.*

In Virginia, as in England, there was much dissatisfaction at the accession of the Roman Catholic James II. Many would have preferred Charles' illegitimate son, the Duke of Monmouth. When news came that he had raised the standard of revolt, had landed in Dorset, had gathered an army of rustics, and was marching on London, some did not hesitate to express their sympathy. Effingham wrote that "so many took liberty of speech upon the rebellion ... that I was fearful it would have produced the same here." [80] But when he issued a proclamation forbidding "false, seditious, and factious discourse and rumors," and made "some examples," quiet was restored. The defeat of the rebels at Sedgemoor, the bloody revenge taken by James, and the execution of Monmouth ended all hope for the time being.

But Effingham's proclamation could not prevent news of what was happening in England from reaching the people. In Ireland James was recruiting a Catholic army under a Catholic general. At home he was replacing civil and military officers by Catholics. To remove all restrictions on Catholics he issued declarations of indulgence, giving freedom of worship to dissenters and Catholics. He converted two Oxford colleges into Catholic seminaries, and ousted the Fellows of Magdalen to make room for Catholic successors.

These events were soon reflected in Virginia. It was noted that when important offices in the government became vacant, Effingham filled them with Catholics. Both of his appointees to the Council were members of the Roman Catholic Church— Colonel Isaac Allerton and Colonel John Armistead. That several justices of the peace refused to take the oath of allegiance "through scruple of conscience" in 1691, after James had been deposed, shows that the Governor tried also to pack the county courts with Catholics.

The people watched these developments with resentment, mixed with fear. The shudder of horror which had gone through England a few years before, when Titus Oates accused the Jesuits of a "hellish plot" to fire London, conquer the country with Irish and French armies, and massacre the Protestants, was still fresh in men's minds. Perhaps his story is not false after all, it was whispered. Perhaps the plan may still be carried out. Think of what has just happened in France, where

[80] *Executive journals of the Council* 1: 75.

thousands of men and women, for refusing to give up their faith were driven into exile or thrown into loathsome prisons with criminals, starved, and beaten. Are we sure that it will not be our turn next?

The Assembly which met in April, 1688, reflected the ugly mood of the people. They were determined to redress the grievances which poured in from one county after another. The Governor's appeal for aid for New York and for a bill to prohibit the exportation of loose tobacco received scant consideration. " Debates of grievances jostled out most other matters," reported Nicholas Spencer.[81] When the Council requested a conference on the tobacco bill, the House countered with a proposal for a conference on the people's wrongs. But their message was couched in such bitter terms that the Council thought " no success could be expected from a conference agitated with heat and resolvedness." [82]

Nor would the Council join the Burgesses in an address to Effingham for redress of " the many grievous oppressions this poor country at present groans under." Thereupon the House drew up a petition to the King which they entrusted to Philip Ludwell to deliver. Before James could reply, he was forced to flee from England, and it was only in February, 1689, that the petition came before the Council of State.

Such was the situation when Effingham left Virginia " for recovery of his health by change of air." He may have realized also that the air of Virginia was becoming unhealthful for him in more sense than one, for had he not left it is possible that the people might have risen in arms and sent him home. Several years later, when Francis Nicholson asked the Council whether " if his Excellency my Lord Effingham had stayed " the country would not have been in trouble? they replied in the affirmative. " The country were in great dissatisfaction . . . and there was great cause to doubt that some disturbance would have been." [83]

But it was only in the spring of 1689, some months after his departure, that an uprising actually occurred. Then it was touched off by a weird story told by a stray Indian to some of the settlers on the northern frontier of a plot by Jesuits and Indians to attack Virginia and Maryland. No less than 10,000

[81] CO5-1357, p. 214.   [83] CO5-1306, Doc. 114.
[82] Ibid., p. 216.

Senecas and 9,000 Nanticocks were under arms, he said, ready to cut off all the Protestants. As the report spread from plantation to plantation, the outlying families fled in terror, while men gathered volunteers by beat of drum. We must defend ourselves in arms, they said, since no reliance can be placed on the Council or even on the county magistrates, for most of them are Catholics.

The Council thought the story of the Catholic plot " only a gloss to their rebellious purposes." In October, 1688, James had sent word to Effingham that William of Orange was preparing to invade England, and had ordered him to place the colony in a posture of defence.[84] It was to seize this opportunity to rise against the government, rather than the imaginary Indian plot, that had made them take up arms, the Council thought. Preferring not to take sides in a matter which could be settled only in England, they arrested some of the ringleaders.[85] But when, apparently on the same day, a letter came to hand from the Privy Council, announcing that William and Mary had been proclaimed joint monarchs of England, order was instantly restored. On April 26, 1688, their Majesties were proclaimed before the courthouse door at Jamestown.

There were two things which the colonial Virginians dreaded —despotism and the tomahawk. And it is significant that both were factors in the two uprisings of the seventeenth century. In Bacon's Rebellion the people demanded, not only protection from the savages, but an end to Berkeley's misgovernment. If the Council was right in their interpretation of the disorders of 1688, they, like the ousting of Andros in New England, were a part of the Glorious Revolution. The Council afterwards took great credit for suppressing the disorders, but one can only surmise whether the people would have remained quiet had not James been overthrown. We must not permit the Indian terror to blind us to the fact that the rebellions of 1676 and 1688 were both in defense of liberty.

[84] CO5-1357, p. 229.
[85] *Executive journals of the Council* 1: 105.

CHAPTER VII

THE GLORIOUS REVOLUTION

THE GLORIOUS REVOLUTION completely changed the relations between the English people and the King. No sooner had James fled than a committee of the Commons drew up a "Declaration of Rights," to secure the liberty of the subjects and the power of Parliament, which was accepted by both Houses and by William. Parliament then declared William and Mary joint monarchs. Mary could argue that as the child of James II she was the rightful heir to the Throne, but William could make no such claim. So the old Tory doctrine of divine right was officially repudiated, and the monarch henceforth ruled by the consent of the nation. The Revolution opened a new epoch of liberty.

The people of Virginia were well aware that they were to share in this liberty. In an address to the King and Queen, the Assembly gave them heartfelt thanks for "so magnanimously exposing" their persons in rescuing them, their religion, laws, and liberties from the twin evils of slavery and popery. They begged them, while extending their justice and goodness over the English nation, not to forget their faithful subjects in Virginia. They, too, were "descended of Englishmen," and had the right to enjoy "the just and lawful liberties and privileges of free born" Englishmen.[1]

In this they were not disappointed. During the next seventy-five years they advanced steadily along the road to liberty. From time to time they had to contend with despotically inclined Governors, but these men, prior to the reign of George III, in assailing the rights of the people acted on their own initiative rather than at the command of the King. By the middle of the eighteenth century Virginia had become in internal affairs practically a self-governing dominion. People began to say openly that final authority rested, not with the King, but with the people, and that governments derived their powers from the consent of the governed.

[1] *Journals of the House of Burgesses*, 1660-1693: 370.

This trend was noted early in the eighteenth century. As early as 1706 Colonel Quary warned the English government of what was coming. A few years later Governor Spotswood wrote: " If the ancient and legal rights of the Crown must give place to the later customs of an infant colony, especially if the practice and usage which . . . men would introduce shall be of greater force, the prince's power and authority must daily lose ground here." [2]

It was a slow, almost imperceptible process. But year after year the Burgesses whittled away at the powers of the Governor, until, after the passage of decades, the change became apparent to all. Berkeley, Culpeper, and Effingham had exercised almost dictatorial powers; Gooch, Fauquier, and Botetourt ate out of the hands of the Assembly. Whereas the Governors of the seventeenth century commanded and threatened, those of the mid-eighteenth century pleaded. On one occasion Governor Fauquier wrote the Lords of Trade that he had signed a bill, not because he aproved of it, but because had he vetoed it he " must have despaired of ever gaining any influence either in the Council or House of Burgesses."

The shouting and firing of guns in celebration of the accession of William and Mary had hardly ended when the Virginians turned their thoughts to the long desired new charter. The Bill of Rights gave them as well as Englishmen residing in England guarantees of liberty, but they had distinctive interests which they thought ought to be protected. Appointing Jeffrey Jeffreys to manage the affair, the Council and Burgesses sent him £200 for expenses and suggested that he call to his support any Virginians who chanced to be in London. That the art of lobbying was as well understood in the seventeenth century as it is today is shown by their instruction " to procure the assistance . . . of the nobility and such as have offices at Whitehall and other men of note . . . to be mediators with their Majesties." [3]

The proposed charter was to confirm the authority of the Assembly. At first sight this would seem to be unnecessary since the Assembly had been in existence since 1619, and had been recognized by James I, Charles I, Charles II, and James II. But the attempts to undermine its authority during the Second

[2] CO5-1318.
[3] *Journals of the House of Burgesses*, 1660-1693: 352.

Stuart Despotism had convinced the people that its very existence might be threatened by some future King.

They asked, also, that in the charter it be promised " that
no tax be made upon this country but by the consent of the
Assembly." The people had been deeply disappointed that a
like promise had been left out of the charter of 1676. They
took for granted that Parliament would not violate their rights
as Englishmen by taxing them, but it would have comforted
them to have it down in black and white. How necessary such
a guarantee was became apparent eighty-five years later with
the passage of the Stamp Act.

The charter was to promise, also, that the King and Queen
would continue to the Virginians and their descendants their
rights as natural born subjects of England, and that as " near
as may be " they should be governed after the same method as
Englishmen, and " have the full benefit of the Great Charter
and all other laws and statutes indulging the liberty of the
subjects." Jeffreys was to ask that " the ancient method " of
making appeals from the General Court to the Assembly be
restored, since appeals to the Privy Council were in most cases
impractical because of the expense involved and the difficulty
of bringing " evidences, papers, and other records " to England.[4]

We do not know why the application for the charter was
dropped. It may have been because Jeffreys found that it would
not meet with success, or the Assembly may have been persuaded that a charter was unnecessary under the liberal administration of the new monarchs.

Francis Nicholson, who had been selected to serve as Lieutenant Governor during Effingham's absence, arrived in Virginia in May, 1690. The choice was unfortunate. This man
was a strange mixture of contrasting characteristics. A devoted
Church of England man and a friend of the clergy, he was at
times shockingly profane. One of the patrons of the College of
William and Mary, and the founder of the city of Williamsburg, he was unscrupulous in trampling on the rights of all
who opposed him. Seeking the admiration of those with whom
he was associated, he alienated his best friends by his fits of
uncontrollable temper. Capable of acts of great generosity, he
was accused of being parsimonious in his private life.

Nicholson's treatment of the Reverend Mr. Slaughter was

[4] *Journals of the House of Burgesses, 1660-1693: 352.*

typical. He and a certain Captain James Moodie had gone to
York to a funeral. "The ceremony and sermon being over,"
Moodie relates, "he went out of church, where he saw and
heard the Governor in the most outrageous passion that he
ever saw, swearing the most horrid oaths and most bitter imprecations against Mr. Slaughter, the minister of that parish,
calling the said Slaughter rogue, rascal, knave, and all the base
billingsgate language that could be in the basest of men's
mouths, shaking his horsewhip and threatening to beat the said
minister therewith, and to pull his gown over his ears." [5]
Apparently Mr. Slaughter had brought on this torrent of abuse
by asking for a fee for the funeral sermon.

Nicholson's conduct as Deputy Governor of New York under
Sir Edmund Andros at the time of the Glorious Revolution was
not such as to inspire confidence that he would do well in
Virginia. With no official orders to proclaim William and
Mary, and with the people ready to rush to arms, what was
needed was tact and conciliatory measures. Instead, Nicholson
flew into a rage and talked about suppressing the "uproar and
rebellion." It was rumored that he planned to burn the city,
and that the people were to be betrayed and murdered. When
some armed men, under the German merchant Jacob Leisler,
seized the fort, Nicholson deserted his post and took ship for
England.[6]

The first meeting of the Council after Nicholson arrived at
Jamestown was held on January 3, 1690. After he had shown
his commission, he and the Councillors went to the courthouse
where it was read to the people assembled there. If the Virginians had been prejudiced against the new Lieutenant Governor by reports of his conduct in New York, they could not
have been reassured by his personal appearance. It was said
that when he made a bow to the ladies, he looked like a goose
picking up straws.

Nicholson began his administration with a due regard to the
influence of the Council. He had noticed that some of them
held large tracts of land for which they paid no quit rents, and
he pointed out, in a letter to the Earl of Nottingham, that it
would strengthen the hands of the Governor if they were forced
to pay up. "But the great men being concerned, I dare not

[5] CO5-1314, Doc. 9.
[6] *Documentary history of New York* 2: 25, 31, 42, 181-183.

venture to put any new method in execution without an instruction." [7]

He was equally cautious at first to defer to the Council in making appointments. When the sheriff of Middlesex died, he asked those Councillors who lived in that part of the country to nominate his successor. When they suggested Mr. Robert Dudley, Nicholson at once gave him a commission. At the same meeting he pointed out that the regular time for naming sheriffs and coroners was at hand, and asked that the Councillors be prepared to make nominations at their next meeting. [8]

But it was not long before he began to use the patronage to build up his own power under the guise of defending the royal prerogative. When the oath of supremacy was tendered the members of the Council, Richard Lee, Isaac Allerton, and John Armistead refused to take it because they were Roman Catholics. Nicholson filled one vacancy by naming Attorney General Edmund Jenings. He then sent a list of four other prominent men to the King and Queen, with the suggestion that they select the other two from it. Three of the four deserved well, he pointed out, because in the House of Burgesses they had been "for their Majesties' interest." Colonel Thomas Milner, the Speaker, behaved very well too, but he hath not estate enough to be a Councillor. But he should have promise of some place of profit." [9]

We have no evidence that Nicholson tried to build up a party in the House of Burgesses by distributing sheriff's places to the members. But he did try to ingratiate himself by hobnobbing with them and "admitting" them daily to his table. This he did, he said, in order to keep a good agreement with them for their Majesties' service and advance the public affairs of the country, and not to propose or gain anything to be done in the Assembly. But the fact that he used the same technique to gain power during his second administration, makes his protestations seem rather hollow.

Nicholson claimed great success for his administration. He had befriended the clergy and bettered their condition, he pointed out, he had "looked after their Majesties' revenue," and left it in excellent condition, he had reorganized the

[7] CO5-1306, Doc. 64.
[8] *Executive journals of the Council* 1: 158.
[9] CO5-1306, Doc. 41.

militia. But he admitted, in fact boasted, that he had defended the royal prerogative on all occasions. He might have added that he had given Commissary Blair his wholehearted support in his efforts to found a college.

When Nicholson heard that Effingham had retired as Governor General of Virginia, and that he had been succeeded by Sir Edmund Andros, he was bitterly disappointed. As Lieutenant Governor under Effingham, he thought that when the government became vacant it was his due. He was especially disgruntled that Andros had been selected since he had against him a long standing pique. Yet he made the best of the situation, greeted Andros upon his arrival, and, at the head of the James City County militia, escorted him to Jamestown "through the several counties which were in his way." [10]

It must have been with apprehension that the Virginians received Sir Edmund, for reports of his despotism in New England had preceded him. They had heard that there he ruled like an Eastern despot, promulgating laws, levying taxes without the consent of the Assemblies, placing men under arrest and denying them the right of *habeas corpus*. And they knew that the Bostonians had at last captured him, put him aboard a vessel, and shipped him back to England. The Virginians were ready to offer stiff resistance should he try to rule them with a harsh hand.

So they were surprised to find Andros a mild mannered man, who not only made no attack on their liberty, but tried to live in peace with both Council and Burgesses. He seems not to have used the patronage to build up his power, nor to have broken the grip of the House on the purse by demanding large fees; he would have allowed the Burgesses to appoint their own clerk had his instructions permitted it, and he carefully kept off the explosive subject of the arrears of quit rents. Edward Randolph summed it up by saying that he had "mightily gained upon the Council and chief men in the country by his even temper." [11]

Nothing can illustrate better the progress made in self-government in Virginia since the overthrow of James II than the Burgesses' cavalier treatment of two bills recommended by the King and Queen. The first, a bill to prohibit the exportation

[10] *Sainsbury papers* 5: 100.
[11] A. T. S. Goodrick, *Edward Randolph* 7: 430.

of loose tobacco, was greatly desired by the English merchants. The other, a bill to establish ports in the Virginia rivers, had been passed in 1688 by the Assembly, and was now returned for certain revisions before becoming law. The Burgesses promptly voted down both measures. " The appointment of ports and enjoining the landing and shipping of all goods . . . from the same will . . . be very injurious and burdensome," they said. There was a long debate on the question of prohibiting the exportation of loose tobacco, but this bill too failed to pass. Andros was deeply concerned at this disregard of the royal wishes, but when the Council advised him that nothing more could be done with the Burgesses, he dissolved them." [12]

The British government also decided that it was best not to press the matter. In 1695 Andros spoke of the King's " goodness in dispensing with his prerogative " to establish ports without the consent of the Assembly, and leaving it to our choice, and also in waiving the prohibition of bulk tobacco so earnestly desired in England because it was found not pleasing here." But the victory of the Burgesses riled Edward Randolph. " They are full of conceit, and fancy themselves as great as the House of Commons in England," he said in disgust.[13]

It is probable that the King was so lenient with the Assembly because he wanted them to vote men and money to assist New York in her struggle with the French and Indians. Andros did his best, pointing out that New York was a bulwark for Virginia, and that if she fell the war cry would soon be heard on the Virginia frontier. The Burgesses were not convinced. The situation in New York was not so desperate as had been represented; they denied that New York was the " bulwark and defense of Virginia "; they were at heavy expense to guard their own frontier. It was characteristic of Andros that he asked the Council to reply for him. The Councillors at heart were no doubt as reluctant as the Burgesses to send aid to New York, but they were in the position of royal advocates and put up the best argument they could. Yet the session ended without anything being done.[14]

When the Assembly met in 1695, Andros had better success. He had been instructed by the King to send a quota of men

[12] *Sainsbury papers* 5: 165.
[13] A. T. S. Goodrick, *Edward Randolph* 7: 448.
[14] *Journals of the House of Burgesses*, 1659-1693: 292, 482-493.

from the Virginia militia whenever the Governor of New York asked for them, he said. This alarmed the Burgesses. They thought it would not only weaken the defense of Virginia by taking away so many men, but would so frighten the young freemen that many would desert their wives and children and leave the colony. In the end they compromised by voting £500 in lieu of men.[15] This Andros was forced to accept, though by so doing he brought on himself a reprimand from the Committee of Trade.[16]

It is strange that Andros, who was so moderate in his dealings with the House of Burgesses, and declared that he never thought himself better than when he had them about him to consult for the good of the country, should have bearded them on one of their most sensitive points—the appointment of a Treasurer. In 1691 the Assembly passed two laws, one for levying a poll tax, and one laying a duty on liquors, both of which were to be " paid by the collectors thereof to the Treasurer." Included in the act was the naming of Colonel Edward Hill as Treasurer.[17]

A year later, when Nicholson gave him a lucrative job as collector, Hill had to vacate this office, since it was unlawful for the same man to hold both. To act as Treasurer until the Assembly convened, the Governor named one of the Council, Henry Whiting. When the Burgesses met they questioned Whiting's authority, but he satisfied them by showing them his commission. They then passed a bill to name a permanent Treasurer, but the Council, probably at Andros' urging, refused to concur. " The Governor would never consent to the Assembly's appointing their own Treasurer but would rather lose a tax than suffer them to do so," James Blair testified. But, he added: " This makes them suspicious and more unwilling to raise money." [18]

Whiting held the office until his death, which occurred probably in September, 1694. Then, for several years, there seems to have been no Treasurer. But the Burgesses were merely biding their time. Their opportunity came in 1699. The old statehouse at Jamestown had burned down, and there was urgent need for an appropriation to build a new one. They passed a bill placing a duty on the importation of servants and slaves,

[15] *Ibid.*, 1695-1702: 9-42.
[16] CO5-1359, p. 79.
[17] *Journals of the House of Burgesses*, 1659-1693: 360.
[18] CO5-1359, pp. 101, 102.

and laying a levy by poll, the revenue from both to be paid into the hands of the Treasurer for financing a new Capitol. Since there was no Treasurer they included in the act the appointment of Colonel Robert Carter to that office. The Governor and Council, realizing that they could not have the Capitol without the Treasurer, yielded.[19]

The undoing of Andros was his quarrel with the Reverend James Blair, Commissary for the Bishop of London in Virginia. When this rugged Scotsman came to the colony he found conditions in the Church far from satisfactory. Since there was no college in the colony the parishes were entirely dependent upon England for their ministers. The dispersal of the people was such that if a parish were large enough to provide the rector with an adequate living, it was too large for him to minister to properly. Some parishes extended forty miles or more along the banks of the great Virginia rivers, the minister was usually too poor to have a library or to marry. Since English clergymen were reluctant to come over under such conditions, there were many vacant parishes. Often the vestries in desperation were forced to accept any that offered themselves, however unsuitable. There were many able and pious ministers in Virginia, but some were of inferior ability, and a few were a disgrace to their calling. And it was inevitable that amid the woods and tobacco fields of a new country they should neglect many features of the liturgy—the use of vestments, the observance of the saints' days, burial in consecrated ground, etc.

With the enthusiastic support of the Bishop of London and of Governor Nicholson, Blair had worked out a plan of reform. He would found a college to educate young Virginians for the ministry; he would secure an act of Assembly increasing the ministers' salary; he would enforce ecclesiastical discipline; he would give the clergy a voice in the government by procuring a seat in the Council for the Commissary. Going to England, he gained the backing of the Archbishop of Canterbury and other prelates, and through them of King William and Queen Mary.[20]

Their Majesties granted a charter for the college, permitted it to be named William and Mary, gave £1,985.14.10 out of the quit rent fund, 10,000 acres of land, the revenue of one pence a

[19] W. W. Hening, *Statutes at large* 3: 197, 198.
[20] T. J. Wertenbaker, *The first Americans*, 133.

pound on tobacco exported from Virginia to any other colony, and a salary for the Commissary from the quit rents. So Blair returned in triumph and took his seat beside the great men of the Council. But it was a triumph which won him the enmity of Andros. The Governor, no doubt, was jealous of his influence in high circles in England, and he viewed with alarm the diversion from the use of the government to the college and the clergy of urgently needed funds. With the opening of the year 1694 the government was facing a deficit with no way of meeting it except by the hated levy by poll, or by drawing on the quit rents.

Soon Blair was complaining that Andros was trying to obstruct his reforms for the clergy. There must have been stormy scenes in the Council meetings, with Blair hurling accusations at the Governor, and the latter denying them. The President of the College " could not be obliged by all endeavors to contain himself within bounds," wrote Andros to Secretary Shrewsbury. " His restless comport I ever passed by till the whole Council . . . faulting him as unfit to be in the Council, I thought it my duty . . . to suspend him." [21]

But Andros did not reckon on Blair's influence in England. Undoubtedly the Commissary wrote the Bishop of London of his suspension, and the Bishop complained to the Lords of Trade. In due time Andros received a rebuke from the King. He had appointed Blair to the Council " the better to enable him to promote and carry on " the " good and useful " work of founding a college. Now he found that his gracious intentions had been discouraged by his suspension. " Our will and pleasure is that forthwith upon the receipt hereof you take off the said suspension." [22] It was a bitter humiliation for Andros when, in August, 1696, Blair produced the King's letter and resumed his seat.[23] So bitter, in fact, that he dared a second time to oust the hated Commissary. At a meeting of the Council in April, 1697, Blair asked whether a recent act of Parliament did not debar him from sitting in the General Court since he was a native of Scotland. Whereupon the Council, with a promptness he probably did not expect, voted that not only did

[21] Sainsbury papers 5: 225, 226.
[22] Ibid., 236.
[23] Executive journals of the Council 1: 350, 352.

it do so, but that it made him ineligible for the Council as well.[24]

Blair's answer was to take ship for England, there to lay his complaints before the English prelates and through them before the Board of Trade. To the Archbishop of Canterbury, the Bishop of Salisbury, and the Bishop of London he undoubtedly poured out his complaints of Andros—that he was an enemy of the college, that he did not support the efforts to secure better livings for the clergy, that he had disobeyed the King's express orders to keep him in the Council. This ecclesiastical lobby was too much for Sir Edmund. Seeing the handwriting on the wall, he wrote that he wished to come home because of ill health. On May 31, 1698, his resignation was accepted and Francis Nicholson named to succeed him as Governor General.[25]

When Andros bade Jamestown goodbye and set sail for England, a full decade had passed since the Glorious Revolution, time sufficient for one to judge its effect upon self-government in Virginia. Some of the losses of the Second Stuart Despotism had not been regained. The act of 1680 giving the Crown a perpetual revenue had not been repealed; the judicial powers of the Assembly had not been restored; the efforts to secure a charter for the colony had been abandoned; the Burgesses had not regained the right to name their clerk.

Yet the gains far outweighed these failures. Of first importance was it that the Assembly itself had been preserved with most of its rights and privileges. It still could initiate legislation, it alone could initiate money bills, it could determine the uses of all appropriated funds, it could appoint the Treasurer. The petitions of the Assembly to the Throne were no longer cast aside with scorn as in the days of Charles II and James II, but were given careful consideration. The battle for liberty had not yet been won, many bitter struggles lay ahead, but the gains made under the mild rule of King William and Queen Mary were vital to the eventual victory.

[24] *Ibid.*, 364.
[25] CO5-1359, p. 208.

CHAPTER VIII

THE VIRGINIA HITLER

IT was James Blair who was chiefly responsible for the appointment of Francis Nicholson as Governor General of Virginia. Nicholson's hearty support for his plans to found a college and better the condition of the clergy when he was Lieutenant Governor, made the Commissary eager to have him back. So when Andros resigned, he used his influence with the Bishop of London, who was one of the Commissioners of Trade, to have him made his successor.

It seems strange that one identified with the interests of Virginia should have foisted on the colony one of the worst Governors in its history. But at the time Blair seems to have permitted the man's good qualities—his undoubted ability, his energy, and his devotion to the Church—to blind him to his many faults. Blair himself admitted this later after he came into violent conflict with Nicholson, and wrote to the Bishop of London in a repentant mood.

The new Governor General arrived in Virginia in the winter of 1698. He found that the personnel of the Council had been greatly changed during his absence. But there were several familiar faces in the group which met in the great hall of the residence of the late William Sherwood. Nicholson then announced the King's appointments to the Council and administered the oath required by Parliament to those who were present. One wonders whether Matthew Page and Benjamin Harrison, in their elation at being elevated to the "Virginia House of Lords," suspected that it would involve them in bitter controversy with the Governor, or that they, together with four of their fellow Councillors, would be responsible for his removal from office.

There was nothing basically despotic in the program Nicholson outlined for himself. He sought to set the finances of the colony in order by eliminating frauds and demanding a strict payment of quit rents so as to increase the royal revenue. He was determined to uphold the King's prerogative against all assaults by the Council or the Burgesses. He wished to put the colony in a state of readiness to repel any attack by hostile Indians, and to aid other colonies who should become involved in Indian wars. He tried to gain permanent tenure for the clergy so as to give them a degree of independence of the vestries. He planned a new city which was to be the seat of government, with broad streets and charming Capitol and Governor's mansion.

Since certain features of this program ran counter to the interests of the Council, and others to those of the people, to carry them through would have required resolution, tact, moderation, and ability to handle men. Resolution Nicholson had in abundance, but in other respects he was entirely unsuited for the task he set himself. To vilify men, to call them rascals, to threaten to lash them with his whip was not the way to handle the liberty-loving Virginians. His attempts to bribe the Councillors and the Burgesses with fat jobs and to pack the courts with favorites, might have been more successful had they not been accompanied with such violent bursts of temper and such threats of ruin against any who opposed him.

It so happened that the Committee of Trade, finding that the amount of tobacco received in England was far greater than that on which the export duty was paid in Virginia, became convinced that there were great frauds in collections. The fault lay with the naval officers and collectors, they thought. They instructed Nicholson not to appoint the same person to both offices, and not to permit members of the Council to hold either. When the Governor, not wishing to offend, at first failed to comply, they gave him a severe rebuke. In June, 1699, he was forced to turn several Councillors out of their lucrative jobs.

This drew from them a violent protest. They denied that they had any knowledge of frauds in the collections. To forbid Councillors to hold these positions was to reverse the custom of many years. The income was their only compensation for their expense in journeying perhaps seventy miles, perhaps one hundred miles, in some cases crossing great rivers, to attend meetings of the Council and the General Court. And though they could not directly blame Nicholson, they probably suspected that it was at his suggestion that the instruction had been made. So it was a soured and discontented group of men who dispersed to return to their homes after the Council meeting ended.

The Old Capitol at Williamsburg, showing the north elevation which is a duplicate of the historic Virginia Capitol originally completed in 1705. Courtesy of Colonial Williamsburg, Inc.

The House of Burgesses in the Old Capitol at Williamsburg.   Courtesy of Colonial Williamsburg, Inc.

Nicholson's efforts to secure more accurate returns of the quit rents did not put them in better humor. It was well known that it was a common practice for men to "conceal" part of their holdings when the sheriff came round to collect the rent, and, if the sheriff happened to be a friend or a relative, he would not look into the matter too closely. As for the great tracts held by the wealthy, the sheriffs dared not demand the rent. To do so would certainly be bitterly resented and might cost them their jobs. Nicholson was convinced that a strict accounting would greatly increase the returns.

When he was Lieutenant Governor he had tried to force the large landholders to pay their rents by taking the matter into the courts. Making a test case of Colonel Lawrence Smith, who had several large properties, he ordered the Attorney General to prosecute him. The case was ready for trial when Nicholson was removed and it was afterwards compounded for a small sum.[1]

At the time Nicholson had had some thoughts of drawing up "an exact, true, and perfect rent roll." But the Council, who had no desire to have their own "concealed" acres exposed, pointed out that it would be a difficult and costly undertaking. So for the time being the matter was dropped. But when Nicholson began his second administration he resumed his efforts. He instructed William Byrd, the Auditor, to order the sheriffs to make accurate rolls of holdings in their counties. But as late as October, 1703, Byrd reported that though he had urged this on the sheriffs he realized that there was "still very great abuse therein."[2] Yet the next year the Governor had in his hands a rent roll, which, however imperfect, must have been of great value in the collection of the rents. Undoubtedly much of the unoccupied lands were not put down on the rolls, yet some of the members of the Council were hard hit. Byrd now had to pay on 20,700 acres, Custis on 12,600, Harrison on 9,100, and the others on holdings ranging from 2,000 to 7,000 acres. Other members of the aristocracy, many of them related to one or more Councillors, were put down for thousands of acres. Lewis Burwell had 7,000 acres in the Isle of Wight County, 4,800 acres in King William, 3,300 acres in Gloucester, 2,100 acres in York, and 1,300 in James City County.[3]

[1] CO5-1309, Doc. 9.   [2] CO5-1339, Doc. 33 V.
[3] T. J. Wertenbaker, *Planters of colonial Virginia*, 183, 247.

Having alienated the Councillors and other influential men by striking at their pocketbooks, Nicholson proceeded to cross swords with another influential group—the vestrymen. The Virginia clergymen had long complained of the insecurity of their tenure, for the vestries who appointed them claimed the right also of dismissing them when they proved unsatisfactory. " They are to their vestries in the nature of hired servants, agreed with from year to year, and dismissed . . . without any crime proved or so much as alleged against them," Commissary Blair complained.

Claiming that whenever a vestry failed to present their minister to him for induction, he had the right to fix him on them for life by collation, Nicholson appealed to Sir Edward Northey, Attorney General of England. Northey's opinion supported him fully, and in triumph the Governor sent copies to all the vestries. But he met with one rebuff after another. We " do not think it proper, neither are we willing to make presentation for induction," replied one vestry. Another declared that the word induction sounded very harsh in their ears, and as for collation they hoped the Governor would not try it. And Nicholson, realizing that, if he should, the vestry would refuse to pay his appointee his salary and so starve him out, was forced to let the matter drop.

Despite his efforts for the clergy, the Governor managed to change the friendship of the man who was so largely responsible for his appointment into bitter hatred. Blair turned against him because he took over many functions rightly belonging to the Commissary and tried to make himself head of the Church. " He has invaded almost all . . . parts of the ecclesiastical jurisdiction," Blair complained, " such as convoking the clergy, . . . appearing himself in their meetings and proposing the subject matter of their consultations, . . . requiring of some ministers canonical obedience to himself as their bishop, taking upon himself to turn out ministers." [4]

This was followed by an attempt to take out of the hands of the Councillors the control of the military forces of the colony. In the summer of 1701, when England was on the verge of war with France, word reached Virginia that a French fleet was preparing to sail for the West Indies. Claiming that there was

[4] T. J. Wertenbaker, Attempt to reform the church of colonial Virginia, *Sewanee Review* 25: 273-275.

danger that they might attack Virginia, " being an open and defenseless country," Nicholson organized a new force to resist them. He ordered the captains of militia to pick out every fifth man in their companies, " being persons young, brisk, fit, and able to go out to war," and organize them into bands of thirty, mounted and fully equipped.[5]

Thus the militia, who were largely under the command of members of the Council, were to be superseded by a new force under Nicholson himself. The people became alarmed when it was rumored that he was trying to persuade the English government to keep a standing army in America with himself as Captain General. If he succeeds, men told each other, we may as well bid goodbye to liberty, for then he will carry out his threats of taking and arming all our servants, of bringing the Burgesses with ropes about the necks, and daring the Assembly to " deny him anything." [6]

When the war with France began and the attack fell, not on Virginia, but on New York, King William asked the Assembly to give financial aid. But the Burgesses refused, pointing out that they needed all their resources to protect their own exposed frontier. It is possible that it was because this answer interfered with his own ambition that it was so displeasing to Nicholson. His Majesty should signify his resentment and order the Burgesses on their allegiance to comply, he thought, " and I hope in God that they will then " do so.[7] Losing his temper, as he always did when opposed, he threatened to draft men, even members of the House, on his own authority and send them to fight in New York. Much more to his credit was his action in advancing £900 to New York out of his own pocket.

It is probable that Nicholson, when he had cooled off, had no real intention of carrying out his threats against the Burgesses, but he did try to control them by a brazen use of the patronage. Of twenty-two sheriffs whom he appointed in June, 1699, no less than sixteen were Burgesses. Ignoring the advice of the Council, he put men in or turned them out as they voted as he directed. During one session of the Assembly, when seven of the Burgesses were county clerks, he had seven blank commissions made out and placed in the Secretary's office where all

[5] CO5-1409, p. 135A.   [7] CO5-1360, p. 117.
[6] CO5-1314, Doc. 35, IIb.

could see them. Then he spread the report that any or all of the clerks who proved to be " bad boys " were to be dismissed and the commissions given to those who behaved better.[8]

" Are not all the places of profit in the hands of the Governor? " it was asked.[9] The sheriff of King and Queen County was arbitrarily removed when he was busy collecting the poll tax. If it happened that one of Nicholson's favorites was legally ineligible for an office he would give him a blank commission and tell him to fill it in with the name of a relative or friend, or even to sell it. Colonel John West was stated to have sold a sheriff's commission for 8,000 pounds of tobacco.[10]

The members of the House who were deaf to his threats and promises, the Governor tried to wheedle. " We have a way of treating three days in a week all the Assembly time," said Harrison, " where some of the House constantly attend to get their bellies full of victuals and too many times their heads full of strong drink." [11]

Fearing that even such measures would not avail if a hostile House were returned, the Governor interfered actively in the elections. " We have had an election of Burgesses . . . in which there hath been . . . promises, threats, spreading scandalous reports . . . browbeating . . . and what not," Philip Ludwell, Junior, wrote his father. Nicholson had been in Charles City County to oppose the election of Benjamin Harrison, promising sheriff's and clerk's places to some and threatening others. " Having rid all through Charles City, from house to house, he went to Surry." Here he commanded the sheriff to draw up a list of those who spoke ill of Major Allen, the candidate he favored. When Major Thomas Swan was elected, he forbade the sheriff " at his peril " to return him. And he told the sheriff of James City County that he could not serve two masters, and if Benjamin Harrison were chosen, he need never expect any more favors from him.[12]

In his dealing with the House of Burgesses, the Governor sacrificed any influence he had built up, by his disregard of their privileges and his violent abuse of individual members and of the body as a whole. His agent in London, John Thrale, saw no reason why the Burgesses should be angered at him

[8] CO5-1314, Doc. D10.
[9] Ibid., Doc. 15G.
[10] CO5-1314, Doc. 36.
[11] Ibid., Doc. 15G.
[12] Ibid., Doc. 15.

for proposing a tax bill. If Mr. Thrale knew how they disliked those levy bills which arose outside the House, he would change his mind, Philip Ludwell pointed out.[13] In one of his fits of temper Nicholson threatened to cut the Speaker's throat.[14]

In the General Court Nicholson made free use of threats and promises to secure verdicts to his liking. Robert Beverley said it was his constant practice to browbeat and vilify both lawyers and their clients. Two cases, especially, he managed with such violence " that there was not one person in court, favorite or foe, but thought it very hard and unjust dealing." One case had to be postponed several times because as soon as it came up he flew into such a rage that the court had to adjourn.[15]

Nicholson threw one suit out of court without even consulting the other judges. In another he pleaded " from the bench more like a party than a judge and flew into great heats and passions." In the case of Swan *versus* Wilson, he grossly abused Swan's attorney. When the verdict went for Swan, Wilson's attorney said there had been an error in form. To this Harrison replied that the form had been in keeping with Virginia practice. Instantly Nicholson turned on him, thundering out: " Sir, you are the Queen's counsel and pretend to set up a precedent in Virginia contrary to the practice in England. You shall not impose upon me with your tricks and equivocations." [16] On another occasion he became so enraged against Mr. Bartholomew Fowler, one of the attorneys, " a very sickly, weak man," that he seized him by the collar and shook him, swearing that his commands must be obeyed without hesitation or reserve.[17]

If we may believe Robert Beverley, the Governor made a habit of packing the grand jury, in order to get flattering addresses from them. He would pick out men whom he knew he could influence, send for them to come to Williamsburg, and order the sheriff to put them on the jury in place of others of whom he was doubtful. Beverley was talking with a man whom the sheriff had summoned and then had discharged, when the sheriff happened to pass. So the man stopped him to ask why he had done it. He replied that the Governor had ordered him to do it. When the jury he had selected for the

[13] CO5-1314, Doc. 17.
[14] *Ibid.*, Doc. 35 II 6.
[15] *Ibid.*, Doc. 10.
[16] *Ibid.*, Doc. 23.
[17] *Ibid.*, Doc. 24.

purpose gave him the address he wanted, he showered them with favors. To the foreman he gave a naval officer's place, others he "favored by barefaced methods" in cases at law in which they were concerned, still others had sheriff's places.[18]

Nicholson's greatest blunder was to antagonize the Council. Its members, representing the Virginia aristocracy, and having influential friends at Court, were not the men to sit quietly and see their hard-earned privileges taken from them. Is the Council so mean spirited as to let a Governor do all the ill things he pleases in their names, and all the while using them like slaves, not suffering them to have any opinion of their own? Philip Ludwell asked. "Arbitrary power is grown to a high pitch among us. Hectoring is the only court language. Our laws and liberties openly trampled upon." [19]

Nicholson should have known that he was in for a fight to the finish when he bearded the Councillors. Prominent among them was the pugnacious Commissary James Blair. Robert Carter, of Corotoman, had been a Burgess at twenty-eight, and had twice been Speaker. A man of great energy, shrewd, and dominating he was dubbed "King Carter." Benjamin Harrison had represented Surry in the House of Burgesses, was a Visitor of the College of William and Mary, was commander of the Surry militia. Philip Ludwell, Jr., Page, Custis, Bassett, Duke, and the others were all men of wealth and influence.

The first open breach between these men and Nicholson came when he began to make appointments to office without consulting them. They were outraged when he removed their friends from lucrative jobs to make room for his own favorites. They protested the issuing of warrants on the revenue and the giving of patents to land without their consent. It was almost an insult for him to prorogue the Assembly on his own authority and without their knowledge.

Later Nicholson put the blame on the Councillors themselves for his failure to get along with them. They hated him, he said, because he would not be guided and governed by them, and turn secretaries, auditors, collectors, naval officers, and others out of their places and put them and their friends in, and would not let them do what they pleased.[20]

The Council meetings became stormy, with the Councillors protesting to the Governor and the Governor flying into a rage.

[18] *Ibid.*, Doc. 10.   [19] *Ibid.*   [20] CO5-1314, Doc. 40.

When the sessions were held in the Wren Building at the college prior to the completing of the new Capitol, passersby could hear Nicholson storming " as loud as he could extend his voice." If any member dared to oppose him in any measure he was sure to bring down on himself a volley of insults.

The Councillors were liable to abuse even when the Council was not in session. One day when John Lightfoot was in Williamsburg, he called on the Governor. He had not been in his presence fifteen minutes before Nicholson began to storm at him, calling him a rogue, a rascal, and a villain. "You have sided with that damned Scotch parson, Blair, and by God, sir, you have shipped yourself in a leaky vessel. . . . You shall be turned out of the Council." Then he flew out against the rest of the Council, saying there was not one of them who was not a rogue and a coward, who did not dare look a man in the face.[21]

The testimony regarding Nicholson's violent temper is so overwhelming as to indicate that the man was unbalanced. On one occasion while talking with Captain James Moodie in an " upper apartment " of the college, he flew into a violent passion against the Commissioners of the Navy, " calling them all the basest names the tongue of man could express." These imprecations were thundered out " with such a noise that the people down in the lower rooms came running up stairs . . . believing that the college had been on fire." Several sea captains, who were lodging in a room some distance away, " came running out of their beds in their shirts," one of them " without his wooden leg, holding himself by the wall." [22]

If Nicholson had contented himself with hurling imprecations at those who offended him, his victims might have been able to endure it. " I must confess I have no reason to be satisfied with the insolent, tyrannical behavior of our Governor, but as long as he is vested with the Queen's authority, I will quietly endure his barbarous usage," wrote Philip Ludwell.[23] But when Nicholson carried his malice so far as to prosecute those to whom he took a disliking, deprive them of their jobs, and imprison them, their safety lay in fleeing the colony.

Clergymen seem to have been especially unfortunate in incurring Nicholson's resentment. At a convocation of the clergy in Elizabeth City church, on October 28, 1702, Commissary Blair asked the Reverend James Wallace, the minister, to deliver a

[21] *Ibid.,* Doc. 14c.　　[22] *Ibid.,* Doc. 9.　　[23] *Ibid.,* Doc. 15.

sermon. The Governor, who claimed to be the head of the Virginia Church and had summoned the meeting in order to secure a flattering address, was present. It may have been this which influenced Mr. Wallace to choose as his text: "Herein do I exercise myself to have always a conscience void of offence toward God and toward men," and to use it to illustrate the duty of both government officials and clergymen.

Shortly after the services were over Nicholson sent for Mr. Wallace. "How durst you preach such a sermon?" he demanded. "How dare you take such a text? How dare you presume to tell me my duty? I will not be told my duty." From that day the Governor pursued him with the greatest malice. He summoned him before the Council, and threatened him with ruin, calling him villain, hypocrite, Jesuit. He went all the way to Elizabeth City to lay charges against him before his vestry. When Mr. Wallace could endure this persecution no longer and prepared to sail for England, he tried to stop him.[24]

If anything else were needed to make Nicholson a ridiculous figure, it was his love affair with Lucy Burwell. Lucy's father, Major Lewis Burwell, was perhaps the wealthiest man in Virginia. Owning many thousands of acres of land, served by scores of slaves and indentured workers, connected by marriage and birth with some of the most influential families in the colony, he was the typical Virginia aristocrat. Carter's Creek, his residence in Gloucester County, remained standing for over two centuries as witness to his lavish style of living. The great halls, the marble mantels, the elaborate staircase, the wainscoting carved to resemble drapery were reminiscent rather of England than of seventeenth-century Virginia. However, Lucy seems to have spent most of her childhood, not at Carter's Creek, but at King's Creek, an historic old estate left to her parents by her mother's uncle, Nathaniel Bacon, Senior. And here it was that Nicholson pressed his suit, riding over to see her whenever there was a lull in the business of the General Court and the Assembly was not in session.

Lucy and her family received him with the courtesy due the representative of the Crown. But they knew of the Governor's fits of anger, of his profanity, and the abuse he had heaped on their relatives. Lucy was not attracted to him and, telling him she did not love him, refused to marry him.

---

[24] *Ibid.*, Doc. 12.

When he was at last convinced that all hope of winning Lucy was gone, Nicholson acted like a madman. He swore that if she married another he would with his own hands cut the throats of the bridegroom, the minister, and the justice of the peace who issued the license.[25] All pretence of friendship for her relatives was thrown to the winds. Every few days he sent Major Burwell such threats of ruin that the poor man was kept in a constant state of alarm. " For what I know not, unless it is because I will not force my daughter to marry utterly against her will, which is a thing no Christian body can do," he wrote Philip Ludwell, Senior. " If it please God I live until the return of our next fleet, I propose for England, for I shall not be able to live here.[26]

Nicholson became violently jealous of young Stephen Fouace, minister of Martin's Hundred parish, in which the Burwells resided. One night, when he was returning from a pastoral call at King's Creek he happened to meet the Governor. Falling into one of his rages, Nicholson, in a thundering voice, commanded him never again to visit the house unless sent for, and never again to speak to Lucy.[27]

" Why, Sir," stammered the frightened pastor, " what is the matter? Does your Excellency take me for your rival? I assure you, sir, I have not that foolish presumption to think to be preferred to your Excellency."

" Hold your prate, sirrah. I have taken good notice of you. You are an impudent rogue, a villain, a rascal."

As they were riding along together Nicholson reached over and pulled Fouace's hat from his head.

" How do you have the impudence to ride with me with your hat on? "

" I hope you will not use me like a footman," said Fouace.

After a pause Nicholson asked: " Is it not a shame for one of your function to suffer me to be ridiculed and railed at in some companies where I know you have been? Is it not your duty to reprove them? "

Fouace replied that the best way to avoid ridicule was to be sure that his behavior was such as not to expose him to odium and contempt, that even the King of France could not hinder many of his subjects from speaking ill of him.

" But seeing your Excellency is pleased to make me mindful

[25] *Ibid.*, Doc. 7.   [26] *Ibid.*, p. 23.   [27] *Ibid.*, Doc. 7.

of my duty to reprove the evil I see done in my presence, I must make bold to reprove your Excellency for using at this rate in the highway, in the woods, and in the night, on a Sunday, a clergyman coming from visiting the sick of his parish."

Nicholson received this in silence. But a few minutes later he ran at Fouace, trying to seize him, and threatening to lash him with his whip. This frightened him, for the Governor had his sword and pistols with him, and they were alone in the night. So he wheeled, set spurs to his horse, and fled.[28]

But he could not escape Nicholson's malice. He soon found that life in Virginia was intolerable, and laid his plans to leave for England. But the Governor had no desire to have him lay charges against him before the Bishop of London and the Lords of Trade and Plantations. After he had gone aboard the tobacco fleet, he tried to bring him back, but by shifting from ship to ship Fouace managed to escape.

Nicholson's folly aroused astonishment even in England, and the gossips in the London Exchange and the coffee houses tittered at his unsuccessful suit. An English clergyman wrote him an anonymous letter. " It is not here as in some barbarous countries where the tender lady is often dragged into the Sultan's arms just reeking in the blood of her nearest relations, and yet must strongly dissemble her aversion. But English women are the freest in the world, and will not be won by constraint, but hate them who use them and theirs roughly."

One day when Nicholson was calling on Lucy, before the final breach had occurred, she happened to drop her handkerchief. He picked it up, slipped several rings in it unobserved by Lucy, and handing it to her mounted his horse and rode away. She sent them back to him, but he returned them. And for a while she kept them. Later he complained of the costliness of his suit. " Though she would not accept him," he told several persons, " she and her friends had taken presents to the value of £500." [29]

When this came to Lucy's ears, she thought it necessary to return everything he had given her. So she, with her mother and brother, together with her uncle, Philip Ludwell, Junior, went to Williamsburg with them. But Nicholson, hearing of their mission, " slipt out in the morning." The little group retired to the nearby Wren building, and waited there until

[28] *Ibid.*   [29] CO5-1314, Doc. 15f.

six o'clock in the evening. Then they went back to Nicholson's house, where Ludwell went in to the "public room" and left the gifts on the table.

Late that night, after he had retired, Ludwell was aroused by two messengers sent by the Governor, one bringing the gifts, and the other a summons in the Queen's name for him to come to Nicholson immediately. Ludwell told the man that he "could not apprehend the Queen had any occasion for his services" just at that moment, and so went back to bed.

But the next morning he went to the Governor's house, taking the gifts with him. He found Nicholson in a towering rage.

"I wonder how you dare come into my house yesterday when I was abroad to offer me such an insult?" he said.

'Sir, I never offered your Excellency an affront in my life that I know of," Ludwell replied.

"Yes you have, several, like the base villain and rascal that you are."

Ludwell bowed and thanked him for this "civil usage." But Nicholson began again to storm, calling him "rogue, lying villain, base rascal, and coward," and declaring that he would teach him his duty. Finally he told him to get out of his house and not return until he was sent for. This Ludwell did with alacrity. But he took good care to leave the gifts. At first this escaped Nicholson's notice, but while Ludwell was putting on his boots he rushed up to him, "calling him all the names the Devil could invent" and commanding him to take the things.[30]

When Ludwell had mounted his horse and started to ride away, the Governor ran out "stark mad," and catching hold of his coat tried to pull him from his horse. Failing in this, he snatched his whip from his hand, and ordered him in the Queen's name to dismount. When he had done so, he shook the whip over his head, and swore that he had a mind to slash him soundly. Ludwell told him that as he was Governor of Virginia he had to take all his ill usage, but if he were in another place he would not dare treat him so. A few days later Nicholson challenged Ludwell to a duel. But Ludwell declined. He had not so much love for the gallows, he said. "But I always wear a sword with which to defend myself, and I am always easily found."

[30] *Ibid.*

When one reads the long recital of Nicholson's misdeeds, one is apt to forget that he conferred one lasting benefit on the colony, a benefit which today is shared by millions of Americans from all parts of the country. He was the founder of Williamsburg. It was on October 21, 1698, that a fire broke out in the statehouse at Jamestown which in a few hours laid the building in ashes. So the old question of moving the capital away from the mosquito-infested town on the banks of the James was again debated. Nicholson favored Middle Plantation. The college was located there, there was ample room for a town, there were several springs of pure water, and the place was healthful. The Assembly voted that a city be laid out there, which, in honor of the "most gracious and glorious King William," was to be named Williamsburg.

Nicholson busied himself with planning the streets, which at first he hoped to lay out in the form of the letters W and M in honor of King William and Queen Mary. When this proved too complicated, he decided to run a central avenue from the college to the site of the Capitol, to be named Duke of Gloucester Street, paralleled by two side streets, one of which was to be called Nicholson and the other Francis. To aid him in designing the Capitol, he called in the ablest architect and builder in the colony, Henry Cary, and day after day the pair pored over the drawings. What book of designs they had before them from which to draw their inspiration we do not know, but it must have been of recent publication, for the building was typical of the late seventeenth-century English houses.

The plan called for a brick structure of two wings, connected by a gallery, the whole to be two stories high, with a sharply rising roof pierced with dormers and surmounted by a high cupola. The floors of the first story were to be laid in flagstones, while the roof was to be covered with cyprus shingles. Inside were to be rooms for the Council, the General Court, the House of Burgesses, and several committee rooms.

The gratitude of the Virginians to Nicholson for founding their new capital and adorning it with beautiful buildings did not blind them to his violence, his injustice, and his persecution of innocent men. Does he think he is governing the Moors or some other slavish people? they asked. He seems to think it a crime in us to demand the liberties of Englishmen. "That which bears up their spirits under all the heavy customs on their commodities, and restraints in point of trade, is that they have the happiness to enjoy the British laws and constitution, which they reckon the best of Governments," said Philip Ludwell, Senior. " But if once their Governors be suffered to break in upon them in this tender point, and to treat them with the arbitrariness of France, or the insolence of Morocco, as this gentleman has done, it is not to be imagined how ill this will go down with Englishmen that have not forgot the liberty of their mother country. The least that can be expected from it is that men of substance, if they find no redress, will remove themselves and their effects out of the colony to any other part of the world where they may enjoy peace and quietness." [31]

At last six members of the Council—Lightfoot, Page, Harrison, Carter, Blair, and Ludwell—drew up charges against Nicholson. Though they were careful to keep the matter secret the Governor suspected that something was up. In July, 1703, he wrote the Lords of Trade: " It hath been industriously reported here that . . . I was turned out of the government for maladministration. . . . I hope in God, I shall not only be able to clear myself, but to make my accusers appear ill people." [32]

Nicholson might have surmised that it was Blair who would present charges against him when, several weeks later, the Commissary left for England. But he could not have anticipated the stratagem which the shrewd Scot was to adopt. Though he arrived in November, 1703, he did not present the charges of the six Councillors to the Queen in the Council until late in the following March, after the tobacco fleet had sailed for Virginia. Thus months would elapse before Nicholson could have word of them and prepare his answers.

The Privy Council referred the charges to the Lords of Trade and Plantations. It must have been with surprise that they listened as the petition was read. We appeal to " your Majesty for relief of ourselves and other subjects of Virginia from many great grievances and pressures we lie under by reason of the unusual, insolent, and arbitrary methods of government, as well as wicked and scandalous examples of life, which have been now for divers years past put in practice by Nicholson, which we have hitherto in vain endeavored by more soft and gentle applications to himself to remedy and prevent.

[31] *Ibid.*, Doc. 17.   [32] CO5-1360, p. 424.

But to our unspeakable grief we have reaped no other fruit . . .
but that thereby we have so highly exasperated the revengeful
mind of Nicholson to the height of implacable malice and
enmity against ourselves and the better part of the people . . .
that without your Majesty's seasonable interposition we fear
the dangerous consequences, not only in fomenting lasting feuds
and acrimonies among the people here, but in endangering
the public peace of Virginia." [33]

During the summer Blair had not been idle. It is probable
that the little colony of Virginians in London got together to
plan their strategy. When the matter came before the Lords of
Trade, the Commissary was armed with affidavits from Fouace,
Captain James Moodie, and others, and letters from Philip
Ludwell, Junior, and Benjamin Harrison to the elder Ludwell,
accusing Nicholson of tyranny. At the hearing Wallace, George
Luke, and Robert Beverley were called on to tell their stories
of perscution and injustice.

Hearing that John Thrale was agent for Nicholson, the Lords
called him in. He made the best defense he could, but he was
ignorant of the whole matter, and he had not witnesses to refute
the charges. When he demanded particular instances of misgovernment and injustice, Blair and Beverley overwhelmed
him with them.[34] To make the Governor's case hopeless, Thrale
died in the midst of the hearings, leaving him without anyone
to defend him.[35]

Late in October, 1704, when the first word of the petition
reached Nicholson he was heard " to make a terrible impreca-
tion, vowing to the living God that he would pursue the peti-
tioners with eternal vengeance." At a meeting of the Council
he glared at the members. " Whoever they were that signed
that petition I hope they will be obliged to stand by it in
England and that such of them as are there will be obliged to
stay and those here to go thither, where it is my desire to come
to a fair hearing," he told them.[36]

He defended himself in several long letters to the Board. He
had done no more than defend the Queen's prerogative against
the assaults of the Council, he said. If everything they asked
were granted them, " her Majesty would have but a skeleton
of a government left, and hardly the power of a Doge of Genoa.

[33] CO5-1660, pp. 463-465.
[34] *Ibid.*, Docs. 23, 24.
[35] CO5-1360, p. 480.
[36] CO5-1314, Doc. 36.

And I think the question may be put to them as the wise King Solomon did to his mother, why don't they ask the kingdom or the government also? " As for Commissary Blair, he " and his little faction now set up to have the power and interest of turning out and putting in Governors, and affect the title that the great Earl of Warwick had." If he were ousted, he would present himself to the Board, " when I hope I shall not be found to have a cloven foot, to be a fury, or to have snakes instead of hair." [37]

If we may credit the reports from Virginia which reached Blair, Ludwell, and Fouace in England in January, 1705, Nicholson began proceedings to " terrify all people " from discussing his conduct. " He sets up inquisition courts, giving commissions to some of his creatures to examine all persons on oath if ever they heard such a man reflect upon the Governor . . . which practice is very terrible to all, there being few in Virginia who have not sometimes in private spoke of him as he deserves. . . . If witnesses are backward they are threatened by the Governor himself and terrified into depositions." When anyone was accused of complaining of him, even in private, he ordered the Attorney General to prosecute him under the law against defaming the Governor passed after Bacon's Rebellion.[38]

The Governor had one warm defender in Colonel Robert Quary. In a letter to the Board of Trade he testified that, when Nicholson was appointed, the Councillors expected to " govern and direct all matters," to monopolize all places of profit and honor, and have him " suppress all that were not of their faction." But when they found that he would not be governed by them, they turned upon him with the greatest malice. " They aspersed and blackened him both in the country and by letters to England, as if he had been the greatest monster in nature." He had been guilty of no maladministration in his government " further than some escapes of his passion, which their injustice often forced him to." [39]

During the first week of March, 1705, Nicholson was busy preparing his defence so that it could get off on the first vessel sailing for England. He penned long letters to the Lords of Trade on the first, the third, and the sixth, and enclosed them with a memorial against Blair, and an address from the Vir-

[37] *Ibid.*, Docs. 43, 44.   [39] *Ibid.*, Doc. 67.
[38] CO5-1314, Doc. 36.

ginia clergy. These papers were received on May 2, and read
May 31. Whether they would have influenced the Lords in
Nicholson's favor we do not know, for on April 2, just a month
before their arrival, the Board received a communication from
Secretary Hedges, advising them that the Queen wished them
to prepare a commission and instructions for Colonel Edward
Nott to be Governor General of Virginia.[40]

It was on August 15, 1705, that the Council met in their
beautiful room in the new Capitol, for Nott's inauguration.
When all had been seated Nicholson entered and read a letter
from the Queen directing him to deliver up the government
and "repair to her royal presence." He must have looked
around at the men who had been his bitter enemies with an
air of triumph as he read a letter from Secretary Hedges, stating
that he was being recalled, not because of the charges made
against him, but merely for her Majesty's service. Then he
handed over the seal of the colony and the charter of 1676. One
wonders whether, as he bowed himself out, he took one last
look at the room for which he had been so largely responsible—
the portrait of Queen Anne, the large oval table, the stiff-backed
chairs, the Queen's arms, the panelling.

Nicholson's administration proved once more that the Virginians could not be governed by illegal and arbitrary means.
That he was not ousted by violence as was Sir John Harvey, or
that he did not drive the people into open rebellion as did
Berkeley, is explained by the difference in the character of the
times. Harvey acted in the spirit of the First Stuart Despotism,
Berkeley of the Second Stuart Despotism; Nicholson was out of
step with his time. To remove him it was not necessary to resort
to violence; an appeal to the Queen was all that was needed.

Perhaps it was fortunate for the cause of self-government that
an experiment in despotism had failed in the opening years of
the eighteenth century. It made succeeding Governors wary of
trampling upon the people's rights, it gave the people confidence. Having won this victory, they went on to others until
their Governors became their servants rather than their masters.

[40] *Ibid.*, Doc. 46.

CHAPTER IX

THE VIRGINIA HOUSE OF LORDS

THOUGH the members of the Council must have been surprised when Nicholson read Secretary Hedges' letter, they did not let it disturb them. They were rid of him, and that was what really mattered. No more could he bully them in the Council meetings, no more could he thwart them in the General Court by packing juries, no more could he ignore them in appointing officers, no more could he insult and revile them. As they sat around the table with the mild-mannered Nott, they realized with satisfaction that his personality was in strong contrast with that of his predecessor. Perhaps it would be easy to control him and keep the power in their own hands.

To a large extent this is just what they did. Though Nott was no weakling, he was anxious to live in peace with both Council and Assembly. It was said of him that his " whole study was to do everybody justice." [1] Like other Governors when they first arrived and were unacquainted with men and conditions in the colony, he was dependent upon the Councillors for advice and guidance. Before he could learn the ropes, he died. Since four years elapsed before a new Governor arrived to take his place, the Council remained for half a decade the controlling power in the colony. From August, 1705, to July, 1710, the government was neither despotic nor democratic, but aristocratic.

Nathaniel Bacon, Nicholson, Spotswood, and others derided the " mighty dons " of the Council, pointing out that they came from humble families in England. These critics did not stop to consider that it was more to their credit to have won by their own efforts positions of wealth and power than to have inherited them. Virginia itself offered them the opportunity, but it was they who seized it.

The group of well-to-do planters whom the Council represented, in the early years of the eighteenth century were far from numerous. " In every river there are from ten to thirty

---

[1] CO5-1315, Bassett to Perry & Co., Aug. 30, 1706.

men who by trade and industry have gotten very competent estates," wrote Colonel Quary. "Out of this number are chosen her Majesty's Council, the Assembly, the justices, and officers of the government." [2]

It must have been a humiliation to such proud men as William Byrd II, "King" Carter, and Benjamin Harrison that they were not admitted to the English peerage. But though there were no dukes, nor lords, nor knights among the Councillors, they had the right to certain titles which carried great distinction. The term "esquire" was given to members of the Council, and was invariably used by them in signing legal documents. If a man were not a Councillor, yet was prominent and wealthy, he had the right to sign himself "gentleman." The holders of high office in the militia—colonels, lieutenant colonels, majors, and captains—prized their titles highly and used them in conjunction with "esquire," or "gentleman." [3]

Nor did the English nobility command greater respect than did the members of the Council in Virginia. When a certain Humphrey Chamberlaine, of Henrico County, became angry with William Byrd I, and, stripping off his coat, drew his sword as if to attack him, he was arrested and clapped into jail. At his trial he excused himself by saying he was a stranger in the country and ignorant of its laws and customs. But the court, ruling that no one "could be insensible of the respect and reverence due so honorable a person as Colonel Byrd," fined him five pounds sterling. [4]

Although the basis of the wealth of the aristocracy was land, the holding of large tracts did not in itself bring riches unless the owner could find the labor necessary to work them. During most of the seventeenth century indentured workers were used extensively. But their cost and the fact that they served but four or five years limited the return they brought their masters. With the importing of slaves in large numbers in the last two decades of the seventeenth century and the first third of the eighteenth century, the cost of raising tobacco was greatly lowered. This not only doubled or tripled existing fortunes, but created many new ones. It is this which explains why the Virginia aristocracy, which so late as the last decade of the

[2] CO5-1314, Doc. 63iv.
[3] Hugh Jones, *The present state of Virginia*, ed. R. L. Morton, 93.
[4] P. A. Bruce, *Social life of Virginia*, 133.

seventeenth century was little more than a group, by the mid-eighteenth century had become a numerous class.[5]

In their mode of life the aristocracy consciously imitated the English country squires. The large libraries which they accumulated served practical as well as cultural ends. The wealthy man who wished to build a residence pored over James Gibbs' *A Book of Architecture*, or Abraham Swan's *The British Architect*. In laying out his garden he consulted Kip's *English Houses and Gardens*, or John James' *The Theory and Practice of Gardening*. On his shelves were English books on law, medicine, religion, agriculture.

Fortunately some of the mansions of colonial Virginia have survived the ravages of time, fires, and wars, to bear witness to the charm and dignity of the plantation life of two centuries ago. Carter's Grove, Mount Airy, Gunston Hall, Westover, Brandon, and others constitute history in brick and wood. The lovely gardens, some of which have been restored in recent years, are in the formal style of Le Notre and Rose. The mansions were furnished with tables, chairs, bookcases by the English masters; on the tables were pitchers, goblets, and candlesticks by English silversmiths. The aristocrat dressed himself and his family in the latest English fashions, owned an English-made coach, imported English race horses, perhaps sent his son to Oxford, when he visited England had his portrait painted by Lely or Kneller.

It was inevitable that in so small a group as the early Virginia aristocracy there should be frequent intermarriages. In 1717 half of the members of the Council were related to each other by blood or marriage. James Blair and Philip Ludwell were brothers-in-law of Nathaniel Harrison; William Byrd's wife was the niece of Ludwell; William Bassett and Edmund Berkeley had married half-nieces of Ludwell; Ludwell's wife was Harrison's sister. Governor Spotswood habitually referred to them as " the family."

It was wrong, Spotswood pointed out, that a group of relatives should wield such power. Since they all sat on the General Court, it was to be expected that they would vote as a unit if the interests of any one of them were involved. " Whoever has lived here and frequented the General Courts held of late in Virginia, has abundant reason to know that there is a strong

[5] T. J. Wertenbaker, *The planters of colonial Virginia*, 155-160.

link of relatives on the bench, who by their majority have the determination of all causes," he wrote in 1718. "When one of their kindred is charged with enormous crimes, clerks may safely keep back the examination, and sheriffs keep back the witnesses. . . . When the King has been plaintiff in a civil action against one of that family, the cause could not be tried for want of judges to make up a bench exclusive of those who were akin to the defendant." [6]

One wonders how long Governor Nott would have put up with this kind of thing had not death overtaken him. Despite his desire to work in harmony with the Council, there is evidence that he had no intention of letting them ride over him roughshod. This became evident when they tried to take the patronage out of his hands. " I do believe the Council have a mind to dispute with me the making of the collectors of the two shillings per hogshead," he wrote the Lords of Trade. " Their pretence is that it is said in my instructions I shall not make them but by advice of Council. Now they have a mind to turn several out and put in their own relatives. And that is not my turn of temper." [7]

When he asked the advice of the Council before reappointing naval officers, they objected to Major Arthur Allen, Colonel Miles Cary, and Colonel William Wilson. But when nothing of consequence was brought against them, the Governor insisted on continuing them. At the same time he shook off responsibility by refusing to renew their commissions until he had instructions to do so from the Lord Treasurer. [8]

Whatever resentment the Councillors bore him for this was forgotten when he championed their plea that they should not be forbidden to become naval officers. " I think this instruction very strange," he wrote the Lords of Trade. " To be deprived of those few places of profit. . . brings the consequence that the good men are very indifferent to being one of the Council. I hope you are of opinion that this restriction may be taken off." [9]

The Governor thought it his duty to defer to the Council in most of his appointments to lesser offices. " I have directed new commissioners of peace," he wrote the Lords of Trade, " and not knowing persons yet, I left the nomination of justices

[6] CO5-1318, Spotswood to Lords of Trade, March 20, 1718.
[7] CO5-1340, Doc. 15.
[8] *Ibid.*
[9] *Ibid.*, Doc. 19.

solely to the Council. I have continued the former escheators since there was no objection to them." [10]

When Nott first took over the government, he found the colony divided against itself. The people as a whole were over-joyed to get rid of Nicholson, but a group made up no doubt of men who had received favors at his hands, resented his removal. When an election was held for a new Assembly, opposing candi-dates were put up by the pro-Nicholson and anti-Nicholson factions. Although the latter won an overwhelming victory, enough Nicholson men were returned to continue the old feuds and hatreds. Governor Nott made his opening address an appeal for peace. It was his earnest hope, he said, that all animosities be laid aside, and that the only contention be as to who should be most obedient to the Queen and most service-able to the country. [11]

Despite this plea the pro-Nicholson faction presented under the guise of a grievance a resolution which was in reality a reproof of the six members of the Council who had presented the charges against the Governor. No one should take upon himself to represent to the Queen the grievances of the colony without the consent of the House of Burgesses, it said. No thanks, but rather a check should be given to those that had done so against the late Governor. But they met with a severe rebuff. So far from approving, the House ordered the so-called grievance to " be burnt under the gallows by the sheriff of York County as a mutinous, seditious, and scandalous paper." [12]

Though there is no evidence that Nott tried to render the Burgesses submissive to his will by bribing them with offices, the Assembly thought this a golden opportunity to weaken the Governor's appointive power. Some could recall Berkeley's Long Assembly, and all had been witnesses of the shameless way in which Nicholson had handed out jobs. So they passed a bill requiring each county court to nominate three men, all of them justices, from whom the Governor was to select one as sheriff, who was to serve not more than two years. Had not Nott been so anxious to avoid any conflict with the Assembly, he would certainly have vetoed this bill, for not only did it restrict his power of appointment, but it infringed upon the royal prerogative.

[10] CO5-1316, p. 450.   [12] Ibid., 147.
[11] Journals of the House of Burgesses, 1702-1712: 131.

But he balked when the House sent up a bill to require the
Governor, in appointing the justices of the peace, to secure the
assent of the Council, or at least five of them. He thought they
were going too far in this attempt to deprive the Governor of
the patronage, leave him at the mercy of the Council and
Assembly, and make him a mere figurehead. When the Lords
of Trade heard that he had vetoed this bill, they wrote congratulating him. " The restraining Governors from making
justices . . . is entrenching on prerogative, and you may be
assured it will not be approved here. In all other plantations
the power of appointing and removing justices of the peace is
solely in the Governor. . . . But it would be prudence in the
Governor to advise for his better information." [13]

When the Assembly met again, in April, 1706, they made a
daring attempt to weaken the Governor's power by passing a
substitute law for the famous Act of 1680 which gave a perpetual revenue to the Crown. The new bill bore the disarming
title of " An Act for raising a public revenue for the better
support of the government . . . and for ascertaining the salary
of the Council." Nott apparently saw nothing alarming in it,
but Colonel Quary at once suspected that it was intended to
weaken the Act of 1680, and perhaps set a precedent which
would eventually give the House control of the revenue from
the export duty on tobacco.

" These topping men " were merely waiting an opportunity
to have the old law damned, he wrote the Lords of Trade.
" Had the Assembly only designed to have augmented and
added to the Queen's revenue, why could they not make an act
of it without damning and destroying the former act? And
that your Lordships may see the snake in the grass, please
observe that the Assembly are pleased to appropriate the
Queen's revenue as they think fit, a thing never pretended to
before, and to limit and confine her Majesty from disposing
of her own money. . . . Whereas in a former act the Queen was
graciously pleased to appropriate £370 to be divided among the
Council for attendance, in this act they have ordered otherwise
. . . by which they have tied up the Queen's hands from giving
any part of her bounty but according to their pleasure." [14]

When this bill came before the Board of Trade they referred

[13] CO5-1362, March 26, 1707.
[14] CO5-1315, Quary to Lordships, Sept. 1, 1706.

it to Attorney General Harcourt and Solicitor General Montague. Although these astute men, as we have seen, gave it as their opinion that the old act had been passed in a way "contrary to the present method," and should be superseded by a new one, the Board decided to let sleeping dogs lie. So they advised the Queen to veto the Act of 1716. "'Tis hoped it will never be revived by any Governor who has at heart the interests of the Crown, and wishes that people should distinguish between what they owe to the indulgence of the Sovereign and what they may claim as their right by the laws of Virginia," wrote Governor Spotswood several years later.[15]

The climate of Virginia, which was fatal to so many newcomers from England, took a heavy toll of Governors. Lord De la Warr fell a victim to the Virginia sickness; Herbert Jeffreys died after having been in the colony only a few months. Now, on August 23, 1706, death ended the brief administration of Governor Nott. He was mourned by the people, and was buried in Bruton Parish churchyard with all the solemnity the colony was capable of. "Had it pleased God to have spared him but a little time longer amongst us, he would have healed all those unhappy differences that have of late made us uneasy, and united us again to be one people," wrote William Bassett.[16]

When the Council met after Nott's death they opened his commission and listened intently as it was read. And there was great satisfaction when they found that in the event of a Governor's death the Council was to take on themselves the administration of the government. But they were far from happy that Colonel Edmund Jenings, as the senior Councillor, was to preside at their meetings with such powers as were necessary in "carrying on the public service." They insisted that the Attorney General of the colony, in drawing up the first proclamation under the new government, should issue it, not under the name of the President alone, but of the President and Council.[17]

Jenings wrote to the Lords of Trade to ask just what his status should be. Their answer was decisive. The instruction that the Council should take over the government upon the death of a Governor had caused many controversies between the President and the Councillors and had greatly hindered public business. So they altered it to read: "The eldest

[15] CO5-1317.　　　　　[17] *Executive journals of the Council* 3: 119, 120.
[16] CO5-1315, Aug. 30, 1706.

Councillor do take upon him the administration of the government . . . in the same manner . . . as other our Governor should do." [18]

Francis Nicholson had written the Lords of Trade some years previously expressing doubts as to the wisdom of making any member of the Council the chief executive. " There may happen great disputes about the person of the President and his powers. And may be when the President and the Council are all natives or else entirely settled here, nature and self-interest may sway them to do some things and pass some acts that may be (as they will imagine) for the good of their country and make and secure an interest with the people. This may be prejudicial to their Majesties' service." [19] No doubt the Lords of Trade saw the force of this reasoning, but they were not prepared to keep a Lieutenant Governor in Virginia whose only function it would be to wait around ready to step in when the Governor died or was recalled.

Although the other members of the Council seem to have regarded Jenings with something like scorn, and one of them had spoken of him as " the right noble little Colonel Jenings," the man had had a distinguished career. He had been clerk of the York County court, collector of the York River district, commissioner for the College of William and Mary, member of the Council, Attorney General, and Secretary. And now, as President of the Council, he seems to have laid aside former animosities, and considered himself merely first among equals.

It was taken for granted that Jenings' administration would be brief, and that a new Governor would come over as soon as one could be appointed. Word had come that a commission had been drawn up for Colonel Robert Hunter, and that he had sailed from Portsmouth in June, 1707. But month after month passed and he failed to appear. As late as March, 1708, the Council was wondering what had become of him. At last they heard that the vessel in which he had shipped had been taken by the French, and that he was held captive in France. So they had to wait two more years before a Governor arrived. [20]

This suited President Jenings and the Council, for it left them in undisputed control of the government. They even refused to hold an Assembly for fear it might question their

[18] CO5-1362, p. 121.   [20] CO5-1362, pp. 336-340.
[19] CO5-1314, Doc. 15.

proceedings. It is true that six times they set the date for a meeting of the Assembly, but six times they postponed it. At last, when people began to question whether these frequent postponements did not put an end to the Assembly, the Council settled all doubts by dissolving them by proclamation.

This was a dangerous thing to do, for it was in the midst of the War of the Spanish Succession, and an Assembly was needed to provide funds for the defense of the colony. But the Council gambled that no French fleet would appear in the Chesapeake Bay. The normal expenses of the government—their own salaries and those of the President, Auditor, Attorney General, and other officials—they paid out of the export duty on tobacco and the quit rent fund. In September, 1708, Jenings wrote that privateers had come in between the capes and had chased a merchant vessel up the York River, that the Indians were threatening the frontier, that the Governor's house was unfinished, and that the quit rent fund was " much drained," but that despite all, the Council would not call an Assembly.[21]

In December, 1709, Lord George Hamilton, Earl of Orkney, was appointed Governor General of Virginia. Orkney had been trained as a soldier, and had distinguished himself at Namur, Blenheim, Malplaquet, and elsewhere. It is probable that it was intended from the first that the office should be a sinecure, and though Orkney held it for years he never set foot on Virginia soil. But Virginia had to pay his salary, for his £1,000 a year was taken out of the export duty on tobacco. To carry on the administration in the colony Colonel Alexander Spotswood was made Lieutenant Governor.

It would seem that in the years from the recall of Nicholson to the arrival of Spotswood, the danger to liberty in Virginia came less from the Throne than from the Council. A free people could not be quiet under the rule of a body of twelve men, not chosen by the voters but appointed by the sovereign.

The average planter, not only the owner of only a few acres, but the man of means had reason to be alarmed. Was it consistent with the principles of English liberty, they must have asked, for a clique of wealthy men, many of them united in one family, to have such power over their lives and their property? If the people were to rule, final authority must be vested in the House of Burgesses, not the Council.

[21] CO5-1362, pp. 318, 325.

CHAPTER X

SPOTSWOOD

A LEXANDER SPOTSWOOD arrived in Virginia June 20, 1710, aboard the warship *Deptford*, and spent the night at Green Spring, with his future enemy, Philip Ludwell. Two days later he met with the Council around the oval table in the beautiful Council Chamber in the new Capitol, and laid his commission before them.

The new Lieutenant Governor was descended from a family of Scottish Anglicans. His great-grandfather had seconded Archbishop Laud's attempt to introduce the Prayer Book in Scotland; his grandfather had been put to death by the Presbyterians. Perhaps it was this tragedy which induced his father to desert his native land and take service in the English army. It was while he was with his regiment in Tangier that Alexander Spotswood was born.

The son chose to follow in the father's footsteps, and in 1693 we find him serving in the Earl of Bath's regiment in Flanders. He fought gallantly, was wounded at Blenheim, and was captured at Oudenarde. It is possible that he served under the Earl of Orkney, also, and that was the reason he named him as his deputy in Virginia. "I must ever own gratefully that to your Lordship's good will I owe my station here," he wrote Orkney in 1718.

Spotswood was one of the ablest Governors sent to America to represent the British Crown. He did much to open the West to Virginia, encouraged settlement in the Piedmont, and erected forts in the passes of the Blue Ridge. He wiped out a nest of pirates under the notorious Blackbeard and strung several of them up at Williamsburg. A man of artistic interests, he was responsible for the beautiful Palace gardens, with their wealth of boxwood, walks, walls, lake, ornate gates, flower beds; and designed charming Bruton Parish Church.

In 1716 he led a party of gentlemen, accompanied by rangers, servants, and Indians, on an exploring expedition to the West. As they rode through the wilderness of the Piedmont, they shot deer and bears, camped in the open, roasted venison on wooden forks. On reaching the Blue Ridge they toiled to the summit, and there, looking out over the Valley of Virginia, drank the health of King George I and the royal family. After descending into the Valley and crossing the Shenandoah River, they turned their horses' heads homeward. Back in Williamsburg, the Governor presented each of his companions with a golden horseshoe, inscribed with *sic juvat transcendere montes.*

Although Spotswood was accused of being haughty and implacable, he lacked the fiery temper of Nicholson or the revengeful fury of Sir William Berkeley. In his conflicts with the Council his astute mind and his knowledge of English and Virginia constitutional law made it easy for him to refute their arguments. Though he defended the powers of the Crown, he was honestly concerned for the welfare of the colony. But he hated democracy, and he had no patience with what he termed the follies of the ignorant multitude. Despite his assaults on the Virginia aristocracy, his ambition was to become one of them, and he used his office to build up one of the greatest estates in the colony.

The instructions given Spotswood by the Lords of Trade were on the whole wise and liberal. The people of Virginia were to have the full benefit of the *habeas corpus*; fees and salaries must be moderate; no one must be deprived of life, member, or property without due process of law; martial law was forbidden; the people were to be supplied with arms. Yet several clauses were loaded with trouble for the Lieutenant Governor—one for appointing courts to try criminals; another for preventing frauds in the accounts of governmental receipts and payments; another for collecting arrears of quit rents; one to prevent the holding of large tracts of unoccupied land.

When this last instruction was read to the Council, they must have shifted uneasily in their seats, for most of them held land which they did not cultivate. Fourteen years earlier Edward Randolph had reported this to the Lords of Trade. The reason the colony was so thinly settled, he thought, was that poor men would not go there " because members of the Council and others who made an interest in the government, have from time to time procured grants of very large tracts of land." Thus newcomers and indentured workers on becoming free were forced to be tenants or go to the utmost bounds of the colony. The remedy, he suggested, was to force payment of arrears of quit rents and prohibit for the future grants of more than 500 acres.[1]

Both Nott and Hunter had been instructed to cancel patents for land of any who neglected to cultivate even a small part of their holdings. So now Spotswood, in the face of bitter opposition, restricted all grants to 400 acres unless the patentee showed that he was able to meet this requirement. In 1710 he tried to satisfy the Lords of Trade by pushing through a law stating what should be considered satisfactory seating, and in 1713 another making the regulations still more specific.[2]

The chief effect of these acts was to arouse the resentment of the Council. They assented to them in their capacity as the Upper House of the Assembly because they dared not flaunt openly the commands of the British government. But they found means to make them inoperative. The rumor was spread throughout the colony that the attorney general in England had ruled that no lands patented prior to the passage of these acts was liable to forfeiture. To ease men's fears, several large landholders purposely refused to pay quit rents. Even John Grymes, the deputy auditor into whose hands the quit rents were paid, himself remained in arrears " to show no danger in that law." [3] Spotswood admitted that the law was a failure when he wrote in 1718: " No man in Virginia has yet had land granted away for non-payment of quit rents."

When Spotswood came to Virginia there were many complaints of hard times. The war in Europe had proved disastrous to the tobacco trade, the flow of hogsheads to the continent of Europe had been reduced to a trickle, tobacco piled up in the British warehouses, the merchants left a part of each crop on the planters' hands, and the price dropped lower and lower. Many of the poorer farmers were in rags, and some began to raise sheep and to spin and weave. The salaried class, especially the clergy, were in dire straits also, since they were paid in tobacco, often of the lowest grade.

The fertile brain of Spotswood now thought out a scheme intended to raise the price of tobacco, give the colony a convenient and stable currency, make the collecting of quit rents easier, and prevent frauds in shipping out tobacco. So he got one of his friends in the Assembly to introduce a bill to require

[1] CO5-1315, Doc. 26.   [3] CO5-1318.
[2] W. W. Hening, Statutes at large 3: 525.

inspection of all tobacco at government warehouses, and the issuing of tobacco notes which were to be legal tender. This plan had much to recommend it, and a similar one was put into successful operation later during the administration of Governor Gooch.

Despite violent opposition in certain quarters, the tobacco bill passed both Houses of Assembly and was signed by the Governor. So now there were sounds of hammering and sawing as warehouses arose on the great rivers. Soon the tobacco vessels were tying up at the adjacent wharves, and the planters were rolling their hogsheads for the inspection. After the agent had examined the leaf, he either rejected it as " trash " and unfit for exportation, or stamped on the hogshead the weight and variety of the tobacco, and gave the owner his certificate.

At first everything seemed to be going smoothly. The quit rents were collected in tobacco notes, the price of the leaf rose in the English market. The clergy wrote Spotswood thanking him for the increased value of their salaries. " Their livings, which by the badness of the pay were sunk to little or nothing, begin now to be much more valuable by your wise and just contrivance to keep up the credit of the public payments." [4]

None the less, the law was unpopular. The debtor objected to paying in appreciated currency. It was a heavy expense for the planter to roll his hogsheads over the bad roads to the warehouses and then pay for inspection and storage. He was resentful if his tobacco was judged to be unfit for export. At the courthouses local politicians began to denounce the act to willing listeners. " He is the patriot who will not yield to whatever the government proposes," complained Spotswood. " Him they call a poor man's friend who always carries stillyards to weigh to the needy planter's advantage, and who never judges his tobacco to be trash." [5]

Spotswood said that the tobacco act was looked upon to be the most extraordinary one that ever passed a Virginia Assembly. When he first outlined his plans for it his friends assured him it would be impossible to persuade the Assembly to pass it. Yet it was adopted unanimously by the Council, and passed in the House " with some address and great struggle."

What the Governor meant by " address " is revealed by an examination of the list of fat jobs that he handed out to indi-

[4] CO5-1406, Dec. 7, 1714.　　　[5] *Spotswood letters* 2: p. 50.

vidual Burgesses. Of the fifty-one members, seventeen were
justices of the peace. Fearing perhaps that this did not assure
the passage of his bill, he was lavish in promising tobacco
agents' places, and no less than twenty-five Burgesses cast their
votes with this job in sight. Only nineteen members failed to
get one or the other of these posts, and some got both.[6] " I
have, in a great measure, I think, cleared the way for a Governor towards carrying any reasonable point in the House of
Burgesses," Spotswood boasted, " for he will have in his disposal
about forty agencies, which one with another are likely to yield
nigh 250 pounds per annum each." [7]

But Spotswood would not have been so pleased with himself
if he had realized the resentment which this open bribery of
the people's representatives caused throughout the colony. The
Assembly " gave him all things asked, and he them agent's
places to pick our pockets," said one disgruntled planter. But
what the officeholder had to expect if he opposed the measures
urged by the Governor is shown by his treatment of Nicholas
Meriwether. When Meriwether not only spoke against the
tobacco bill in the Assembly, but by " many seditious speeches "
denounced it to the people of New Kent County, Spotswood
promptly removed him from his place as justice of the peace.
This, he thought, would discourage others from following his
example.

Having corrupted the Burgesses and made most of them his
henchmen, Spotswood would have no doubt continued them
indefinitely by successive adjournments, had they not been
automatically dissolved by the death of Queen Anne. " By a
good providence we were delivered from them, else they would
have continued as long as he," wrote Joshua Gee.[8] Just how
passively the people would have submitted to another long
Assembly must remain a matter of speculation, but their resentment against both Spotswood and his puppets is shown by
their selections for the House of Burgesses in 1715. Of the
twenty-five members who had accepted agents' jobs, only one,
William Armistead, of Elizabeth City, was returned. And the
voters of New Kent showed their anger at Spotswood's treatment of Meriwether by returning him to the House. Alto-
gether only sixteen Burgesses of the old House had seats in the
new, and of these eleven had been neither agents nor justices.

[6] *Virginia Magazine* 2: 2-15. [8] CO5-1319.
[7] *Spotswood letters* 2: 49.

Spotswood was deeply resentful. The new Burgesses, he thought, were a set of ignorant demagogues, determined to oppose anything he suggested. It was all the fault of the law which permitted any man to vote who owned any real estate, even half an acre. Just before an election reports were spread that the country was on the verge of ruin, and no one was qualified to save it but "some of their own mobbish politicians." It was no wonder that some of the Burgesses could not write grammatical English, since the ignorant people insisted on electing men of their own stamp.[9]

The new Assembly was as hostile to the Governor as their predecessors had been subservient. Everything he proposed they objected to, in some cases for no other reason than to thwart him. They were egged on by Gawin Corbin, who had been ousted from his job as naval officer; George Marable, whom Spotswood had removed from the James City County court; and Edwin Conway, of Lancaster County. But the whole atmosphere of the House was one of hostility.

No sooner had the House been organized than grievances from various counties poured in, most of them complaining against the tobacco law. The people of Surry prayed that the law be repealed, the people of Henrico wanted it repealed, the people of Essex wanted it repealed, the people of Warwick complained of the hardships of the law. It seemed that no more than two counties in all Virginia were satisfied.[10] Spotswood claimed that these grievances did not represent the views of a majority of the people. Many of them were drawn up by members of the House, some were signed at election fields, horse races, and drunken meetings. "Nor shall a seditious paper, signed by five obscure fellows who must have a scribe to write all their names, ever pass with me for a county grievance."[11]

When Richard Littlepage and Thomas Butts, two of the justices of New Kent, refused to certify the grievances of that county, they were arrested under the Speaker's warrant. Though the House voted them guilty of high misdemeanor and contempt, they refused to appear, claiming that the Burgesses had no legal authority over them. Thereupon the House appealed to the Governor to arrest them. " The freedom and privileges

---

[9] CO5-1318.   [11] *Ibid.*, 167.
[10] *Journals of the House of Burgesses*, 1712-1726: 132, 133.

of this House are in danger of being utterly subverted," they said, "when justices . . . assume a jurisdiction and by their judgment debar the people and their rightful representatives of the rightful ways . . . for redressing their grievances . . . we believe that such matters do concern the Burgesses in Assembly." [12] But Spotswood rebuffed them. They were exceeding their authority, he told them, when they persecuted justices and tried to punish them for their proceedings on the bench.

In his anger at not being able to control the Burgesses, Spotswood tried to make the House less democratic by restricting the right to vote. But not daring to reveal his intention, he approached the question in a roundabout way. In September, 1715, he sent out a printed letter to all of the county courts, questioning whether the justices should levy a tax to pay the Burgesses' salaries when no law existed empowering them to do so.[13] To the Lords of Trade he explained that if the justices declined to pay the levy, "the Burgesses must have become suitors for an act wherein might properly have been described the qualifications of the electors and elected." [14] In other words, he was prepared to veto any bill to legalize the collecting of salaries that did not disfranchise the small landholder and restrict the right to sit in the House to the well-to-do. So he kept mum on the fact that the salaries could be assessed by the sheriffs on a writ, as was the practice in England.

But in this matter he was balked by the members of the Council. Carter, Blair, Ludwell, and the others no doubt guessed what Spotswood was aiming at, and they were unwilling to have him undermine the very foundations of liberty in Virginia. So in the General Court they passed "an unpreceded sentence " to levy the Burgesses' salary on the private estates of the justices if they refused "to levy it on their counties." [15]

The House asserted in no uncertain terms its right to judge of the election and qualifications of its members. When they heard that William Cole and Cole Digges, of Warwick County, had promised the voters that if elected they would serve without salary, they refused to seat them. A new election was held in which, presumably, no such promise was made, and Cole and Digges were again elected, and this time permitted to take

[12] *Ibid.*, 147, 148.   [14] *Ibid.*
[13] CO5-1318.   [15] *Ibid.*

their seats.[16] Spotswood taunted the House for not grasping at this opportunity to reduce the heavy burden of the poll tax, and the Council thought there was neither law nor practice to justify their action.[17] Yet the Burgesses were right, not only in regarding Cole and Digges' offer as bribery, but in claiming that it was contrary to a law passed in October, 1705.[18]

The House now made a major assault upon the powers of the Governor. The time had come, they thought, to put an end to the bribing of its members with lucrative jobs, which had been done with such pernicious consequences by Berkeley, Nicholson, and others. They passed an act making it unlawful for any Burgess to be also a naval officer, tobacco agent, clerk of a county court, or hold any other office of profit in the government. They next tried to put an end to long Assemblies by prohibiting their continuance for more than three years. A third measure " for ascertaining secretaries', sheriffs', clerks' and constables' fees " was designed to make the bait of office less attractive. These bills aroused Spotswood's ire, for he saw immediately that they were designed to strike the vital power of patronage from his hands and the hands of his successors. So he vetoed all three.

The Governor's main purpose in calling the Assembly of 1715 was to have them vote assistance to South Carolina in that colony's bloody struggle with a powerful confederation of Indians. " We must appear to have neither policy nor bowels of compassion, if this government can remain unconcerned while savage pagans are overwhelming one of our adjacent provinces, and inhumanly butchering and torturing our brethren," he told the Burgesses in his opening address.[19] To them South Carolina seemed a long way off. They had troubles enough at home without sending men and money there, but, since the Governor was so set on it, they would yield if he would consent to something they wanted.

They passed a bill to raise £450 for the purchase of supplies for South Carolina, but tacked on a rider for the repeal of the hated tobacco act. This, of course, Spotswood vetoed. To let it pass, he thought, would be an act of high injustice, since upon the faith of the tobacco law at least £7,000 had been

[16] *Journals of the House of Burgesses*, xxxiii.
[17] *Ibid.*, 153, 165, 168.
[18] W. W. Hening, *Statutes at large* 3: 243.
[19] *Journals of the House of Burgesses*, 1712-1726: 122.

spent in erecting warehouses and wharves, and in the purchase of scales.[20] Neither he nor the Burgesses realized that the law was under attack in England. The merchants were dissatisfied with it, and Solicitor General William Thompson held that it was an act in restraint of trade. In July, 1717, the act was vetoed by King George I.[21]

Spotswood closed the session with an ill-natured and bitter denunciation of the Burgesses. "The true interest of your country is not what you have troubled your heads about," he said. "All your proceedings have been calculated to answer the notions of the ignorant populace, and if you can excuse yourselves to them, you matter not how you stand before God, your Prince, and all judicious men or before any others to whom you think you owe not your elections. . . . In fine, I cannot but attribute those miscarriages to the people's mistaken choice of a set of representatives whom Heaven has not generally endowed with the ordinary qualifications requisite to legislators, for I observe that the grand ruling party in your House has not furnished chairmen for two of your standing committees who can spell English or write common sense. And to keep such an Assembly on foot would be discrediting a country that has many able and worthy gentlemen in it. And therefore I dissolve you." [22]

Having insulted the Burgesses and the people who had elected them, Spotswood next incurred the enmity of a majority of the Council. The trouble started when he laid before them the instruction requiring him to see that fair books of accounts be kept of the Crown revenues.[23] Since only the gross sums had been reported and itemized accounts kept only on "loose papers," he demanded that the Auditor and the Receiver General adopt more businesslike methods. To this Receiver General William Byrd and Auditor Ludwell replied that they kept their accounts as their predecessors had kept them and in accordance with instructions from the Auditor General for all the colonies.

Soon after this Byrd left for England, taking with him, if we may believe Spotswood, "all the books of the revenue." The Governor then demanded of Ludwell whether or not he in-

[20] *Ibid.*, 169.
[21] CO5-1313.
[22] *Journals of the House of Burgesses*, 1712-1726: 170.
[23] CO5-1416.

tended to comply with the instruction to keep account books. Ludwell replied that he could not change the old method without orders from the Auditor General. Since this was nothing less than setting up the authority of this officer against that of the King, the Governor thought the excuse a very poor one. So, in January, 1716, he ousted both Ludwell and Byrd from office.[24]

No doubt there had been confusion in the accounts, and no doubt Spotswood's insistence on having account books would have done much to bring them into order. It is possible, also, that there had been much remissness in paying taxes and some fraud. The Governor wrote the Lords of Trade: "Notwithstanding all the contrivances of the family to justify the late officers of the revenue, here is now demonstration, not only of darkness and confusion in the manner of collecting the quit rents, but likewise of frauds and errors in accounting for the King's revenue." [25]

Realizing that he had brought down on himself the hostility of the Councillors, Spotswood now tried to undermine their power by setting up courts of oyer and terminer to which he appointed persons other than themselves. The General Court, on which all members of the Council and none else sat, had long been the court of last appeal in the colony. The Councillors prized their seats in this court not less than their seats in the Upper House of Assembly or around the Council table. Spotswood claimed that their power over the lives and property of the people made all regard them with awe, and "kept the country in subjection to their party." [26] "They know that they have now lodged wholly in their hands that power that Absalom wanted for effectually securing the people in his interest, when he longed to be the judge of every man's cause." [27]

It was to be expected, then, that they should insist that none but themselves should sit on the new court of oyer and terminer. In May, 1717, eight of them met in secret and drew up a letter to the Lords of Trade defending their position. The charter of 1676 expressly stated that the Governor and Council had authority to try "all treasons, murders, felonies." The laws of Virginia made the Governor and Council the supreme court.

[24] *Executive journals of the Council* 3: 437.
[25] CO5-1318, Spotswood to the Lords of Trade, March 20, 1718.
[26] *Ibid.*
[27] *Ibid.*, Spotswood to Orkney, July 1, 1718.

They could not believe that a Governor could " break through laws and charters and alter all the ancient usage and tradition of the government." [28]

Spotswood also appealed to the Lords of Trade. And he was overjoyed when this body wrote him that they could not see what reason the Council had to insist upon being the sole judges of the new court since his commission empowered him to " appoint judges." [29] They were backed by Attorney General Edward Northy in his opinion of December 24, 1717. Northy advised, however, that Governors be instructed not to hold courts of oyer and terminer except in cases of extraordinary emergency." [30]

The test came in December, 1718, when the court of oyer and terminer was about to begin its session. Several Councillors had taken their seats when Spotswood announced that he was joining with them Mr. Cole Digges and Mr. Peter Beverley. Since neither was a member of the Council, Ludwell and four others got up and left. The five then drew up a remonstrance, which Ludwell presented to Spotswood in court, with a " long harangue." Noticing that people were gathering, he turned around, and raising his voice, addressed them. " The Governor's power of naming other judges than the Councillors in life and death cases is of dangerous consequence to the lives and liberties of free subjects," he said. " For that reason I refuse to sit in the court of oyer and terminer with those gentlemen." [31]

In London, Byrd pleaded the cause of the Council before the Lords of Trade. It would be fatal, he argued, to permit a Governor to try any person by what judges he thought proper. " Whoever has had the fortune to live in the plantations knows that Governors are not in the least exempt from human frailties, such as passionate love of money, resentment against such as presume to oppose their designs, particularly to their creatures and favorites." [32] To this Spotswood retorted: " What else could tempt the ruling party in the Council so strenuously to insist on a right, never claimed before, of being judges of oyer and terminer, but the desire of gaining to one family an

[28] Ludwell, Smith, Lewis, Bassett, Harrison, Berkeley, Carter, and Blair.
[29] CO5-1364.
[30] CO5-1318.
[31] CO5-1318, Spotswood to the Lords of Trade, March 5, 1719.
[32] *Ibid.*, Byrd Concerning Courts.

entire power over the lives, as they now have over the estates, of the people of Virginia? [33]

To the Earl of Orkney, Spotswood wrote bitterly. If he lost his battle with the Council, future Governors would think it folly to oppose them. " I take the power, interest, and repu- tation of the King's Governor in this dominion to be now reduced to a desperate gasp, and if the present efforts of the country cannot add new vigor to the same, then the haughtiness of a Carter, the hypocrisy of a Blair, the inveteracy of a Lud- well, the brutishness of a Smith, the malice of a Byrd, the conceitedness of a Grymes, and the scurrility of a Corbin, with about a score of base disloyalists and ungrateful Creolians for their adherents, must for the future rule the province." [34]

Since the Virginia treasury was now overflowing as a result of peace in Europe and the shipping out of vast quantities of tobacco, Spotswood managed to get along without an Assembly for three years. He would probably have continued to do so indefinitely, had he not wanted an act to reimburse the Indian Company which had been dissolved by order of the King. The trade with the Indians had recently become a mere trickle, because South Carolina had confiscated the goods of some Virginia traders, and lawless savages had robbed others. So an act was passed in 1714 under which a monopoly of the trade with the southern tribes was lodged in the Virginia Indian Company.

In return the company was required to contribute £100 towards building a public magazine at Williamsburg, to garri- son and keep in repair a fort at Christanna on the frontier, and erect a schoolhouse there for Indian children. Some of the leading men in the colony became stockholders, among them William Cocke, Mann Page, William Cole, Nathaniel Harrison, and Cole Digges. They had spent large sums " in purchasing servants, taking up land and making settlements on the frontier, clearing roads, and building warehouses," when word came that the act under which they operated had been vetoed by the King.[35] Since they were now left holding the bag, they asked that the Assembly reimburse them.

The election which followed was one of the bitterest in Vir-

[33] *Ibid.*, Spotswood to the Lords of Trade, Dec. 22, 1718.
[34] *Ibid.*, Spotswood to Orkney, Dec. 22, 1718.
[35] CO5-1317, Memorial of the Virginia Indian Company.

ginia history. Spotswood made full use of the patronage.
"Commissions flew about to every fellow that could make two
or three votes," wrote Joshua Gee. "He gave the power to
his friends to make a discreet use of [them]. And indeed never
fouler play was by men, than at most of our elections." [36]
Political pamphlets were distributed at every courthouse. One
of them began: "Having seen a rascally paper which contained advice to freeholders in favor of a court party and tools
of arbitrary power to enslave and ruin a free born people . . .
to prevent which I thought it my duty to open your eyes. . . .
You are to know, brother electors, that this Assembly is called
for no other reason but to pay to the Indian Company their
charges on Fort Christanna, if they can get a set of men fit for
that purpose to gull into that unjust payment." [37]

The outcome of the election was another defeat for the
Governor. No less than thirty-four members of the hostile
House of Burgesses of 1715 were returned. Of the new members Gawin Corbin, John Grymes, Archibald Blair, and others
were bitter enemies of Spotswood. During the session the
Governor kept his temper, since he had been ordered to do so
by the Lords of Trade, but the Burgesses, remembering his
former insults, did everything they could to annoy him. Though
his opening address was conciliatory, it was greeted with "violent censures." One wrathful member "shot his bolt" and
cried out: "It is all stuff and calculated only for the latitude of
Whitehall." When Spotswood laid before the House several
letters from New York in regard to renewing a treaty with the
Indians, "they made it their jest, and setting up a great laugh
. . . cried out in their vulgar language, ' A bite! ' " [38]

Needless to say, Spotswood got practically nothing out of this
Assembly. They refused to repay the Indian Company for what
they had laid out for the defense of the colony. They refused
to pay for a proposed trip to New York by Spotswood to renew
the treaty with the Iroquois. To his request for payment of his
expenses in making fatiguing journeys in the service of the
country, they replied, " we hope they will give you the satisfaction of reflecting that you have deserved the salary allowed by
his Majesty." [39]

[36] CO5-1319, Letter of Mr. Gee, Oct. 5, 1721.
[37] CO5-1318, " Advice to Freeholders."
[38] CO5-1318, Answer to Lieutenant Governor Spotswood.
[39] *Journals of the House of Burgesses*, 1712-1726: 213.

But the Burgesses were not yet done with him. Late in the session, when it seemed that nothing more of importance was to come before them, and some had gone home and others were at the race track, the "party managers" brought in an address to the King with a long string of accusations against him. Spotswood intimates that Blair and Ludwell were responsible for this maneuver in order to have the House second the complaints of the Council. Blair made his influence felt through his brother, Archibald Blair, and Ludwell through his son-in-law, John Grymes. "As during the last two sessions the one has scarce let a day pass without dropping in the Assembly some scurrilous reflection upon me," Spotswood wrote, "so the other can't keep his temper when he perceives any matter agreeable to me is likely to be carried." [40]

The accusations, which were embodied in instructions to William Byrd II as agent for the House, were carried by a vote of twenty-two to fourteen. But when they were considered one by one most of them were struck out. In their final form the accusations boiled down to little more than that the Governor had misconstrued the laws, that he had tried to keep the justices from levying the salaries of the Burgesses, and that he had by provoking speeches and messages abused the House.[41] Spotswood, in two long papers, had no difficulty in answering the charges, but they remained as convincing evidence that there existed widespread dissatisfaction with his administration.

To counteract this impression he now followed the precedent set by Nicholson of seeking flattering addresses. "To support his cause tools were picked to make up grand juries to deliver fulsome addresses to the Governor and abuse the Council and Assembly," Joshua Gee tells us. "The same tools made addresses from the courts and even engaged every barefooted fellow to sign addresses from the counties." [42] The address from Middlesex spoke of Spotswood's wise and moderate government; that of the "justices, clergy, and principal inhabitants" of New Kent declared that his character had been traduced; that of King and Queen County that the charges against him were false. All in all, the addresses came from twenty-one of the twenty-five counties.[43]

[40] CO5-1318, Spotswood to Orkney, Dec. 22, 1718.
[41] *Journals of the House of Burgesses*, 1712-1726: 230, 231.
[42] CO5-1319, Letter of Mr. Gee.
[43] CO5-1318.

This deluge of praise must have had its influence with the Lords of Trade and the Earl of Orkney. But more convincing was the logic of Spotswood's letters in which he answered the charges against him. He had brought down on his head the hostility of the Councillors and Burgesses through his efforts to carry out their Lordships' orders and uphold the prerogative of the King, he said. To remove him for doing his duty would render the situation hopeless for future Governors.

So, despite the arguments and pleading of William Byrd, both Orkney and the Lords of Trade gave Spotswood their support. Orkney thought that no essential complaint had been brought against him, and praised him for putting the government of Virginia upon a much improved footing.[44] The Board of Trade wrote Spotswood, in June, 1719: "You may depend upon all the countenance and support which we can give you which we think you have deserved." [45] It was rumored in Virginia, also, that the Board was considering removing from the Council some of the Governor's bitterest enemies.

Yet at the moment of triumph, Spotswood, instead of lauding it over the Councillors and forcing them to submit, seemed anxious to compromise all differences. The key to his moderation is found in his opening address to the Burgesses in November, 1720: "To consider the stake I have among you and the free choice I've made to fix it under this government, you have not surely any grounds to suspect me of injurious designs against the welfare of this colony." [46] Then he indulged in a metaphor to show that the interests of Virginia and Great Britain did not conflict. " I look upon Virginia as a rib taken from Britain's side, and believe that while they both proceed as living under the marriage contract, this Eve must thrive as long as her Adam flourishes."

In other words, Spotswood did not want to continue his differences with the planter aristocracy because he planned to become one of them. In 1716 he had acquired 3,229 acres on the Rappahannock, known as the Germanna Tract, and peopled it with German tenants. Three years later he granted 3,065 acres, the so-called Wilderness Tract, to a certain Richard Hickman, who transferred it to him. He next acquired the

[44] *Board of Trade journal,* 1715-1718: 425, 426.
[45] CO5-1365, Lords of Trade to Spotswood, June 26, 1719.
[46] *Journals of the House of Burgesses,* 1712-1726: 250.

Fork Tract, the Barrows Tract, the Mine Tract of 15,000 acres, the Lower Massaponax Tract, and the Upper Massaponax Tract. In 1729, when the new county of Spotsylvania was created, the Governor owned 25,000 acres within its borders.[47] On his Mine Tract he had invested so heavily in an iron foundry that Byrd called him the Tubal Cain of Virginia.

So, when Nathaniel Harrison approached him with proposals for a reconciliation, Spotswood was quite willing to do his part. But there were long negotiations before peace was concluded. On May 16, 1718, when the Governor made new overtures, they were greeted by stiffness and reserve. Yet the Councillors at his invitation, went from the Capitol to the Palace, and there gathered around a bowl of arrack, drinking until midnight. On the other hand, the hostile eight shunned Spotswood's celebration of the King's birthday, " got together all the turbulent and disaffected Burgesses, had an entertainment of their own in the Burgesses House, and invited all the mob to a bonfire, where they were plentifully supplied with liquors." [48]

In the end the Councillors came to terms. Smith and Berkeley were dead, while Carter, Blair, Ludwell, Lewis, Byrd, and Harrison had seen the handwriting on the wall. At a meeting in the Council Chamber of the Capitol, in April 1720, with Spotswood at the head of the table, it was agreed that all past controversies be forgotten, and that in the future there should be no other contention than who should most promote the King's service and the public benefit of the colony.[49]

For some months there was comparative quiet in Virginia. But in 1721 Spotswood became uneasy when James Blair decided to visit England. " He is continually assuring me of all the service he can do me at home," the Governor wrote to the Bishop of London, " but . . . I shall be contented with his not offering to do me any disservice." [50] These fears were well-grounded, for there is reason to think that the Commissary was instrumental in having him removed from office, just how is not known. It is significant that when it was rumored that a new Governor was coming over, " it was understood that Parson Blair was likely to act as prime minister." Significant, also, is it that Hugh Drysdale, who succeeded Spotswood early

[47] Leonidas Dodson, *Alexander Spotswood*, Chap. XIII.
[48] *Spotswood letters* 2: 284.
[49] *Executive Journals of the Council* 3: 524.
[50] Rawlinson manuscript.

in 1722, came to Virginia on the same vessel as Blair, and remained on the most intimate terms with him throughout his short administration.[51]

Spotswood's last act as Lieutenant Governor reflects no credit upon his character, and did disservice both to the Crown and colony. Upon hearing that he was to be removed, he made out patents for huge tracts of land in Spotsylvania County to certain persons who immediately conveyed them to him.[52] He later adopted a system of tenantry, leasing land in small parcels for two generations, a system which was copied in the huge Virginia manors developed in western Virginia late in the century. Although tenantry hastened settlement, it was inconsistent with the democratic spirit of the frontier, and was largely abolished by the Revolution.

Nathaniel Blakiston said of Spotswood: " That gentleman has real capacity and talents to manage in a high sphere, but he adheres too much to his own sentiments, and thinks himself ill-treated if everybody does not think as he does." [53] This weakness accounts in part for his inability to get along with either the Council or the Burgesses. Many of the policies which he advocated were wise, but his attempts to force them through were unwise. When the Council opposed him he tried to break their power; when the Burgesses thwarted him, he tried to bribe them into submission.

Spotswood's administration was marked by several years of great prosperity, by the expansion of the frontier, by the attempts to develop manufactures, by the regulation of the tobacco trade; but more important was the demonstration that the people would no longer permit their representatives in the Assembly to be made submissive to the Governor by the use of the patronage. The punishment which they meted out to the faithless in the Assembly of 1714 marked a notable advance along the road to liberty, and was a warning to future Governors not to attempt to rule by corruption.

[51] CO5-1319.
[52] Ludwell papers 2 (40).
[53] Ibid.

CHAPTER XI

PEACE AND PROSPERITY

A S the first quarter of the eighteenth century was a period
of bitter contention between the Governors of Virginia
and the Council and Burgesses, so the second quarter was
marked by peace and harmony. In England the government,
under the leadership of Sir Robert Walpole, adopted a conciliatory policy toward the colonies, the famous policy of letting
sleeping dogs lie. Great Britain was reaping huge profits from
the trade with America, and the chief concern of the Board of
Trade was to see that no laws were passed by the Assemblies to
lessen them. On the other hand, the colonies were permitted
to govern themselves to a degree that would not have been
tolerated under the Stuarts.

Possibly it was by chance that the two Lieutenant Governors
whose administrations covered this period—Hugh Drysdale and
William Gooch—were admirably suited to carry out this policy.
Or they may have been selected because of their winning per-
sonalities, their ability to see both sides of a question, their
desire to do justice to all men, their lack of greed and ambition
to dictate. We know that Drysdale was recommended to the
Earl of Orkney by Walpole himself.[1] At all events, after contending for years with the implacable Nicholson and the dictatorial Spotswood, Drysdale and Gooch must have seemed gifts
from Heaven to the Virginians.

Drysdale arrived in Virginia on September 25, 1722, and two
days later was sworn in in the Council Chamber. He was heartily welcomed. A few months later he could report that there
was " universal contentment on the change made in the government," and that his administration had the approbation of all
ranks of people.[2] In marked contrast to their wordy war with
Spotswood, the Burgesses showed him only respect and affection.
" We must acknowledge the present calm and tranquility to be
the consequences of your prudence and moderation," they told

[1] Leonidas Dodson, *Alexander Spotswood*, 270, 271.
[2] *Sainsbury transcripts* 9: 74, 75.

him.[3] When he was planning to leave for England because of ill health, they addressed the King to say that his speedy return would be a great happiness to the people of the colony.[4]

Drysdale's popularity was based more on what he did not do than what he did do. He made no attempt to undermine the judicial power of the Council, he seems not to have used the patronage to control the House of Burgesses, he did not try to make the colony less democratic by restricting the right to vote, he did not deny to the Burgesses their ancient privileges, he did not use his office for personal gain.

He was at first critical of the policy, favored by the Council, of issuing patents for huge tracts of land. His predecessor had granted some for 10,000 acres, some for 20,000 acres, some for 40,000 acres despite the order that 1,000 acres should be the limit. " Thus the intention of the government to make Spotsylvania a well inhabited frontier is frustrated," he said.[5]

But the Councillors and other men of wealth persuaded him that large holdings which could be cut up into small farms and leased to tenants hastened rather than retarded settlement. " The Council are of opinion that the limiting the quantity of land to be taken up in the new counties is prejudicial and a discouragement to their speedy settlement," he wrote in July, 1724.[6] He did not stop to consider that the growth of tenantry would be a blow, not only to economic democracy, but political democracy as well, since tenants, unless they were also freeholders, had no right to vote.

Drysdale called for an election for a new Assembly who met in the Capitol on May 9, 1723. The Burgesses had hardly settled themselves in their seats when they took up two cases which concerned the rights of the people and their privileges. In Essex County grievances had been presented to the court for certification to the Assembly, charging Colonel Joseph Smith, commander of the county militia, with harsh and illegal conduct while a member of a court-martial. Colonel Smith, himself a member of the court, refused to sign this paper, so that it failed to reach the House. Thereupon the Burgesses declared him " guilty of a breach of his duty," and ordered the Speaker to reprimand him.[7] In striking contrast to Spotswood's up-

---

[3] *Journals of the House of Burgesses*, 1712-1726: 402.
[4] *Ibid.*, 419.   [6] *Ibid.*, 134.
[5] *Sainsbury transcripts*, **9**: 121.   [7] *Ibid.*, xlix, 1.

holding of Littlefield and Butts in a similar case, Drysdale backed the House by removing Smith from the county court.[8]

In the other case a certain William Hopkins was accused of " rude, contemptuous, and indecent " language in the House about one of the members—Mr. Matthew Kemp. When he was adjudged guilty and ordered on his knees to ask the pardon of the Burgesses and Mr. Kemp, he flatly refused. It was then ordered that he be led through the Duke of Gloucester Street, from the Capitol to the college gate and back, with a placard pinned to his breast bearing the following inscription: " For insolent behavior at the bar of the House of Burgesses, when he was there as an offender and with obstinacy and contempt disobeying their order." This prospect was too much for Hopkins, so, no doubt with inward curses, he made the apology.[9]

There was universal grief in Virginia when Drysdale died, on July 22, 1726. He was buried with elaborate ceremonies, to the booming of cannon. The Council wrote Mrs. Drysdale expressing " the just sense " of " the public loss," and giving her permission to remain for the time being in the Palace.[10] Pending the appointment of a new Lieutenant Governor, they voted to make Robert Carter President. The selection normally would have gone to Edmund Jenings, as the senior member of the Council, but he had just been suspended because of his age and because he was much " decayed in his understanding."

William Gooch, who was appointed to succeed Drysdale, took the oath of office on September 11, 1727. It must have been with apprehension that the members of the Council greeted him. It would be too much to expect that the colony would have in succession two Governors of the stamp of Drysdale. Might not the new arrival be another Spotswood, or even another Nicholson?

They were not long kept in doubt. Gooch proved to be one of the most popular Governors in the history of the colony. Sincerely interested in the welfare of the people, conciliatory in his dealings with both the Council and the Burgesses, he brought internal peace and contentment. The story was told of him that one day when in the company of several gentlemen, he happened to pass a Negro slave. When the Negro lifted his hat, Gooch lifted his in return.

[8] *Executive journals of the Council* 4: 40.
[9] *Journals of the House of Burgesses,* 1712-1726: 1.
[10] *Executive journals of the Council* 4: 114.

"What, Governor Gooch, do you lift your hat to a slave?" one of his companions asked.

"I would be deeply humiliated to be surpassed in courtesy by a slave," was the reply.

Throughout Gooch's administration there was practically no friction between the Governor and the Assembly. The public affairs were carried on in perfect harmony and good understanding, he reported in 1734. The address of the Speaker of the House of Burgesses, Sir John Randolph, to Gooch is one of the most remarkable in Virginia history. "You have shew'd how easy it is to give universal satisfaction to the people under your government. . . . You have not been intoxicated with the power committed to you by his Majesty, but have used it like a faithful trustee for the public good. . . . You never propose matters without supposing your opinion subject to the examination of others, nor strive to make other men's reason blindly and implicitly obedient to yours. . . . You have extirpated all factions among us . . . and plainly proved that none can arise, or be lasting, but from the countenance and encouragement of a Governor." [11]

Both the Council and the Burgesses expressed their gratitude to Gooch by gifts of money, the former voting him £300 to cover the expense of his voyage to Virginia, and the latter giving him £500. Although his instructions forbade his acceptance, he pocketed the money. "I thought it would not become me to refuse this extraordinary instance of their regard," he wrote the Lords of Trade. There was a precedent for his acceptance, for Nicholson had had £300 when that sum was worth £600 in the present currency. And though the Board censured him, they did not make him refund the money.[12]

It was typical of Gooch that he was willing to yield in matters of which he did not fully approve in order to carry points which he had very much at heart. He had not been long in the colony when he came to the conclusion that it would greatly benefit the planters if the tobacco inspection act of 1713 could be revived. But he was well aware that the people had not forgotten the use Spotswood had made of it to gain control of the House of Burgesses, or his veto of the bill to prohibit Burgesses from holding places of profit in the government. So, in return

[11] *Journals of the House of Burgesses*, 1727-1740: 242.
[12] Gooch to the Lords of Trade, Feb. 12, 1728; Aug. 9, 1728.

for the passage of a new tobacco law, he assented to an act to keep officeholders out of the House. "The Burgesses were for this bill," he wrote the Lords of Trade, "and my desire to keep them in good humor while matters of greater moment were under their deliberation, prevailed with me to assent to it." [13]

But he thought that the act had nothing in its favor, except that it was an imitation of the laws of England made for securing the freedom of Parliament. "In my humble opinion this country is yet too young for so refined a regulation. Places of profit are indeed but few, but men of capacity for the discharge of them do not much more abound; therefore either the government must be ill served, or the House of Burgesses meanly fitted if men of capacity and integrity must be shut out either of the one or the other." [14]

Gooch either did not understand the importance of this bill, or deliberately concealed it from the British Government. Had he known of the use of the power of appointment by former Governors to gain control of the House of Burgesses, he could not have dismissed the measure so lightly. Nor could he have realized what a major victory it was for liberty. Henceforth no Berkeley could bribe the Burgesses into submission and so rule the colony like a despot; no Nicholson could hand out commissions as sheriffs, or collectors, or officers in the militia in exchange for votes in the House; no Spotswood could create tobacco agents' jobs to tempt the people's representatives.

Though Gooch was solicitous for the welfare of the poor planter, he was not in favor of manhood suffrage. So he affixed his signature to a bill limiting the right to vote to freeholders owning 100 acres of unoccupied land or twenty-five acres with a house.[15] Had he had his way the limitation would have been greater. "Yet as the former laws had allowed any kind of a freehold to give that right, and all attempts made heretofore to exclude the mob of the populace . . . had proved vain, it is much better to have that point fixed on some certain basis, than to leave all persons indefinitely at liberty to have a vote. . . . After such a beginning it may be hoped a further regulation will follow to remove from the House such members as have

[13] W. W. Hening, *Statutes at large* 4: 292.
[14] July 23, 1730.
[15] W. W. Hening, *Statutes at large* 4: 475.

little recommended them to the people's choice besides the art
of stirring up discontents." [16]

Though Gooch thus frankly avowed his dislike of democracy,
he promoted its growth by encouraging the westward expansion
of settlement, not only in the Piedmont, but in the Shenandoah
Valley. In 1736 he wrote the Lords of Trade: " Great numbers,
as well of his Majesty's natural born subjects as foreigners, . . .
have removed into this colony on the west side of our mountains." This he pointed out would be a protection to the older
parts of the colony by heading off any attempt of the French
at penetration.

Perhaps it had not occurred to Gooch that expansion would
divide the colony into two parts—the democratic up-country,
and the aristocratic tidewater. Spotsylvania, Brunswick, Gooch-
land, Amelia, Caroline, and other counties in the Piedmont
were filling up with small farmers from the east, Frederick
with poor Germans and Swiss. It is true that some well-to-do
planters established "quarters" managed by overseers above
the Fall Line, and later invaded parts of the Valley, but even as
late as the French and Indian War frontier conditions persisted
in the regions on either side of the Blue Ridge. The influence
of the west grew steadily as each new county sent its two
representatives to the House of Burgesses. Whereas in 1727
when there were 65 members of the House, only 10 were from
the west, in 1752, when the members numbered 104, 46 were
from the western or southwestern counties. The time was not
distant when the up-country members would count a majority.
A bewigged Carter, or Harrison, or Wormeley, in his broad-
cloth suit with silver buttons, may have been resentful when
a roughly clad delegate from Albemarle or Frederick took a seat
beside him, but he dared not show it.

But in the first test of strength the newcomers lost because
the east still dominated the Council. In 1749, after the burning
of the Capitol in Williamsburg, the western Burgesses proposed
that the seat of government be moved to a site on the Pamunkey, in Hanover County, which would save them many miles
of travel in attending meetings of the Assembly. The feeling
on each side ran high. Mr. John Blair, a member of the Council, in conversation with one of the Burgesses, pointed to the
Speaker, saying: "There goes the man who is at the bottom

---

[16] Gooch to the Lords of Trade, Oct. 5, 1736.

of this hellish scheme." The House was deeply offended, and was appeased only when Blair apologized. After much hesitation the bill for the removal was passed by a vote of forty to thirty-eight, but it was promptly rejected by the Council.[17] So the Capitol was rebuilt on the old foundations, but with the proviso that this would not fix the seat of government permanently in Williamsburg. It did, however, fix it there until the Revolution, when, in response to the wishes of an overwhelming majority of the people, it was moved to Richmond.

During most of Gooch's administration the two Houses worked in harmony. But occasionally there was friction. At the close of the session of 1728 the Burgesses passed a resolution to pay their own salaries out of the fund raised by the duty on liquors in order to lessen the hated poll tax. But the Council refused to concur. The Burgesses then voted that they be paid from funds in the hands of the Treasurer. Again the Council demurred. They argued that the salaries of the Burgesses was the concern of the counties. "It would be an unequal distribution of the public money to allow the same share of it to a county which has a thousand tithables as one that has three thousand." [18] This reasoning was based on the assumption that a Burgess represented only the interests of the county which elected him and not those of the colony as a whole, an assumption contradicted by the whole history of the House. Yet the Burgesses, though with some bitterness, were forced to yield for the time being.

Gooch was much concerned over the dispute, for he was convinced that it was not ended. He was right. At the very next session a bill was passed to pay the Burgesses out of the money in the Treasurer's hands, provided this should not reduce the fund below £1,500.[19] The Council consented, under Gooch's urging, because the bill allowed the Burgesses only ten shillings a day instead of thirteen as formerly, and nothing when not actually in attendance, but "at home about their private affairs or perhaps in pursuit of their pleasures." Gooch wrote the Lords of Trade congratulating himself on having reduced salaries, but this does not obscure the fact that the act was a victory for the House.[20]

[17] *Journals of the House of Burgesses*, 1742-1749: xxvii, xxviii.
[18] Gooch to the Lords of Trade, June 8, 1728.
[19] W. W. Hening, *Statutes at large* 4: 279.
[20] July 23, 1730.

In fact, the House of Burgesses, like the House of Commons, was becoming the dominating body, and the Council, like the House of Lords, was growing weaker. With the multiplying of the number of wealthy planters through the use of slave labor, the twelve men who made up the Council ceased to be the sole representatives of their interests. Many aristocrats were honored to have a seat in the Lower House. One has only to glance down the list of Burgesses to find many of the proudest names in colonial Virginia—Page, Harrison, Fairfax, Randolph, Burwell, Carter, Ball, Wormeley, Digges, Spotswood, Lee, Byrd, Claiborne, etc. So the aristocrat as well as the small farmer, the wealthy easterner as well as the pioneer of Orange or Albemarle, or the German of Frederick looked to the House to protect their interests.

While the leadership of the House continued to be aristocratic, the rank and file grew more democratic. The open spaces of America fostered a spirit of independence. When men had gone into a wilderness, cleared openings in the forest, built their simple houses, laid out crops, fought the Indians, they became impatient of control by a group of eastern aristocrats, or by a government three thousand miles away in which they had no voice.

Nor was democracy confined to the west, for the small farmer class of the east persisted despite the importation of thousands of slaves. It is true that many, finding it difficult to compete with slave labor, sold their little holdings, packed up their few household goods, and set out for the West or for one of the northern colonies. But others kept their heads above water by producing only the highest grades of tobacco, for which the blacks at first were not suited. " I must beg you to remember that the common people make the best," Gooch wrote in 1731.

But this reprieve was only temporary, for in time the wealthy planter taught the Africans to produce even the high priced Orinoco. Then the poor planter had to join the class of slaveholders by making a few purchases, or sink into abject poverty. That thousands did buy slaves we know from an examination of the tax lists. In 1716, in Lancaster County, of some 200 slaveowners, 165 had from one to four only. The only large owner was the wealthy Robert Carter who had 126.[21]

The replacing of the Virginia yeomanry, the men who cul-

[21] *William and Mary Quarterly* 2: 106-122.

tivated their holdings with their own hands, by small slaveholders was in many ways a development to be deplored, but
it saved the small farmer class from extinction, and democracy
from a fatal blow. Without it all the eastern part of the colony
and part of the Piedmont would have become a land of wealthy
proprietors and their slaves, and ignorant, degraded, poverty-
stricken whites.

The small slaveholders were fiercely jealous of their rights,
both social and political. From the proud aristocrat they demanded courtesy and respect. And these the aristocrat thought
it wise to accord them, for he knew that they constituted an
overwhelming majority of the voters. Nor were there anywhere,
in the northern colonies or in the West, more ardent upholders
of self-government. In the long struggle for liberty it was
usually the aristocrats who led the way, but they would have
been powerless had they not had the loyal support of the small
eastern farmer as well as the western frontiersman.

And the climax of this struggle was not distant. Walpole
resigned in 1752, and his successors were not inclined to let
the colonies become semi-independent little republics. Had
their attention not been diverted by European wars, they would
probably have come to grips with the colonial governments
sooner than they did.

At the moment, however, the chief differences between Virginia and the mother country seemed to be economic rather
than constitutional. The planters had long protested against
the Navigation Acts, but they had in time adjusted themselves
to them. To the merchants of England they were tied by the
bonds of mutual interest, for they were dependent upon them
for transporting and disposing of their tobacco, and for bringing them manufactured goods in return.

But there developed various points of difference. And it
became a bitter grievance to the planters that when these differences were placed before the British government, the decision
always favored the merchants. In fact, so great was the influence of certain traders that at times their recommendations
to important posts in the colonies were decisive. Among the
best known of these men was Micajah Perry, whose opinion the
Board of Trade frequently sought on matters affecting commerce. It was rumored that it was he who persuaded the
Auditor General to appoint Philip Ludwell Auditor of Virginia. And when the British government turned down the

recommendation of a Governor in filling a vacancy in the
Council in favor of one by the merchants, it was deeply resented in the colony. "Your Lordships cannot but be sensible
that little regard is likely to be paid a Governor who shall be
supposed to have no interest at your Lordships' Board," Gooch
wrote in 1747.

The people were even more resentful at the insistence of
the merchants in blocking any measure by the Assembly, no
matter how beneficial, if they thought it would lessen their
profits. Many of them had invested in the Royal African Company, and the slave trade to Virginia was booming. It was
stated that black workers were coming in at the rate of 1,500
or 1,600 a year, and at every landing place scores were sold to
the highest bidders. In 1730, out of a total population of
114,000, no less than 30,000 were Negroes.[22] With profits piling
up, the merchants wanted no interference with this trade, however inhuman it was, and however harmful to the economic and
social structure of the colony.

Many thoughtful men in the colony viewed the situation
with alarm, not only because the importation of so many blacks
was drying up the stream of white immigrants from England,
but because it was driving out of the colony poor men who did
not want to compete with slave labor. And the planters had
reason to dread slave insurrections. Some of the Africans were
docile enough, but a few resented their bonds fiercely. In 1710
a conspiracy was discovered in Surry and James City Counties,
in which the Negroes planned to rise, kill all who opposed
them, and escape out of the colony. Several were tried in the
General Court, convicted and executed.[23]

There was much satisfaction when the Assembly, in the
revenue act of 1723, tried to stem the tide by placing a duty
on the importation of slaves. But when the act came before
the Lords of Trade, the merchants opposed it vigorously. John
Cary, who had lived in Virginia, and later went to England to
enter the tobacco trade, when summoned before the Board,
argued against it. It would ruin the poor planters, he said,
because it would run up the cost of slaves, and they would not
be able to buy enough to cultivate their plantations.[24] This
argument, as we have seen, was not entirely misleading, but

[22] CO5-1322, Report of Gooch.
[23] *Executive journals of the Council* 3: 234, 235.
[24] *Sainsbury transcripts* 9: 112.

it ignored the predicament of the thousands who could afford not even one, no matter how cheap, and so sank into great poverty, became " poor white trash." Yet the Board sided with Cary and his fellow merchants, and in January, 1724, advised the King to veto the act.

The Assembly, greatly disappointed, five years later made another attempt, placing a duty of forty shillings a head on the importation of slaves. Gooch gave them his full support. The merchants would not be injured by the law, he argued, since the purchasers had to pay the tax.[25] But the importers did not see it that way, and at their urging the King disallowed the act.

How bitterly these vetoes were resented in Virginia is shown by a statement of Thomas Jefferson in his " A Summary View of the Rights of British America," written in 1774. " The abolition of slavery is the great object of desire in those colonies, where it was, unhappily, introduced in their infant state. But previously to the enfranchisement of the slaves we have, it is necessary to exclude all further importations from Africa. Yet our repeated attempts to effect this, by prohibitions, and by imposing duties which might amount to a prohibition, having been hitherto defeated by his Majesty's negative: thus preferring the immediate advantages of a few British corsairs to the lasting interests of the American States, and the rights of human nature deeply wounded by this infamous practice. Nay, the single interposition of an interested individual against a law was scarcely ever known to fail of success, though, in the opposite scale, were placed the interests of a whole country.[26]

The merchants opposed, not only the duty on slaves, but any other duty which they thought might lessen imports. The Assembly repeatedly passed laws to place duties on rum, brandy, wine, cider, beer, and ale, not because they thought they would debauch the people, but to raise revenue to meet the needs of the government without resorting to the hated poll tax. They finally persuaded the merchants that light duties on liquors would do them no harm. And perhaps the King was persuaded to give his assent by the urgings of Gooch. " The revenue arising from the duty on liquors is the best expedient to raise money for defraying the contingent charges of the government and the chief support of the College of William and Mary," he

[25] June 8, 1728.
[26] *The writings of Thomas Jefferson*, A. A. Lipscomb, ed., 1: 201.

wrote. " By it most of the public debts are paid and the people eased of an intolerable poll tax, which many of the poorer sort would be unable to pay."

But in 1730 the Assembly went too far when, in the revenue bill of that year, they exempted Virginia owners from half the tax in a rather forlorn attempt to build up local shipping. The merchants were indignant. It was a very partial procedure, they thought, for the colonists to tax his Majesty's subjects at large to a higher degree than themselves. Moreover, it set up the shipping of Virginia in opposition to and in great prejudice to the navigation of Great Britain. Needless to say the act was disallowed.[27] It was now the turn of the planters to be indignant. Gooch wrote the Board: " I cannot conceal from your Lordships the resentment of the people against the merchants." [28]

The Virginians, like the peoples of the other colonies, were angered at the passage of the Molasses Act, which placed prohibitive duties on the trade between the British colonies on the American continent and the foreign West Indies. Virginia's stake in the trade to the French and Spanish islands was much less than that of New England, but it was great enough to draw a protest from Gooch. And the good Governor seems to have winked at the violations of the act. In 1734 he wrote the Lords of Trade: " As to trade, upon the strictest inquiry I can make I can find none . . . but with Great Britain, the British islands in the West Indies, and the island of Madeira." [29] The Board might well have asked why it was, if this were true, that so many Spanish pieces of eight and so many pistoles and French guineas and crowns were circulating in the colony.

Even more serious than the conflict between planters and merchants over the restrictions of trade, was the quarrel over debts. The trade with Great Britain was carried on chiefly by credit, and in times when the price of tobacco was high and profits good the planters lived well and spent freely. Then it was that they made heavy purchases of silverware, handsome furniture, or even blooded horses. And only too often, when prices of tobacco fell, they could not bring themselves to curtail expenditures in proportion. In fact, when they placed their orders they could not foresee just what their year's crop would

[27] CO5-1322, pp. 287, 317.　　　　[29] May 24, 1734.
[28] Oct. 22, 1731.

yield. Many of them became involved in debt. When they
could not meet their obligations, the merchants demanded that
their lands be forfeited. On the other hand, the planters, from
time to time, tried to lessen the burden by paying their creditors
in depreciated paper money.

When the merchants appealed to the Virginia courts to force
payment of debts they found them usually sympathetic with
the debtors. Moreover, in most cases they could not appeal to
the British courts for there was a law forbidding it in cases
involving less than £300. For larger suits the shoe was on the
other foot, for when they were taken before the Privy Council,
the advantage was all with the merchants. Residing in Great
Britain, most of them in London, they could appeal in person
to present their cause. Since the prosperity of the kingdom was
so dependent upon its commerce, they always received a sympathetic hearing.

Typical was the suit of the executors of Micajah and Richard
Perry to recover debts from the estate of Colonel William
Randolph, who had had a long-standing account with them.
When the Virginia courts decided in favor of the defendants,
the executors of the Perrys appealed to the King. The Privy
Council referred the matter to a commission of four merchants,
three of whom gave it as their judgment that with compound
interest and insurance charges the defendants owed £2,460. So
the verdict of the Virginia court was reversed.

The Council and Burgesses protested in an address to the
King. They were alarmed that this case had been decided without a legal trial by jury, they said. It had never been the practice
to charge " interest upon interest " in " open running accounts." They thought it wrong that " the reports of merchants
who were not under oath and were inclined to favor one
another, should be permitted to overrule the verdict of legal
juries. If the planters were to be loaded with whatever charges
their factors thought fit, it would greatly discourage trade and
industry.[30]

But they were unprepared for the extreme lengths to which
the merchants would go. At a meeting of the Council in October, 1731, they could hardly credit their ears when Gooch read
them a letter stating that they were about to present a petition
to Parliament concerning the colonies. They wanted first a

---

[30] *Journals of the House of Burgesses, 1712-1726:* 422-424.

law prohibiting the Assemblies from passing any acts affecting trade and navigation, second, a law making real estate liable for debts, and third, a law permitting appeals from the Virginia General Court to the Privy Council in suits involving £100 or more.[31]

Gooch wrote at once to the Board denouncing this attempt to muzzle the Assembly. " When I considered, my Lords, how long and happily the British subjects have traded to America and acquired great riches under the ancient establishment made in these points by the Crown, set forth in the royal charters and instructions, without seeking to abridge the people of the plantations of their birthright as Englishmen, or limiting the Crown in the methods of government, I must confess I was somewhat startled." [32]

The Council also protested vigorously. It was impossible for the Assembly to avoid all legislation affecting trade, they said in a letter to the Board, since it might prohibit certain vitally necessary laws. If the merchants objected to any act of Assembly, they could lay the matter before the King. As for making the land of the planters liable for debts, it was pointed out that there was no law making the lands of the merchants liable to the demands of the colonists. Yet the factors were as often in the planters' debt as the planters in theirs. It would create uneasiness in the minds of a loyal people to find they had not equal justice. And to allow appeals to the King in cases involving as little as £100 would be a heavy burden; for the expense of the planter, who would have to make a voyage to England to defend his rights, would be as great as the sum involved.[33]

It was no doubt to anticipate any action to forbid legislation in the colony affecting trade that a clause was added to certain acts suspending their operation until the King had given his assent. During Gooch's administration the first such act appropriated £1,000 for the erection of a lighthouse of brick and stone on Cape Henry, provided Maryland appropriate a like amount and the King gave his assent. A duty of one penny a ton was to be levied on all vessels passing the light. Gooch urged the Lords of Trade to influence Lord Baltimore to recom-

[31] *Executive journals of the Council* 4: 252.
[32] July 10, 1731.
[33] Council to the Lords of Trade, Jan. 1, 1732.

mend the matter to the Maryland Assembly. But he was tread-
ing on dangerous ground when he suggested that if the Marylanders balked, the Board secure an act of Parliament " to bind
both governments to do that good to themselves and the trade
of Great Britain." [34] Fortunately the Board refused to take
such a drastic step, and it was only in 1772 that the lighthouse
was erected.[35]

Knowing that the King had vetoed the tobacco act of 1713,
Gooch took pains to prepare the minds of the Board of Trade
to consider favorably the new one he was contemplating. The
government was being defrauded by running tobacco into Great
Britain without paying the duty there, he wrote them. It was
the practice for sailors to buy " mean and trash tobacco," and
sell it to agents who knew how to dispose of it. " Thus is the
market for the good tobacco damped by the fraudulent importation of the bad." The remedy was to bring all the tobacco
under strict inspection by sworn officers, all the bad destroyed,
and the weight of every hogshead reported to the commissioners of the customs.

The tobacco act of 1730 provided for warehouses to which all
tobacco must be brought in hogsheads for inspection, where it
would be burnt if of low grade, or stamped if good, and the
owner paid in notes which circulated as money. At the time
the price of tobacco was low, and the planters, especially the
small farmers, were in dire need. Gooch contended that the
law would stimulate trade and bring relief.

His arguments were set forth in a printed pamphlet entitled
*A Dialogue between Thomas Sweet-scented, William Orinoco,
Planters, both Men of Good Understanding, and Justice Love-
Country.*

Will opened the discussion: " I am sure I have heard a great
many speeches against it at the race-grounds and at the county
courts. . . . Why, pray is it not a clear case, don't we see our
tobacco burnt? . . . T'was constantly buzzed about as if by this
law the rich intended to ruin the poor."

Justice: " None but the worst villains could suggest such a
reflection."

And so the arguments went, with Justice answering every
objection.

Gooch claimed that the law in operation benefited the poor.

---

[34] June 8, 1728.   [35] W. W. Hening, *Statutes at large* 6: 227.

It was the rich man with his slave labor who was responsible for most of the "trash" which the inspectors burnt. The small farmer who planted, tended, and cured his own tobacco produced the best.[36] In fact, he added, "the greatest encouragement is given to the common people to make tobacco that could be thought of, for . . . they take as many notes for it as they please, i. e. notes for fifty or a hundred pounds . . . [which] will be accepted as payment at any store or shop." In other words, it gave them a far more convenient currency than their bulky tobacco. More convincing to the small farmer than these arguments was the rise in the price of tobacco which followed the passage of the act. But it must have been obvious to thoughtful men that no regulation of the tobacco trade could better the condition of the poor man so long as he had to compete with slave labor. It was slavery which created a trash far more harmful than poor tobacco—poor white trash.

Gooch's success in securing the King's assent to the tobacco law was matched by his success in persuading the Assembly to assist with men and money in an expedition against New Granada on the northern coast of South America. In May, 1740, an act was passed to impress men, and in a few weeks about four hundred had been raised. A ragged, motley crowd they must have been, for no one was taken who had any lawful occupation or who had a right to vote.[37] But the officers were from the best Virginia families, among them Lawrence Washington, half-brother of George Washington. Later the Assembly voted £5,000 to cover the cost of feeding and transporting the troops as far as Jamaica, where they were to join the forces sent out from England.

Former Governor Spotswood had been appointed to lead the colonials, but when he died before the ships sailed, Governor Gooch, leaving the government in the hands of the senior Councillor, Commissary Blair, took over the command. The attack on Cartagena proved a failure. The British ships could not get near enough to shell the town. When the troops tried to storm the walls the ladders proved too short, and they were repulsed with heavy losses. Gooch himself was wounded.

Gooch was knighted in 1746, and made a major general in the British army. He seems never to have recovered fully from

[36] Gooch to the Lords of Trade, Feb. 27, 1731.
[37] W. W. Hening, *Statutes at large* 5: 94-96.

his wound, and from an illness contracted during the New Granada campaign. Complaining that he had grown old and infirm, he asked the King for permission to " go home " to recover his health. To the universal regret of the people of Virginia, he left for England in the summer of 1749. He died December 17, in London.

Gooch himself gave the key to his administration when he wrote: " The condition of affairs in this colony may be summed up in two words, peace and plenty." With many families becoming rich through the settlement of the West and the growth of the tobacco trade, with many hundreds of small farmers acquiring a degree of well-being by the purchase of a few slaves, with no immediate threat from the Indians on the frontier, with Governor and Council maintaining cordial relations, with the Governor cooperating with the Assembly and not trying to dominate it, with rapid strides being made toward the goal of self-government, the years of Gooch's administration may aptly be termed the golden era of Virginia colonial history.

Many of the addresses of various bodies to the Virginia Governors lack the ring of sincerity, because they were obtained by bribery or threats. But the Council, in 1736, seem to have spoken from their hearts when they told Gooch: " As for us, Sir, who have the honor to be the near witnesses of the prudence, moderation, and justice of your administration, we should be unjust to ourselves, as well as ungrateful to your character, if we . . . did not declare that we esteem the quiet and tranquillity which this colony has enjoyed under your government as one of the greatest public blessings."

The Burgesses were even more articulate: " We are very sensible how much the colony owes to your good conduct in the government, and that all your actions are directed to a faithful discharge of your duty to his Majesty and to promote our common good. And should we distrust so just and upright a magistrate it would be discountenancing a virtuous administration, and making no difference between that and the greatest enormities, tyranny, and oppression. Or should we withhold our confidence from a person who for so many years has never once abused it, we might justly be reckoned an unworthy representative of a grateful people."

CHAPTER XII

AT STAKE—LIBERTY AND A CONTINENT

WHEN Robert Dinwiddie stepped ashore at Yorktown on
November 20, 1751, he was greeted by Secretary Thomas
Nelson and two members of the Council—Colonel William
Fairfax and William Nelson. Hastening on to Williamsburg,
he was met on the road by Commissary William Dawson, John
Blair, and Philip Ludwell. When the little cavalcade reached
the outskirts of the town, they found the Mayor, Aldermen,
and other prominent citizens waiting to welcome them. At
the Palace, Dinwiddie took the oath of office. He and the
members of the Council then went to Wetherburn's tavern for
dinner, where they were guests of the town. As the cannons at
the powder horn roared their approval, they lifted their glasses
to drink the " royal healths."

The inauguration of Dinwiddie brought to an end the custom of appointing military officers as Governors or Lieutenant
Governors of the colony. Nicholson, Andros, Spotswood, Hunter, Drysdale, and Gooch had all been soldiers. One wonders
why the policy had persisted so long, for there would seem to
be little in the training of an army officer to fit him for the
duties of a colonial administrator. The habit of issuing commands and expecting instant obedience might easily cause
failure in dealing with a liberty-loving people. Yet in practice,
it seems to have been the personal character of the Governor,
rather than his training, which determined his conduct. Nicholson and Spotswood were by nature dictators, Drysdale and
Gooch had no desire for power for power's sake.

Yet the Virginians were no doubt pleased with the appointment of a man from civil life. Dinwiddie came from a family
of Glasgow merchants, and as a young man had been engaged
in the pottery business. At the age of twenty-eight he was made
Collector of Customs in Bermuda, in which office he won the
approval of the Lords of Trade by uncovering serious frauds in
the collecting of customs in the West Indies. In 1738 he was
advanced to the important post of Surveyor General of the
southern ports of the North American continent. Additional

responsibilities were placed upon him a few years later, when he was made Inspector General of the Customs. In 1749 he resigned this office, probably in order to engage in trade.

The painting of Dinwiddie in the National Portrait Gallery, London, shows a rather stout, middle-aged man. The face which looks out from beneath a large wig, despite the placid expression, shows strength in the lines of the mouth and the steady gaze of the eyes. Dinwiddie, throughout his career did not willingly provoke a conflict, but when the conflict was started he fought stubbornly. Yet when necessity dictated he knew how to yield. The first of these qualities made him an important factor in preserving the most important part of North America for British civilization. The other contributed greatly to the triumph of self-government in Virginia.

The new Lieutenant Governor's administration began auspiciously. In his opening address to the Assembly he expressed his pleasure at being in Virginia, where he had so many friends. He realized it would be difficult to equal the record of his predecessor, but he hoped, with the advice of the Council and the Burgesses, to serve the colony well. One wonders whether he had in mind some of the former Governors of Virginia when he pointed out that indolence, avarice, and ambition were responsible for many public calamities.

The spirit of good will to the Governor ripened into gratitude when he sided with the Assembly in their protest against an action of the King in Council. This was almost unprecedented, for a Governor was supposed to defend anything the royal government did, no matter how harmful to the colony or unjust.

It seems that the Assembly, in 1748 and 1749, had made a laborious revision of the laws. The completed work, in sixty-seven acts, they sent to the King so that he could review them. But it was not anticipated that he would either veto or sign any of them. So there was consternation when Dinwiddie reported that the King in Council had signed fifty-seven of the revised laws and vetoed ten. Of the latter, two—one declaring slaves personal property and the other setting up the General Court—were of great importance. Each House drew up an address to the King pleading with him to reconsider his action. When Dinwiddie promised to endorse and deliver them, Councillors and Burgesses alike were grateful. Before dispersing they voted him a gift of £500, which Dinwiddie, despite his instructions seems to have accepted.[1]

But the honeymoon was of short duration. Before Dinwiddie left England he was entrusted with a new seal for Virginia. It was this, no doubt, which gave him the idea of adding to his income by charging a pistole for signing patents for land and affixing the seal. Had he been aware of the storm raised by the similar attempt by Lord Effingham sixty-four years earlier, he would have known what was in store for him. The Council, too, seem to have been forgetful in this matter, for when the Governor asked their opinion, they advised him to go ahead.[2]

When the Assembly met in November, 1753, Dinwiddie told them that a large body of French regulars, accompanied by Indian allies, had marched down from Canada into the Ohio region and had built a fort there. The King had commanded him to lay before them a request for funds to defeat their designs, and to purchase gifts for the friendly Indians.

The Burgesses were fully aware of the danger. For the French to build a chain of forts on the Monongahela and the Ohio to connect with those on the Mississippi would make a barrier to further expansion of the English colonies to the west. It would also constitute an ever present threat to their frontier, since in future wars the way would be open to forays of hostile Indians. Such men as Joshua Fry, Edmund Pendleton, John Robinson, and Benjamin Harrison may have realized that the fate of Virginia and of all English North America hung in the balance.

But for the moment the Burgesses were more interested in preserving their liberty than their safety. They began by considering the complaints of several counties against the pistole fee. Dinwiddie accused the Reverend William Stith, President of the College of William and Mary, of inciting the people against the fee. Stith was his personal enemy, he thought, because he had opposed his appointment as Commissary of the clergy.[3] So he wrote to the Bishop of London suggesting that if he would advise Stith " to be peaceable and quiet and teach the doctrine of love," it would make him more easy in his government.[4] If it was Stith who aroused the people against

---

[1] *Journals of the House of Burgesses*, 1752-1758: 99.
[2] *Executive journals of the Council* 5: 385.
[3] Dinwiddie to the Lords of Trade, Jan. 22, 1754.
[4] Jan. 22, 1754.

Governor Dinwiddie. Portrait in the National Portrait Gallery of London.
Reproduced by permission.

The General Court in the Old Capitol at Williamsburg. Courtesy of Colonial Williamsburg, Inc.

the pistole fee, he made a good job of it. Henrico County protested, Chesterfield protested, Albemarle protested, Cumberland, Amelia, Dinwiddie Counties protested.

The Burgesses were deeply concerned. In an address to the Lieutenant Governor they declared that their duty in the discharge of the trust reposed in them by the people required them to ask him by what authority he demanded the fee. He replied that he had acted on his own authority, with the advice of the Council. And he intimated that the taking of the fee was a thing that did not concern them.

The Burgesses were indignant. In an address of historic significance they told Dinwiddie " in the strongest terms " that it was their undoubted right to enquire into the grievances of the people. To question it was to threaten the liberties of his Majesty's subjects and the constitution of the government. " The rights of the subject are so secured by law that they cannot be deprived of the least part of their property but by their own consent. Upon this excellent principle is our constitution founded, and ever since this colony has had the happiness of being under the immediate protection of the Crown the royal declarations have been: ' That no man's life, member, freehold, or goods be taken away or harmed but by established and known laws.' " [5]

Well would it have been if the King and his advisers had pondered well this declaration when it came before them, for it gave in unmistakable language the principle in defense of which the American Revolution was fought. And it would have been well for Dinwiddie had he bowed to the wishes of the Burgesses at a time when their cooperation was needed to save the British colonies from French aggression.

But in the meanwhile he had placed the matter before the Board of Trade, and the Board had asked the opinion of Attorney General Sir Dudley Ryder.[6] When Dinwiddie received word that Sir Dudley thought the assent of the Assembly unnecessary, he was resolved not to yield. The fee relates solely to the disposal of the King's lands, he told the Burgesses, which is a matter of favor from the Crown.

The Governor's plea that the fee was necessary in order to bring thousands of occupied, but unpatented acres, under the

[5] *Journals of the House of Burgesses,* 1752-1758: 143, 144.
[6] CO5-1328, pp. 85, 86.

rent roll seems to have been an afterthought. " On my arrival
I found in the Secretary's office a list of lands taken up near
1,000,000 acres, which, most of them, should have been patented," he wrote the Board of Trade, " which is an annual
loss to the quit rents." [7] But he did not explain how the charging of a pistole fee would have been an incentive to the holders
of these lands to have them patented.

The Burgesses were by this time thoroughly aroused. The
Governor said it was only " some hotheaded young men " who
had stirred up all the trouble, but when it was resolved that
his answer was unsatisfactory, there was not one dissenting
voice. The demand for the fee, they insisted, was illegal and
arbitrary, contrary to the charters of the colony, to King William's express order, and tending to the subversion of laws and
constitution. They were determined to place the matter before
the King in a " dutiful and loyal address." [8]

At the close of the session, after the Governor's speech proroguing them, the Burgesses refused to budge from their seats
until they had passed still another resolution which breathed
the spirit of revolution: " That whoever shall hereafter pay
a pistole as a fee to the Governor for the use of the seal to
patents for land shall be deemed a betrayer of the rights and
privileges of the people." This Dinwiddie thought tended to
" sowing sedition and rebellion among the people." [9]

In the meanwhile, the Burgesses had drawn up the address to
the King and appointed Attorney General Peyton Randolph
their agent to take it to England. To defray his expenses and
pay him for his services, they voted him £2,500 out of the funds
in the hands of the Treasurer. When this came before the
Council, they rejected it. The Treasurer then declared that he
would pay the money without their consent, but he refrained
when the Governor told him it would not be allowed in his
accounts.

" I am sorry to find them very much in a republican way of
thinking," Dinwiddie wrote to the Earl of Halifax, " and indeed they do not act in a proper constitutional way, but making
encroachments on the prerogative of the Crown, which some
former Governor submitted too much to them, and I fear

[7] June 16, 1753.
[8] *Journals of the House of Burgesses*, 1752-1758: 155
[9] Dinwiddie to Holdernesse, Dec. 29, 1753.

without a very particular instruction it will be difficult to bring them in order." [10]

When Randolph asked Dinwiddie for permission to go to England, he met with a prompt refusal. "You have not acted agreeable to your duty and your office," he told him. When Randolph insisted upon going, the Governor assumed that he had vacated his office and appointed George Wythe Attorney General in his place.[11]

Soon after Randolph's arrival in England articles began to appear in the gazettes intended to arouse sentiment against the pistole fee, which Dinwiddie wrongly attributed to him. The fee was no less than a tax levied on the people without their consent, they said. Foreign Protestants and others were leaving the colony rather than pay it. To this Dinwiddie replied that any thinking man could distinguish between a fee and a tax. And he denied flatly that one person had left Virginia to avoid the pistole fee.[12] But he was sorry that the affair had made so much noise in the English coffee houses.

The Board of Trade considered the pistole dispute most inopportune. At a time when the French were challenging the right of Great Britain to the vast trans-Allegheny region, it was unfortunate that the Governor should have aroused the bitter resentment of the Assembly. " It is necessary that harmony and mutual confidence be established between the Governors and people in all the colonies," they wrote, " but especially in Virginia, on the frontier of which the French are carrying on their encroachments." [13]

But they could not desert Dinwiddie entirely since the issue involved the royal prerogative. The King rejected the address of the Burgesses, and the Board confirmed the Governor's right to the fee. But they hedged it about with several restrictions. There must be no fee for grants of less than one hundred acres, or for lands granted for importing settlers, or for lands west of the mountains. They reproved Dinwiddie for proposing that the fee be established by act of Assembly, in violation of the King's rights. The making out of surveys for land and neglecting to pass patents was clearly " in the Governor's power to prevent." " We expect you to do your duty . . . even though no

[10] *Official records of Robert Dinwiddie*, ed. R. A. Brock, 1: 100, 101.
[11] Dinwiddie to the Board of Trade, Jan. 29, 1754.
[12] *Official records of Robert Dinwiddie*, ed. R. A. Brock, 1: 153.
[13] CO5-1367, pp. 94-101.

pecuniary advantage should arise from it." And they recommended that he reinstate Randolph as Attorney General. "This may quiet the minds of the people and stop this unjust clamor." [14]

Dinwiddie was far from happy about this report. The proposal to establish the fee by act of Assembly had come from the Council, not from him, he wrote in reply. As for not taking a fee for patents west of the mountains, he wanted to know which mountains. He had taken no fee for lands beyond the Alleghenies. The suggestion to reinstate the Attorney General was especially displeasing. However, when Randolph arrived at Williamsburg with many letters of recommendation from men of influence in England, denying that he had written the attacks on the Governor in the press, and promising " to conduct himself more regularly in future and with more regard to his Majesty's service," he reinstated him.[15]

One wonders just how many pistoles Dinwiddie pocketed for the use of the seal in the six and a half years of his administration. A few months after he had left Virginia for good there were no less than 1,360 applications for patents waiting to be sealed. Governor Fauquier, Dinwiddie's successor, stated that this was costing the Crown £1,000 a year in quit rents. It would seem to indicate that Dinwiddie, ignoring the positive orders of the Board of Trade, had appeased the people by permitting 1,000,000 acres of occupied land to remain unpatented. Thus the Governor's victory was a hollow one, and the Burgesses, without acquiescing in the decision of the Board, were content to let the matter drop so long as the fee was not collected.

Fauquier, on his part, handled this hot potato with care. " Being extremely desirous to keep peace and harmony in this country," he wrote the Lords of Trade, " and that his Majesty's revenue should not suffer . . . I have made a declaration in Council that I would be willing to acquiesce in anything that should be thought reasonable to procure both these advantages. This affair has formerly raised a great flame in this country which is not yet quite subsided, and . . . I am endeavoring to quench it entirely that the Assemblies may the easier be prevailed upon to give what is necessary." [16]

In the meanwhile the storm of war had broken over the

[14] *Ibid.*
[15] *Official records of Robert Dinwiddie*, ed., R. A. Brock, 1: 507.
[16] Sept. 23, 1758.

colonies. A terrible war it was. It lacked the wholesale devastation of the atomic bomb and the hydrogen bomb, but it was marked by infinite cruelties. Dinwiddie described it vividly. "Think you see the infant torn from the unavailing struggles of the distracted mother, the daughters ravished before the eyes of their wretched parents, and then, with cruelty and insult, butchered and scalped. Suppose the horrid scene completed, and the whole family, man, wife, and children murdered and scalped by these relentless savages, and then torn in pieces." [17]

To Dinwiddie goes the credit of warning the British government that the French were trying to confine the English to the region east of the Alleghenies. In December, 1752, he wrote the Board of Trade that they had built a string of forts from Canada to the mouth of the Mississippi, that they had 5,000 soldiers at New Orleans, and 1,600 elsewhere in America. When he heard that a force of French and Indians had built a fort on the Allegheny River, and were preparing to descend on the Ohio, he sent young George Washington to warn them to leave. This proving ineffectual, he came to the Assembly for funds to finance an expedition to drive them out.

This was the first of a series of appeals for money which gave the Assembly a golden opportunity to weaken the power of the Governor and the royal prerogative. Yet it was an opportunity full of danger. If they clogged their grants with such conditions that Dinwiddie would not accept them, they ran the risk of having the colony overrun by the enemy. At times the Governor was in despair. "The French could have cut off every one of our men and marched down to Hampton without the least danger," he wrote in July, 1754.

When the Assembly met in February, 1754, Dinwiddie told them that Washington had seen a large body of the enemy on the upper Allegheny. Give me men and supplies to oppose them, he pleaded. The safety of Virginia depends on you at this critical juncture.[18] In reply to this appeal they did vote £10,000 but Dinwiddie was far from happy about it because the bill named a committee of the two Houses to supervise its expenditure. "This bill takes from me the undoubted right I have of directing the application of the money," he com-

---

[17] *Journals of the House of Burgesses,* 1752-1758: 176.
[18] *Journals of the House of Burgesses,* 1752-1758: 176.

plained. But since funds could be had on no other terms he gave his assent. " I assure you it was contrary to my inclination, but necessity has no law," he wrote James Abercrombie.[19]

So men were raised and equipped and sent out to the junction of the Allegheny and the Monongahela. Here, under the command of George Washington, they were fortifying themselves when they were attacked by the French and Indians and forced to retire. Again Dinwiddie pleaded for a grant large enough to meet the emergency. When the Assembly responded by voting £20,000, he was delighted until he discovered a rider to pay Peyton Randolph the £2,500 they had promised him for representing them in England in the pistole affair. This was too much for Dinwiddie to swallow, so he vetoed the bill.[20]

In his perplexity the Governor now made a radical suggestion to the Board of Trade. " I think it impossible to conduct any expedition in these parts with a dependence on the Assemblies for supplies, without a British act of Parliament to lay a poll tax on the whole subjects of these provinces, to bring them to a sense of their duty to the King, to awaken them from their insolence, to take care of their lives and fortunes." [21]

It is easy to imagine the storm of indignation this would have raised in Virginia had the people known of it. Why, no such thing had been done in the century and a half of the colony's existence. Charles I had not dared tax the colonists without their consent; Charles II, though he obtained a revenue in Virginia by threatening the Assembly, had not acted without their consent. Over and over the people had sought guarantees that they should enjoy the inherent right of all Englishmen of being taxed only by their own representatives.

Dinwiddie's suggestion undoubtedly reflected the changed attitude of the British government. He would hardly have dared make it if he had thought it would shock the British Ministry. On the other hand, the violent reaction of the people of the colony to the pistole fee should have made it clear to him that they would resist taxation by Parliament fiercely. In other words, his action was revealing of how far apart Britain and her colonies had grown, and prophetic of the clash that was to come.

But now Dinwiddie was cheered by word that the King had

---

[19] *Official records of Robert Dinwiddie*, ed. R. A. Brock, 1: 157.
[20] *Ibid.*, 328.   [21] *Ibid.*, 329.

promised £20,000 and 2,000 stand of arms from the royal stores
to aid in the war. With this evidence that Great Britain was
willing to do her part, he again appealed to the Assembly. He
was overjoyed when they granted £20,000. " I parted with the
Assembly on good terms. I shall try to keep them in good
humor," he wrote the Board. When he heard that two regiments of British regulars were on their way to Virginia, he
confidently expected that the French would soon be driven
from the Ohio region. All Virginia was elated when the troops
arrived at Alexandria in their brilliant red coats. The Assembly voted an additional £22,000.

Then came disaster. General Braddock, who commanded the
British, knew nothing about Indian fighting, and scorned the
advice of those who did. " These savages may, indeed, be a
formidable enemy to your raw American militia, but upon the
King's regular and disciplined troops, sir, it is impossible that
they should make any impression," he told Benjamin Franklin.
So his advanced regiment, as it was filing through the woods,
was attacked and cut to pieces. The Virginia contingent fought
bravely, but could not stem the tide. Braddock himself was
killed. Colonel Dunbar, in command of the other regiment,
though his men had taken no part in the battle and still out-
numbered the enemy, marched them off to Philadelphia, and
left the Virginia frontier open.

The dismay of the people when the news of this unexpected
defeat reached them was tempered by their pride in the heroism
of the Virginia troops, " who purchased with their lives im-
mortal glory to their country and themselves on the banks of
the Monongahela." So when Dinwiddie asked for more funds,
the Assembly voted £40,000.[22] To raise this sum they levied
heavy taxes on the people and placed a five per cent duty on
imports. In times of peace no Governor would have consented
to an import duty on British goods, for it would have brought
immediate protests from the merchants. But Dinwiddie signed
the bill and praised the Assembly for its " unanimity " and
" martial spirit." [23]

When they met again in October, 1755, they forgot for the
moment the Indian terror and spent their time on a project to
emit £200,000 in paper and set up a loan office. To this the

[22] *Journals of the House of Burgesses*, 1752-1758: 301.
[23] *Ibid.*, 315.

Governor would not assent, and after a session of only twelve days, he dissolved them to take his chances on a new election. The Board of Trade praised him. " Their availing themselves of this time of danger and distress to establish a paper currency, so destructive of credit, justifies your dissolving them." [24]

Dinwiddie was now so out of patience that he suggested once more that Parliament pass the Assembly by and itself levy a tax on the people of the colonies. He recommended a poll tax of twelve pence for two years, and a permanent tax of two shillings on every one hundred acres of land. " I know our people will be inflamed if they hear of my making this proposal, as they are averse to all taxes," he wrote the Board of Trade.[25] One wonders what the Americans would have done had the British Government followed this suggestion. It might have alienated their affection at the very moment when it was most needed. It would probably have been as impossible to collect the taxes as it was to enforce the Stamp Act a decade later. Fortunately, the Board of Trade decided that this was not the proper time to start a controversy with the colonies over this vital matter.

The new House of Burgesses who met in March, 1756, while showing a willingness to support the war, were just as independent, just as jealous of their privileges as former ones. When some of their members were absent from their seats while attending the General Court, they sent their mace-bearer within the bar to bring them back. This Dinwiddie resented as an indignity to the court. The orderly administration of justice was just as important as the enacting of laws, he told the House.

Their audacity was shown at the same session in the matter of the Acadian exiles. Governor Charles Lawrence, of Nova Scotia, on the advice of his Council, had decided to distribute these unfortunates throughout the British colonies. When the people of Virginia heard that a fleet with over eleven hundred had arrived in their waters, they were deeply concerned. No Governor had a right to unload on them such a number of French Roman Catholics, they said. Their remaining in the colony at a time when Great Britain and France were at war would be very dangerous. So they passed a bill, to which the Governor assented, to ship the exiles to Great Britain.[26]

But while the Assembly was sitting, the Indians were making

[24] Board of Trade to Dinwiddie, Feb. 17, 1756.
[25] *Official records of Robert Dinwiddie*, ed. R. A. Brock, II: 341.
[26] *Journals of the House of Burgesses*, 1752-1758: 351.

a series of murderous raids in the Valley of Virginia. Washington, who was left in command of the Virginia forces after Dunbar withdrew, wrote Dinwiddie in April, 1756, to describe the plight of the people. " I see their situation, know their danger, and participate in their sufferings, without having it in my power to give them further relief than uncertain promises. . . . The supplicating tears of the women, and moving petitions from the men melt me into such deadly sorrow that I solemnly declare . . . I could offer myself a willing sacrifice to the butchering enemy provided that would contribute to the people's ease." [27]

Nor were the Burgesses deaf to the sufferings of these poor people. Although the burden of taxation was very heavy, they voted £60,000 for the erection of forts and the sending of the militia into the Valley. Part of this sum they provided for by the emission of treasury notes. " In the situation I was obliged to give my assent or disband our forces and leave our frontier unguarded and exposed to the incursions of a merciless foe," Dinwiddie wrote the Board of Trade. But he assured them that the merchants would not be losers since the notes bore interest at five per cent, and would be redeemed in 1760. Virginia had voted in all £150,000 for the war, he pointed out, which was much more than any other colony had done.[28]

At a short session in September, 1756, Dinwiddie told the Assembly of the surrender of Oswego. All realized that it was a crushing blow, since it cut off the English from the Great Lakes, made a deep impression on the Indians, and opened New York to invasion. When the Governor asked for men and money as Virginia's contribution to the Royal American Regiment, which the Earl of Loudoun, Commander-in-Chief of the British forces, was recruiting, they voted £8,000. This the Earl promised to report to the British government " in the very handsome manner " it deserved.[29]

But when they met in April, 1757, they did not permit this compliment to keep them from taking issue with Loudoun for laying an embargo on commerce in order to put an end to the sending of supplies by the colonists to the French. It was obvious to all that this would do more harm than good, they said. Wheat stored in vessels ready to set out for Great Britain was

[27] *Writings of George Washington*, J. C. Fitzpatrick, ed. 2: 324, 325.
[28] *Official records of Robert Dinwiddie* 2: 464.
[29] *Journals of the House of Burgesses*, 1752-1758: 413.

" likely to perish." And unless the planters could sell their tobacco, it would be impossible for them to pay their taxes. After all, men asked, what authority had Loudoun to give such an order? The Burgesses petitioned Dinwiddie to rescind it so far as Virginia was concerned. They were determined to vote no more supplies until he did so.[30] Dinwiddie was forced to yield, and the fleet waiting in Virginia waters cleared for Great Britain.

As one vessel after another sailed out between Cape Henry and Cape Charles, the Assembly acted quickly to support the war. They raised £6,000 to send out rangers against the Indians, £25,000 to pay arrears due officers and men of the Virginia forces, and issued £80,000 in non-interest bearing notes, renewable in seven years.[31] At once the old " heats and disputes " with the Governor were resumed. Dinwiddie was opposed to paper money, but the Burgesses, knowing that they had the whip hand, would not yield. " They took advantage of the emergency of our affairs, when without money every operation must be stopped, and the protection of the country, the lives and properties of these very people [have] been exposed to the barbarous enemy," the Governor complained. " I was obliged at last, much against my judgment, to assent." [32]

In one vital matter the Burgesses themselves had to yield. The expenditure of money appropriated during previous sessions had proved so unsatisfactory that they left all new disbursements to the Governor. They appointed three commissioners to examine such accounts as he should turn over to them, but they were merely to assist, not control him.[33]

Despite the one point of difference, Dinwiddie, in proroguing the Assembly, praised them for their " dutiful obedience to his Majesty's commands," and their compliance with what he himself had recommended. He had told them earlier in the summer that his health had been failing and that he had asked permission to resign his office and return to Great Britain. Now he said goodbye. " I shall always retain a sincere regard for the prosperity of this dominion," he said.[34] He sailed from Yorktown in January, 1758.

[30] *Ibid.*, 448.
[31] *Journals of the House of Burgesses, 1752-1758:* xxviii.
[32] Dinwiddie to the Lords of Trade, Sept. 12, 1757.
[33] *Journals of the House of Burgesses, 1752-1758:* xxviii.
[34] *Ibid.*, 492.

To Robert Dinwiddie goes a large part of the credit for saving the major part of North America for British civilization. It was he who saw the meaning of the encroachments of the French in the Ohio Valley; it was he who sounded the alarm in both Great Britain and America. And when the fateful struggle with France was under way, his appreciation of what was at stake made him subordinate other issues to it. He broke his instructions repeatedly because he thought it necessary in order to win the war.

This resulted in substantial gains for self-government in Virginia. In voting funds, not only did the Assembly specify the uses to which they should be put, but tried to supervise each disbursement. In sending the Acadians to England and forcing Dinwiddie to raise Loudoun's embargo they showed their spirit of independence. The issuing of paper money was in direct conflict with the Governor's instructions. And the British government dared not take steps to curb them so long as the French threat remained.

But there is abundant evidence that the King's Ministers were merely biding their time. The old laissez-faire policy of Sir Robert Walpole was giving way to a closer scrutiny of colonial affairs. When the Earl of Loudoun was made Governor General of Virginia, he received more than a hundred instructions. He must guard zealously the prerogative of the Crown, he must permit no riders to acts of Assembly, he must accept no gifts from the Assembly, he must not permit the issuing of paper money. The twenty-fourth instruction is especially revealing of the accepted view in Great Britain that American interests must be disregarded if they clashed with those of the mother country. The Governor was not to assent to any act putting duties on slaves to "the great discouragement" of British merchants, or duties on felons, since this was contrary to the act of Parliament for "preventing robbery, burglary, and other felonies, and for the more effectual transportation of felons."

It has often been said that had the French power in America not been broken, the colonists would not have dared to rebel against Great Britain. It would be more to the point that if the French threat had not been removed the British government would not have dared to drive the Americans into rebellion. So long as the war with France lasted the colonial Assemblies were masters of the situation; when it was over the assault on their liberty was not long delayed.

Perhaps it is not too much to say that the war called the attention of the British Government to the colonies. They could not have overlooked such letters as that from Dinwiddie to Pitt on June 18, 1757: " I am convinced if alterations are not made in the present constitutions of the colonies, and have a general mode of government under his Majesty's immediate directions, and a coalition of the whole, it will be impracticable to conduct his Majesty's affairs with that spirit which the present emergency requires." [35]

---

[35] *Official records of Robert Dinwiddie* 2: 642, 643.

CHAPTER XIII

THE WIDENING RIFT

FRANCIS FAUQUIER, who succeeded Dinwiddie as Lieutenant Governor, is described as "a gentleman of most amiable disposition, generous, just, and mild, and possessed in an eminent degree of all the social virtues." When Thomas Jefferson was a student at the College of William and Mary, he, together with Professor William Small and George Wythe, dined with him frequently. "At these dinners I have heard more good sense, more rational and philosophical conversations than in all my life besides," Jefferson said many years later.[1] Fauquier, who was an accomplished musician, delighted in joining with Jefferson and several others in weekly concerts in the lovely ballroom of the Palace. He was a member of the Royal Society, and, if we may judge from the presence in his library of a set of Palladio, a student of architecture.

When Fauquier arrived, on June 5, 1758, he found the colonists absorbed in preparations to send strong forces to join General Forbes in his expedition against Fort Duquesne. Ever since the French had established themselves there it had been a nest from which swarms of Indians had made raids on the frontier. "I found this colony zealous in his Majesty's service, and very strenuous to support the common cause," Fauquier wrote the Lords of Trade.[2]

Secretary Pitt and General Abercrombie had written urging the Virginians to exert themselves to the utmost. John Blair, President of the Council and Acting Governor pending Fauquier's arrival, had called the Assembly together and asked them to vote funds for a new regiment. The vote was unanimous. They were eager to help in any attack on their "cruel neighbors of Fort Duquesne." So now the colony resounded to the beat of drums as officers brought in the recruits. Some ensigns raised ten, some lieutenants twenty, some captains seventy. To supply the men with arms, Blair stripped the magazine at Williamsburg and even took the muskets from the

[1] *The writings of Thomas Jefferson*, ed. A. A. Lipscomb, 14:231.
[2] CO5-1329, June 11, 1758.

Governor's Palace. Tents and kettles he ordered from Philadelphia, pledging the credit of the colony to pay for them.[3]

This was the situation when Fauquier landed, and it gave
him reason to hope that Fort Duquesne would be in English
hands early in the autumn. When long delays made this un-
likely, he summoned the Assembly to ask for more funds. But
now he was confronted with a perplexing problem. It had long
been the practice for the House of Burgesses to make their
Speaker the Treasurer of the colony. Dinwiddie, probably because of a grudge against John Robinson, who held these two
offices, had recommended their separation. The Board of Trade
approved and directed Fauquier to see that this was done.[4] But
the Governor held back. He was not long in finding that
Robinson was the most popular man in Virginia, the idol of
the people whether rich or poor. Had he insisted that someone
else be made Treasurer, the Burgesses would not have voted a
penny for the expedition. Fearing that the Board's instruction
might be whispered around and come to Robinson's ear, he
decided to take him into his confidence and place the whole
matter before him. The Speaker was much gratified. " I am
told by those who know his character that I have attached him
to me in the strongest manner by the openness of my behavior,"
Fauquier wrote the Board.[5] So the supply bill went through
with a rush. But the Board must have realized that their authority in the colony had sunk to a new low when the Governor
not only ignored their orders, but thought it necessary to apologize for them in order to curry favor with the Speaker of the
House.

In the meanwhile, things were going well in the war. Under
the able leadership of Pitt, Great Britain had poured men and
money into the colonies, and replaced the incompetent Loudoun with the able General Jeffrey Amherst. A blow of great
importance for Virginia was struck when a small force captured
Fort Frontenac at the outlet of Lake Ontario. This cut the
French line of communication with the west and made Fort
Duquesne untenable. So this key position fell without firing
a shot. As Forbes' army approached, the garrison blew up the
fort, and taking to their canoes fell down the Ohio.

[3] CO5-1329, Blair to Lords of Trade, June 20, 1758.
[4] *Official records of Robert Dinwiddie* 1: 375.
[5] CO5-1329, June 28, 1758.

Fauquier congratulated himself for his part in this success. He had kept the Burgesses in good humor; he had obtained the funds needed to keep the Virginia troops in the field. If he had been lax in defending the King's prerogative, surely the end justified the means. So he was not a little piqued when he received a reprimand from the Board of Trade.

The trouble stemmed from the fact that tobacco provided a very poor standard of value. When the crop was bountiful its purchasing power fell, if the summer were dry and the leaves withered in the field, it doubled or tripled. In the first case debts and taxes could be paid at a low value, in the other the value might be so great as to threaten widespread injustice and suffering.

In 1748 by an act of Assembly the salary of the clergy had been fixed at 16,000 pounds of tobacco. This law had received the King's assent, and according to the "ancient constitution," could not be repealed without his approval. Yet, seven years later, when there had been a severe drought, the Assembly passed an act permitting payment of all obligations in money at the rate of two pence a pound. The law was to continue in force for ten months only, and there was no clause suspending its operation until the King had given his assent.

The clergy were bitter. They thought it hard that when the price of tobacco was low they were forced to accept it, but when it was high they were to be paid in money at one third the market price of tobacco. In a petition to the House of Burgesses they pointed out that their average income was so inadequate that they found it difficult to support their families. It was this which explained why so few graduates of Oxford and Cambridge entered the ministry in Virginia, and why so few in the colony thought it worth while to study divinity.[6]

A delegation of four ministers called on Governor Dinwiddie to urge him to veto the bill. But Dinwiddie, who was begging for funds and troops, had no stomach for a conflict with the Assembly over this affair. "What can I do?" he told them. "If I refuse to approve the act, I shall have the people on my back." So he signed the bill.

Unwilling to let the matter rest here, ten of the ministers, among them the Reverend Patrick Henry, uncle of the statesman, appealed to the Bishop of London. The unjust Two-

[6] Charles Campbell, *History of Virginia*, 508.

penny Act would lower them in the eyes of the people, it would discourage them in the discharge of their duty. And, to clinch their argument, they pointed out that their cause was also the cause of the King. " Our salaries have had the royal assent and cannot be taken from us or diminished in any respect by any law made here without trampling upon the royal prerogative." [7]

Three years later, when again there was a " prodigious dimunition " in the tobacco crop, the Assembly acted to give relief to debtors and taxpayers by again making obligations payable in money at tuppence a pound. This time the clergy made no appeal to the Burgesses, but Commissary Dawson, John Camm, and Thomas Robinson went to the Palace to urge Fauquier to veto the bill. Note that it has no suspending clause, they said. Note that it alters a bill to which the King gave his assent. If you let it pass, will you not be ignoring your instructions? [8]

But Fauquier was as much in need of funds as Dinwiddie had been. He answered that that was not the point to be considered. What was important was what would please the people. So he gave the act his approval. " The bill was a temporary law to ease the people from a burden which the country thought too great for them to bear," he wrote the Lords of Trade. " A suspending clause would have been to all intents and purposes the same as rejecting it. . . . The country were intent upon it . . . and I conceived it would be a very strong step for me to take . . . to set my face against the whole colony. . . . I am persuaded that if I had refused it, I must have despaired of our gaining any influence either in the Council or the House of Burgesses." [9]

But the clergy were determined to bring the matter to an issue. Commissary Dawson advised caution, but pressure from other ministers forced him to call a convention. When they met they not only vented their indignation in many denunciations of the Two-penny Act, but drew up an address to the King entitled " The Representation of the Clergy." In it they hammered on the point that their cause was his cause. The act was as injurious to the royal prerogative as to the rights of the Church. " It gives us great concern that an ancient, standing law of this dominion, confirmed by the sanction of the royal assent, is no security to our livings." [10]

[7] *Journals of the House of Burgesses*, 1761-1765: xlii-xlvi.
[8] *William and Mary Quarterly*, First Ser. 19: 16.
[9] CO5-1329, Jan. 5, 1759.   [10] CO5-1329. Read May 23, 1759.

This appeal they entrusted to the Reverend John Camm with instructions to place it in the King's hands. Camm, who later became Commissary, President of the College of William and Mary, and a member of the Council, was a man of great ability, but according to Fauquier, turbulent and delighting " to live in a flame." On his arrival in England he obtained an interview with the King and delivered the " Representation." His Majesty referred it to the Privy Council, who, in turn, handed it on to the Board of Trade.

This suited Camm exactly, for his trump card was the Bishop of London, and the Bishop's influence with the Board was great. His Lordship was exasperated at the presumption of the Virginia Assembly. " To make an act to suspend the operations of the royal act is an attempt which in some times would have been called treason, and I do not know any other name for it in our law," he told the Board. " To assume a power to bind the King's hands, and to say how far his power shall go and where it shall stop, is such an act of supremacy as is inconsistent with the dignity of the Crown of England." It manifestly tended to draw the colonists from their allegiance to the King for them to find that they had a higher power to protect them. " Surely it is time for us to look about us, and to consider the several steps lately taken in the diminution of the prerogative and influence of the Crown."

The Bishop denounced Governor Fauquier for signing the Two-penny bill. " What made him so zealous in this cause I pretend not to judge, but surely the great change which manifestly appears in the temper and disposition of the people of this colony in the compass of a few years deserves highly to be considered, and the more so as the Deputy Governors and the Council seemed to act in concert with the people." [11]

The Board was duly impressed. They denounced the Two-penny Act as a usurpation and advised the King to declare it null and void. Not only did the King do so, but he gave Fauquier a stunning rebuke. " We do . . . strictly command and require you for the future, upon pain of our highest displeasure, and of being recalled from the government of our said colony, punctually to observe and obey the several directions contained in the 16th article of our said instructions, relative to the passing of laws. . . ." [12]

[11] *Ibid.*, " Thomas London on the Clergy Bill," June 14, 1759.
[12] G. M. Brydon, *Virginia's Mother Church* 2: 318, 319.

Camm sent copies of these papers to Virginia, and when they were handed around among his friends the clergy rejoiced. The King was on their side, all would be well. Camm wrote to his attorney in Virginia to bring suit in the General Court against the vestry of his parish for his salary in tobacco. On the other hand, the people of the colony were highly resentful against the clergy, and especially against the Bishop of London. Colonel Landon Carter and Colonel Richard Bland wrote pamphlets defending the Two-penny Act and denouncing his Lordship. To the Bishop's contention that the act tended to draw the people from their allegiance, it was answered that nothing was more apt to estrange them than to deny them the right to protect themselves from distress. His Lordship had called the act treason. " But were the Assembly to do nothing? This would have been treason indeed." In case of an eventuality which the Governor's instructions could not provide for, which could bring ruin before relief could come from the throne, it was the duty of the Assembly to deviate from the fixed rules of the constitution. The preservation of the people could not possibly be treason.[13]

In the meanwhile Fauquier had been waiting impatiently for his copies of the King's veto and his instructions in the matter. Month after month passed and nothing came. Finally, late in June, ten months after they had been written, Camm appeared with them at the door of the Palace. Fauquier took them, and then denounced him for slandering him in England. Then he called out in a loud voice for his Negro servants, and when they had assembled, pointed his finger at Camm. " Look at that gentleman and be sure to know him again, and under no circumstances permit him to revisit the Palace," he said.[14]

As time passed the war of pamphlets was renewed. In 1763 Camm wrote assailing Carter and Bland and trying to answer their arguments. But so unpopular was the cause of the clergy that no one in Virginia would publish what he wrote, and he had to have it done in Maryland. Bland retorted in a letter in the *Virginia Gazette*, and Camm came back in a letter which he called " Observations." [15]

Interest now centered on a test case in which the Reverend James Maury brought suit for his salary in tobacco in the

[13] Charles Campbell, *History of Virginia*, 509-511.
[14] *William and Mary Quarterly*, First Ser. 19: 19.
[15] *Ibid.*, 21.

Hanover County court, in November, 1763. The court declared
the Two-penny Act no law, since it had been vetoed by the
Crown, and ordered that at the next court the jury should
determine how much damages, if any, should be paid. Maury's
case seemed as good as won, and the attorney for the defendants,
Mr. John Lewis, retired from the case. In his place they engaged a young, little-known lawyer, named Patrick Henry.

It was on December 1, 1763, that a great crowd assembled at
the Hanover courthouse, filling the little room and overflowing
into the yard. Among them were twenty clergymen. But when
Henry saw his uncle there, he persuaded him to leave. John
Henry, Patrick's father, presided. When several gentlemen
refused to serve on the jury, the sheriff was forced to fill their
places with men of the small farmer class. Several were dissenters.

The case was opened by Mr. Peter Lyons, attorney for the
plaintiff. When he had concluded, Henry rose to reply. At
first he seemed hesitant and awkward. But soon he warmed up
to his subject. His eyes kindled, his gestures were bolder, he
seemed to grow more erect, his voice resounded through the
room. His audience were spellbound, and on every bench, at
the door, in every window people leaned forward, their eyes
fixed on the youthful orator.

Henry contended that there was a contract between King
and people. The King owed the people protection; the people
owed the King obedience and support. But should either violate the contract, it released the other from the obligation. The
Two-penny Act was good and essential, and its disallowance
was a breach of the contract. It was an instance of misrule, a
neglect of the interests of the colony. The King, from being
the father of his people, became a tyrant who had forfeited
the obedience of the subjects. At this point Mr. Lyons cried
out: "The gentleman has spoken treason." And from various
parts of the room arose a murmur of "treason! treason!"

But Henry turned to the ministers seated before him and
denounced them and the rest of the clergy in blazing words
for trying to triple their salaries at the expense of the people.
"Do they manifest their zeal in the cause of religion and hu-
manity by practicing the mild and benevolent precepts of the
Gospel of Jesus? . . . Oh no! Gentlemen. Instead of feeding
the hungry and clothing the naked these rapacious harpies
would . . . snatch from the hearth of their honest parishioner

his last hoe-cake, from the widow and her orphaned child their last milch-cow." [16] At this the ministers got up and left the room. When the jury brought in a verdict of one penny damages, the throng shouted their approval. Strong arms lifted Henry aloft and bore him out of the courthouse.

Henry's contention in essence was that the people of the colonies had a right to govern themselves. And in this he was but finding legal arguments for the existing state of affairs. The Assembly, after a century and a half of battling with Kings and Governors, had made itself to all intents and purposes supreme. In annulling the Two-penny Act the King crossed lances with the representatives of the people and had come off second best. The jury, sitting in the little country courthouse, under the urging of an obscure lawyer, had defied him. Thus, two years before the Stamp Act, Virginia inaugurated the policy of resistance. Most of Henry's arguments were borrowed from the Carter and Bland pamphlets, but whereas they pleaded, he secured positive action. In so far as the Two-penny Act was concerned, the King's veto power was annulled.

Bland summed up the constitutional argument behind this action in a pamphlet written at the time of the trial but published only eight months later. " Under an English government all men are born free, are only subject to laws made by their own consent. . . . If then the people of this colony are free born, and have a right to the liberties and privileges of English subjects, they must necessarily have a legal constitution, that is a legislature, composed in part of the representatives of the people, who may enact laws for the INTERNAL government of the colony, . . . and without such a representative I am bold to say no law can be made." [17]

But the stubborn Mr. Camm was determined not to give up. In April, 1764, his cause came up in the General Court after a delay of five years. The case against him was argued by Robert Carter Nicholas, who claimed that when the Governor had approved a law it was legal, even though in so doing he broke his instructions. A majority of the court [18] were convinced and voted that the Two-penny Act of 1758 was valid despite the King's veto. [19] Camm appealed the case to the Privy

[16] W. W. Henry, *Life, letters, and correspondence of Patrick Henry* 1: 39-41.
[17] *William and Mary Quarterly*, First Ser. 19: 33.
[18] Blair, Tayloe, Byrd, Thornton, and Burwell.
[19] CO5-1330, Fauquier to the Lords of Trade, May 9, 1764.

Council. It came up in 1767, and was thrown out on a technicality. In this way they avoided giving further offense to the colony without admitting the validity of their claims.

The controversy over the Two-penny Act came at a time when the Board of Trade was at odds with the Virginia Assembly over the repeated issues of paper money. Had Dinwiddie and Fauquier not assured them that without these issues there would have been no funds with which to carry on the war, they would certainly have put a stop to them. As it was, all they could do was to urge that steps be taken to prevent the paper from declining in value and to protect the interests of the British merchants.

Prior to 1757 each issue had borne five per cent interest, and taxes had been voted for their redemption. But in April of that year the notes were all called in and new ones issued in their place bearing no interest. This, with a new issue of £80,000 brought the total to £179,962.10.0. This was more than was needed to carry on the business of the colony, and the value of the notes began to sink.[20] In 1748 an act had been passed declaring that debts contracted in sterling could be paid in Virginia currency at a twenty-five per cent advance, or one pound five shillings for one pound sterling. But as the rate of exchange was not long in rising above this figure, the merchants feared large losses.

The London merchants, speaking not only for themselves, but for those of Bristol, Liverpool, and Glasgow, laid their complaint before the Board of Trade. The issuing of large amounts of paper money could be most injurious to trade by putting it upon an uncertain basis, they said. And to pay debts contracted in sterling in depreciated colonial currency was as unjust as it was unwise. So they asked the King to instruct the Governor to urge the Assembly to amend the act of 1748 to make all debts due to persons in Great Britain payable according to the real difference in exchange.[21]

It seems strange that the merchants and the Board of Trade did not know that what they asked for had already been done. In 1755 the act of 1748 had been amended so as to direct the courts in cases where contracts had been made in sterling, to order payment in Virginia money at the rate of exchange they

[20] CO5-1330, Glasgow Merchants to Board of Trade, Jan. 10, 1764.
[21] *Journals of the House of Burgesses*, 1758-1761: 40, 41.

thought just.[22] " The merchants do not know the law," Fauquier wrote the Board. " Let the value of paper currency fall
as much as they please . . . exchange will rise as fast, and they
will obtain for a sterling debt just as much of the paper currency as will purchase a good sterling bill of exchange. And
what injury is done them unless . . . the whole court combine
in a barefaced villainy to defraud them? " At the last court the
exchange had been fixed at 35 per cent.[23]

The amendment to the law of 1748 had had no clause suspending its operation until the King had given his assent, and,
like the Two-penny Act, was a clear infringement on the royal
prerogative. But since it had merely anticipated the King's
wishes, it drew no rebuke from him. None the less, it was one
more step toward autonomy, one more demonstration that in
internal affairs the Virginians were a self-governing people.

The fixing of the rate of exchange quieted the merchants for
the time being, even though they looked on uneasily as Fauquier assented to further emissions, for £57,000 in September,
1758; £52,000 in February, 1759; £10,000 in November, 1759;
£20,000 in March, 1760; £32,000 in May, 1760; and £30,000 in
March, 1762. The whole totalled nearly £413,000, and William
Hunter's printing press at Williamsburg was kept busy stamp-
ing out notes of £10, £15, £3, 10 shillings, 3 shillings, etc. In
the meanwhile, only £51,156. 10.0. had been retired and burnt,
leaving £362,000 in circulation.[24]

Long before this figure had been reached, opposition to
paper money had grown within the colony itself. The law
which protected the British merchants did not apply to Virginia
creditors, since their contracts usually had been made in the
local currency. So, as the flood of paper continued to mount,
the small farmer or shopkeeper who had borrowed from his
wealthy neighbor, could pay him back in depreciated notes.
And as they were legal tender, he had to accept them. " Debtors
pursued their creditors relentlessly and paid them without
mercy."

In 1762, though a bill to issue £30,000 in paper money passed
the House by a vote of 66 to 3, it hung fire in the Council. At
the time there were only six members in attendance, three of
whom opposed any further emissions, so Fauquier got the

---

[22] W. W. Hening, *Statutes at large* 6: 478-483.
[23] CO5-1329, Jan. 5, 1759.
[24] *Ibid.*, June 1, 1763.

Speaker to hold back the bill while he sent out a hurry call for the others. In the end the bill passed by a vote of five to four. " On this occasion I have stretched my influence to the utmost pitch," the Governor wrote the Board.[25] The four dissenting Councillors—William Nelson, Thomas Nelson, Richard Corbin, and Philip Ludwell Lee—all of them rich men, made a vigorous protest, which was entered upon the Journal.[26]

Not satisfied with this, Corbin took the step, unusual for a member of the Upper House, of complaining to the Board of Trade against an act of Assembly. He was astute enough to base his case, not on his personal losses, but on the losses to the revenue and to the merchants. Taxes had been paid in the depreciated currency. In turn this had made it impossible to meet the needs of the government and at the same time sink the outstanding notes. As for the merchants, though it was true that sterling contracts were to be paid at the current rate of exchange, and though the judges who determined it seemed to be impartial, the rate might rise from five to fifteen per cent between the date of their decision and the date of settlement, to their great loss.[27]

When the British merchants heard that some of the most prominent men in Virginia had sided with them in urging that an end be put to currency inflation, they were encouraged to renew their complaints to the Board of Trade. The Board, in turn, wrote Fauquier to urge the Assembly to give them satisfaction. So the Governor, on May 19, 1763, addressed the House, pointing out that common justice required that every man should receive full payment for debts due him. And the support of the public credit, so vital for a trading country like Virginia, made it absolutely necessary to redeem the paper in circulation at the dates fixed by law.[28]

The Burgesses responded by adding to the fund for sinking the paper money by laying additional taxes on slaves, wheel carriages, licenses, etc.[29] But they would not budge from their determination to keep all the notes legal tender. And they made a long and able reply to the Governor, drawn up by Charles Carter, Edmund Pendleton, Wythe, and Richard Henry

[25] CO5-1330, April 8, 1762.
[26] Legislative journals of the Council 3: 1281.
[27] CO5-1330.
[28] Ibid.; Journals of the House of Burgesses, 1761-1765: xxvii.
[29] W. W. Hening, Statutes at large, 7: 639.

Lee, justifying their proceedings and claiming that the merchants had no just grounds for complaint. In it they inserted a declaration of American rights which the British Ministry would have been wise to take to heart. Their dependence upon Great Britain they acknowledged as their greatest happiness and only security. But this was not the dependence of a conquered people, but of sons sent out to explore and settle a new world for the mutual benefit of themselves and their common parent. It was the dependence of the part upon the whole, which, by its admirable constitution, diffused a spirit of patriotism which made every citizen, however remote from the mother kingdom, zealous for the King and the public good.[30]

But the merchants were far from being satisfied, and a group in Glasgow sent another appeal to the Board of Trade. They thought that part of the trouble came from the ease with which paper money could be counterfeited. And they were sure that the hundreds of counterfeit notes, passing from hand to hand in Virginia, partly accounted for the enormous heights of exchange. But they supported the Assembly in continuing the legal tender clause. To take it off might make the currency debts "more fluctuating, uncertain, and less valuable." The only effectual remedy was to forbid further issues of paper money, to see that notes as they were brought into the treasury were duly burnt, to order that circulating notes bear five per cent interest, and to remedy any deficiency in the taxes.[31] When Parliament passed an act to prohibit future emissions in the colonies, they seemed satisfied.

But there was a strong underlying sentiment in the colony against burning the notes. The soil of tidewater Virginia, after a century and a half of cultivation, was beginning to wear out, and thousands of acres were gradually reverting to forest land. This, with war taxes and an occasional drought, had brought hard times. But the planters, instead of tightening their belts, continued the old extravagant mode of living by borrowing money. "I fear they are not prudent enough to quit any article of luxury till smart obliges them," observed Fauquier.[32] So for many cheap money meant salvation from ruin.

These men made their influence felt in the House when a scheme for borrowing £240,000 from the British merchants

[30] *Journals of the House of Burgesses*, 1761-1765: xxx-xxxiv.
[31] CO5-1330, Jan. 10, 1764.
[32] *Ibid.*, Fauquier to the Lords of Trade, Nov. 3, 1760.

was passed in May, 1765. Of this sum £100,000 was to be used for a new currency to replace old notes, and £140,000 to be lent out at five per cent interest. But when the bill came up to the Council it was bitterly opposed by Corbin and finally defeated.[33]

In the meanwhile, people were wondering why the rate of exchange did not drop. They were not ignorant of the quantative law of currency, and they knew that the amount of paper in circulation ought to have been reduced each year. So they were surprised to find it remaining between sixty and sixty-five per cent. Behind this apparent contradiction of economic law there must be some mystery.[34]

The mystery was explained in May, 1766, when a bomb exploded which shook the colony from the capes to the Alleghenies. That month the beloved John Robinson, Speaker and Treasurer, died. Fauquier had called him "the darling of the country." The Gazette lamented his loss and praised "the many amiable virtues which adorned his private station."

So there was universal astonishment when the examiners of his accounts found a deficit of £100,000. Robinson had not taken the money for his own use. Even had he been dishonorable enough to do so, there would have been no need for it, since he was one of the richest men in the colony. What he had done was to lend his friends thousands of pounds from the public funds.[35] In this he was guilty of two serious breaches of his duty. Since the Assembly had refused to establish a public loan office, he must have known that he had no right to do so on his own responsibility. And there could be no excuse for his disregard of the law which required that he burn the paper money as it came in.

But when his friends came to him in distress begging loans to save them from ruin, he did not have the strength of character to refuse them. Thousands of pounds went out to men in all parts of the colony, among them members of some of the oldest and most distinguished families—William Byrd III, Charles Carter, Jr., George Braxton, Henry Fitzhugh, Lewis Burwell, etc. Robinson's estate was large enough to cover all these loans, but it took many years for his executors to recover even part of what was due him.

[33] Journal of the House of Burgesses, 1761-1765: 350.
[34] Virginia Gazette, P. and D., June 27, 1766.
[35] D. J. Mays, Edmund Pendleton 1: 174-208.

Robert Carter Nicholas, Robinson's successor as Treasurer, was bitter in condemnation of what he had done. " The seeming mysteries of our exchange now begin to unfold themselves," he wrote in a letter to the *Gazette*. " It comes out that a great part of the money squeezed from the people for their taxes, instead of being sunk . . . was thrown back into circulation." The Assembly had given their word that they would protect the interests of the British merchants by burning the paper promptly on the dates of their retirement. What must the world think when these good intentions had been in part defeated by a strange kind of misconduct? What made it worse was the need the colony had for the friendship of the merchants at a time when the great men in England had their eyes fixed upon all the Assemblies. " The consequences are as glaring as the sun in the meridian." [36]

Nicholas saw to it that the law was obeyed. As the notes came in they were burnt. As a result the exchange began to drop until in a few months it became normal. The day of easy money was over, and the host of debtors faced ruin. For many months the pages of the *Gazette* were crowded with notices of slaves and plantations for sale.

In the meanwhile, the century and a half old struggle between mother country and colonies was rapidly approaching a crisis. The issue had long been postponed because of the inactivity of the King's ministers, who were content to close their eyes to what was going on across the Atlantic. But the time was at hand when the question of whether the Americans should be governed from London or should govern themselves had to be settled.

This was in part due to the fact that as time passed Parliament had grown less and less representative of the people. In Great Britain there was no provision, as there is in the Constitution of the United States, for periodic reapportionments of the people's representatives to keep step with changes in population. For centuries most of the Commons had been elected under a very restricted franchise by certain old boroughs. Though with the passing of the decades many of these boroughs, once centers of population and wealth, had fallen into decay, they still sent their representatives to the House of Commons. Perhaps the most notorious was Old Sarum, a city of Norman

---

[36] *Virginia Gazette*, P. and D., June 27, 1766.

times, whose castle and cathedral and crowded houses overlooked the Salisbury plain, but which for centuries had been
deserted. Unless the ghosts of men long dead were to have a
voice in running the nation, it was absurd for these old ruins
to be represented in the Commons. In practice the rotten
borough system, as it was called, tended to perpetuate the
ascendency of the landed proprietors.

And the country squires wanted no change. They thought
the British Government the best in the world, and were determined to defend their privileges. It never occurred to them
that duty required that they should try to alleviate the miseries
of the poor people; they were too intent on enjoying their great
manor houses, their formal gardens, their stately dinners, their
fox hunts, to heed the voices which were pleading for social
and political reform.[37]

But it would be a mistake to assume that Great Britain had
become static in intellectual, social, and institutional matters.
On the contrary, the first seven decades of the eighteenth century was a period of tremendous activity. It was the period of
Richardson and Fielding in literature, of the great religious
revival led by Wesley and Whitefield, of renewed interest in
Shakespeare, of the birth of industrial Britain, of the bold
defiance of authority by John Wilkes. Had Parliament truly
reflected the spirit of the age, had it not revered the old system
of government as the best attainable by man, it would have
attuned itself to these changes.

If the Commons were out of step with the march of events
in Great Britain, they were far more so with developments in
the colonies. They knew nothing of the influence of the vast
natural resources and the limited supply of labor in lifting
the level of the common man and giving him a sense of self-
respect, nothing of the democratizing power of the frontier.
And what little they saw they disliked. No doubt some would
have applauded Samuel Johnson when he said of the Americans: " Sir, they are a race of convicts, and ought to be thankful
for anything we allow them short of hanging."

With such irreconcilable differences between the ruling
group in Great Britain and the people of the colonies the
conflict was inevitable. The King, the Privy Council, the Board
of Trade, the Commons construed the many instances of colon-

[37] Charles M. Andrews, The American Revolution, *American Historical Review*
31: 219-232.

ial disobedience as attacks on the foundations of the established order, as revolutionary innovations. To Americans they seemed no more than the assertion of rights inherent in all free men. And though many of their claims had no precedent in English experience, they began to speak of them as ancient and necessary for the existence of representative government.

That the clash came when it did was in part due to the passing of the laissez-faire period in the British Government. New figures had made their appearance at Whitehall, who had no patience with the old slipshod way of doing things. They wanted a consolidated empire, ruled from London, rather than a loose federation of semi-independent states. To them it seemed intolerable that the colonial Assemblies should defy the King at will. " Must we and America be two distinct kingdoms, and that now immediately? " asked George Grenville.

The French and Indian War revealed much concerning conditions in the colonies which surprised and alarmed the Ministry. They had found it impossible to get the colonies to act in unison, they had defied the King's wishes repeatedly, the Governors were kept busy explaining why they had to disregard one instruction after another, they were disgusted at the pouring out of paper money, and they must have been influenced by the warnings that the Americans were too much of a republican way of thinking. The advice to have Parliament lay a general tax on the colonies had come, not only from Dinwiddie, but from various parts of America.

The determination of the Ministry to follow this advice was based ostensibly on the reasonableness of requiring the colonies to bear their share of the burden of the expense of the war. It may be argued that Virginia and some of the others, because of the disruption of trade, the very heavy taxes, the devastation on the frontiers, and their heavy losses in men, had already paid more than their share. But that there was something deeper, more vital, behind the resolve to tax than a mere matter of finance, is obvious. It was a demonstration of policy, a manifesto that Great Britain was determined to govern her colonies.

When word reached America that the Ministry planned to tax the colonies by a stamp Act, there was general dismay. There were many grave faces among the Burgesses as they took their seats in November, 1764. Some of the ablest men in Virginia, among them Peyton Randolph, Edmund Pendleton, George Wythe, and Richard Henry Lee, drew up a protest to the King and Parliament. They begged the King to protect the people of the colony in the enjoyment of their ancient right of being governed in internal affairs by laws derived from their own consent, with the approbation of their sovereign or his substitute. This right, as men and descendants of Britons, they had possessed ever since they left the mother kingdom to extend its commerce and dominion.

To the House of Lords they pointed out that, as their ancestors had brought with them to America every right and privilege they could claim in the mother kingdom, their descendants could not justly be deprived of them. It was a fundamental principle of the British Constitution, without which freedom could nowhere exist, that the people are not subject to any taxes except by their own consent or by those who were legally appointed to represent them.

They reminded the Commons that this principle had been recognized ever since the founding of the colony. During the reign of Charles II, when the British Government sought a revenue to support the government of Virginia, they had tacitly admitted that Parliament had no right to levy the tax. Instead they drew up a bill in England and sent it over to be acted on by the Assembly.[38]

As they penned this protest the thoughts of Wythe and the others must have reverted to the part played by the control of taxation in winning self-government for the colony. They spoke of their rights as ancient, yet they must have known that the Virginia of their day was far freer than it had been under the Stuarts. And there could be no doubt as to how this great change had come about. They and their fathers and their great-grandfathers had used the control of the purse to whittle the royal prerogative until little was left. For Parliament to strike this weapon from their hands would be to nullify the gains of many decades and leave them defenseless.

When the bill to tax the Americans came before the Commons, on February 7, 1765, a lengthy debate followed. It was on this occasion that Colonel Isaac Barré retorted to Charles Townshend's assertion that the Americans had been " planted by our care, nourished by our indulgence." " Your oppressions planted them in America," he shouted. " They grew up by your neglect of them. . . . They protected by your arms! They

[38] *Journals of the House of Burgesses*, 1761-1765: liv-lviii.

have taken up arms in your defence." [39] But when the Virginia memorial was presented it was rejected by an overwhelming majority.[40] The bill passed the Commons by 205 votes to 49, and the House of Lords without a division. The measure required the colonists to use stamps, purchased from the British Government through royal agents, on newspapers, almanacs, pamphlets, advertisements, and various kinds of legal documents.

It was with heavy hearts that the Assembly met in May, 1765. Edmund Pendleton, when news of the passage of the Stamp Act reached him, had exclaimed, " Poor America! " As he, George Wythe, Richard Bland, Robert Carter Nicholas, Henry Lee, Peyton Randolph, and other leading statesmen took their seats, they had no thought of resistance. They proceeded with routine business—the authorizing of a ferry over the Potomac, giving rewards for killing wolves, opening a road through the Swift Run Gap, preventing escapes from debtors' prisons, etc. Probably none of the aristocrats from the tidewater paid any attention to young Patrick Henry when he joined the House late in the session. When most of the bills had passed the third reading many of the members left, and mounting their horses rode out of town, leaving only thirty-nine to wind up business.

This was Henry's opportunity. Opening an old law book he wrote down seven resolutions. Then, rising, he introduced them in the House. In substance the first four declared that Virginians from the first settlement had possessed all the privileges of the people of Great Britain, that these privileges had been confirmed to them by two royal charters, that the taxation of the people by themselves was the distinguishing characteristic of British freedom, and that the people of the colony had never forfeited the right to be governed by their own Assembly in the articles of taxation and internal policy.

When Henry came to the fifth resolution there must have been a gasp of surprise. It held that any attempt to vest the power to tax the colonies in any other body than the Assembly was illegal, unjust, and unconstitutional, and tended to destroy British as well as American liberty. Henry did not introduce the other two resolutions, probably because of the uproar which the reading of the fifth occasioned.

A violent debate ensued. George Wythe, John Robinson,

---

[39] *Parliamentary history of England*, ed. T. C. Hansard, **16**: 38, 39.
[40] L. P. Gipson, *The coming of the Revolution*, 81.

Peyton Randolph, and others thought the language too extreme. But what Fauquier described as " the young, hot, and giddy members," were carried along by Henry's eloquence. " Tarquin and Caesar each had his Brutus, Charles I his Cromwell, and George III. . . ." At this point he was interrupted by the Speaker who declared that he had spoken treason. Henry denied that he advocated treason. If he had said anything wrong, it should be attributed to his concern over his country's dying liberty.[41]

The first four resolutions passed by safe margins, but the fifth barely got by, by a vote of twenty to nineteen. In alarm the more conservative members sent out a hurry call for such absent Burgesses as were still in or near Williamsburg. When several had come in an attempt was made to have the resolutions struck off the journal. They succeeded with the fifth, Fauquier reported, " which was thought the most offensive," but failed with the other four.[42]

Perhaps Henry, himself, as he left Williamsburg, wearing a pair of leather breeches and leading his bony nag by the bridle, did not realize that his resolutions would be the alarm bell of revolution. The *Maryland Gazette*, the *Newport Gazette*, the *Boston Gazette*, and other papers published them, not only the four which passed in the House, but the other three as well. And the sixth and seventh were radical indeed. They declared that the people of the colony were not bound to obey any laws to tax them other than those passed by the Assembly, and that any person who should uphold such laws " by speaking or writing " should be deemed an enemy of the colony. It was the policy of resistance.

Virginia was now aflame. It was rumored that groups of men from all parts of the colony were preparing to march on Williamsburg to seize and destroy the stamps as soon as they arrived. Many justices declared that they would resign rather than use the stamps in the processes of their courts, and it seemed certain that others would follow their example. From Westmoreland came word that a mob had burned in effigy the stamp distributor for Virginia, Colonel George Mercer, a native

[41] William Wirt, *Sketches of Patrick Henry*. The eyewitness account by a French traveler throws doubt on the long accepted statement that Henry replied to the Speaker's charge: " If this be treason make the most of it." *American Historical Review* 25: 745.
[42] CO5-1330, June 5, 1765.

Virginian who had served in the French and Indian War.[43]
Fauquier waited anxiously for his arrival with the stamps,
praying that adverse winds would delay him until the session
of the General Court was over and the crowds of merchants,
persons involved in suits, debtors, witnesses, and others had
left town.

But the Fates were against him. Mercer arrived on October
30, and at once went to his father's house. Having word of this,
a crowd of men, some of them leading citizens in their home
counties, started off to find him. As they approached the Capitol
they met him and asked him whether he intended to retain
his office as stamp distributor. To this he gave an evasive
answer, and continued to the coffee house nearby where Governor Fauquier, Speaker Robinson, and several members of the
Council were seated on the porch. The crowd, which had
followed him, pressed toward them and a cry was heard, " Let
us rush in." But when Fauquier and the others advanced to
repel them, someone called out, " See the Governor, take care
of him." Upon this they fell back. And when Mercer promised
that he would give his answer at the Capitol the next day at
five, they seemed satisfied and permitted him to walk through
them side by side with the Governor to the Palace.[44]

In the meanwhile, word of Mercer's arrival had spread
through the countryside, so that the next day hundreds of
persons poured into town. As five o'clock approached a vast
crowd assembled in the Capitol yard. There Mercer spoke
to them. His appointment had been unsolicited, he said. He
had not, as had been rumored, urged the passage of the Stamp
Act. "And now," he added, " I will not, directly by myself or
deputies proceed in the execution of the act . . . without the
assent of the General Assembly of this colony." At this there was
a great shout of approval, and those near him raised him aloft
and bore him out through the gate to a nearby tavern. As they
entered, the huzzas were redoubled, while drums rattled, and
horns blared. That night the town was illuminated and bells
rang out. The following night the occasion was climaxed by
" a splendid ball." [45]

As for the stamps, they never touched land. They were transferred to a warship, " it being the place of the greatest, if not

---

[43] *William and Mary Quarterly*, First Ser. **18:** 162n.
[44] CO5-1330, Fauquier to the Lords of Trade, Nov. 3, 1765.
[45] *Virginia Gazette*, Oct. 25, 1765. Supplement.

the only security for them." If the mob could have laid their hands on them they would certainly have gone up in flames.

Now in various parts of the colony men met to organize what they called Sons of Liberty. The merchants of Norfolk, native-born Scotsmen many of them, had a double grievance, since the Sugar Act threatened their trade and the Stamp Act their liberty. In March about thirty leading citizens met at the house of Mayor Calvert, where " they brought daylight on " debating the best way to resist both acts. At their call the people crowded into the courthouse to protest. " We will . . . defend ourselves in the full enjoyment of . . . those inestimable privileges of freeborn British subjects of being taxed only by representatives of their own choosing. . . . If we quietly submit to the execution of the said Stamp Act, all our claims of civil liberty will be lost, and we and our posterity become absolute slaves." [46]

A few days later, when word went round that a certain Captain William Smith had been responsible for the seizure of several vessels in the Elizabeth River, he was arrested by a group of leading citizens. Hurrying him to the County Wharf, they tarred and feathered him, set him in the ducking stool, and pelted him with stones and rotten eggs. They next marched him through the town with drums beating, ducked him again, and at last threw him headlong into the water. Had not a passing boat pulled him out, more dead than alive, he would have been drowned. [47]

At Hobb's Hole, Essex County, a merchant named Ritchie barely escaped similar treatment. A number of men, hearing that he had boasted that he could secure stamps and was deter-mined to clear his ship with them, marched on the town and drew up along the main street. They brought Ritchie out and threatened to strip him to the waist, tie him to the tail of a cart, and then fix him in the pillory. This was too much for him. Reluctantly he swore on " the holy Evangels " that no vessel of his would clear " on stamped paper." Thereupon most of the crowd dispersed, and those living nearby went to the tavern " where they spent the evening with great sobriety." [48]

The people of the colony were encouraged in their resistance to the Stamp Act by articles in British gazettes and magazines,

[46] *Virginia Gazette*, April 4, 1766.
[47] CO5-1331, J. Morgan to Fauquier, April 7, 1766.
[48] *Tyler's Magazine* 16: 111-114.

which were reprinted in the *Virginia Gazette*. A writer in the *Gentleman's Magazine* contended that the act violated the British constitution, which "declared that no Englishman is to be taxed without his own consent." "I know very well I shall be told that though the Americans are not immediately represented in the English Parliament, they are nevertheless represented virtually. . . . But why, in the name of common sense, if the mother country judged herself the virtual representative of all her various dependencies, did she grant a provincial legislature to her colonies, and from the time of their first existence invest this legislature with the sole power of internal taxation?" For the colonists to yield, he thought, would be to confess themselves slaves.[49]

And when the Virginians read the *Gazette* they noted with satisfaction that the disruption of trade was causing great distress in England. A dispatch from Birmingham stated that unless the Stamp Act were repealed twenty thousand persons would be out of work.[50] The merchants of London petitioned the Commons for relief. Their trade with the colonies, which was of such great importance to the nation, faced utter ruin, they said. They could not collect debts due them in America, because the Sugar Act and the Stamp Act had thrown the colonies into confusion and brought on many bankruptcies. Unless these acts were repealed a multitude of workers would become a burden on the community or else seek their bread in other countries.[51]

It was late in May, 1766, that a vessel arrived in Virginia waters bearing the news that the Stamp Act had been repealed. As horsemen galloped along the roads and boatsmen in their shallops ascended the great rivers, the word was passed from mouth to mouth. Everywhere there was joyous celebration. At Great Bridge the people listened to a patriotic sermon in St. Giles Church, and then went to the Banqueting Room, where they raised their glasses in a series of toasts—to the King and Queen, Colonel Barré, and others. At Hampton there was a banquet at the Bunch of Grapes, followed by a ball at the King's Arms Tavern, while outside there was a great bonfire.[52] The people of Williamsburg waited for their celebration until

[49] *Virginia Gazette*, P. and D., Apr. 4, 1766.
[50] *Ibid.*
[51] *Ibid.*, Apr. 25, 1766.
[52] *Ibid.*, June 13, 1766.

the convening of the court when the town was crowded. Then every house was illuminated, and there was " a ball and elegant entertainment at the Capitol," marked by " much mirth " and the drinking of toasts.[53]

With the French and Indian War brought to a successful conclusion, with the problem of currency inflation settled, with the Stamp Act repealed, it seemed that Fauquier might look forward to a period of harmony and prosperity. But fate soon struck a cruel blow. In the summer of 1767 the Governor became ill with a very painful disorder. And though, under the care of Dr. Matthew Pope, of York, he became better, he never fully recovered his health.[54] He died in the early hours of March 3, 1768. In his will he directed that if the nature of his illness should not be understood by his physicians, an autopsy be held on his body, so that he might become more useful to his fellow creatures in death than he had been in life. He desired, also, that he be buried " without any vain funeral pomp." [55]

Francis Fauquier was an able, just, tactful Governor, who tried to do his duty both to the King and to the colony. His was an extremely difficult task. His sympathies seem to have been with the people. Living among them, knowing their views, he must have deplored the policy of the Ministry in trying to deprive them of the cherished right of self-government. Great Britain's strongest link with America was not the link of government, not even the economic link, but the link of affection. And nothing tended more to strengthen it than the appointment of such a man as Fauquier to be Lieutenant Governor of the largest of the colonies. It would have been a lasting grief to Fauquier had he lived to see the final separation of mother country and colonies.

[53] *Ibid.*, June 20, 1766.
[54] *Ibid.*, July 16, 1767.
[55] *William and Mary Quarterly*, First Ser., 8: 173-177.

CHAPTER XIV

INDEPENDENCE

IT was in October, 1768, when news reached Virginia that Norborne Berkeley, Lord Botetourt, had kissed the King's hand as Governor General. The unrest in the colony had convinced the Privy Council that the government "should no longer be administered by a substitute." So when Sir Jeffrey Amherst declined "going over to America," it was decided to appoint one who would go. For the first time since the death of Nott, Virginia had a resident Governor General. The people of the colony regarded this as a singular honor. When Botetourt arrived in Williamsburg, he found the members of the Council, the Speaker of the House, the Attorney General, and other prominent men waiting to receive him at the gate of the Capitol yard. After they had gone in to the Council Chamber, where the new Governor administered the oath, they stepped over to the Raleigh Tavern for supper. Then Botetourt was escorted to the Palace through the illuminated Duke of Gloucester Street and the Palace Green.[1]

If the British Government had hoped to please the people of Virginia in sending them a Governor General, they were not disappointed. "All ranks vied with each other in testifying their gratitude and joy that a nobleman of such distinguished merit and abilities is appointed to preside over and live among them."[2] But it was not so much his rank as his personality which won all hearts. He was easily accessible, affable to the humblest visitor, sympathetic with the people's grievances.

The new Governor was at once confronted with grave issues. In May, 1767, Charles Townshend had secured an act of Parliament placing duties on glass, lead, painters' colors, and tea imported into the colonies. It was expressly stated that the revenue was to be used to pay the salaries of British officials in America. Another act was passed to enforce the trade laws, and still another to suspend the New York Assembly for its defiance of the Billeting Act.

[1] *Virginia Gazette*, P. and D., Oct. 27, 1768.
[2] *Ibid.*

Again all America seethed. It is obvious, men told each other, that the British Government will not be content until they have made slaves of us. At first they claimed that they were seeking nothing more of us than a revenue. Now they openly avow that these new duties are to be used to make British officials in America independent of the Assemblies. That would be the final triumph of royal authority.

So when Botetourt dissolved the old Assembly and called for a new election, the people selected their ablest and most patriotic men. Among them were George Washington, Thomas Jefferson, Patrick Henry, Richard Henry Lee, Henry Lee, and Edmund Pendleton. When they met, in May, 1769, Governor Botetourt entered an elegant coach which had been presented to him by King George III, on it the insignia of royalty, drawn by six milk-white horses, and drove from the Palace to the Capitol. After the usual address to the Assembly and the replies of the Council and the Burgesses, Botetourt entertained many of the members at dinner.

In the previous February the Governor had written the Lords of Trade warning them of the temper of the people. " I must not venture to flatter your Lordships that they will ever willingly submit to being taxed by the mother country. The reverse is their creed. They universally avow a most ardent desire to assist upon every occasion, but pray to be allowed to do it in consequence of requisition." [3]

It seems strange, then, that he should have been surprised to hear that the Burgesses had passed several resolutions asserting the rights of the people. They declared that the sole right of imposing taxes " is now, and ever hath been " constitutionally vested in the House of Burgesses; that the people have the right to petition the sovereign for redress of grievances; and that trials for crimes committed in the colony should be tried in the Virginia courts.[4]

The next day the Governor summoned the Council and Burgesses to the Council Chamber, where he said he had heard of the resolutions, that he predicted they would have an ill effect, and that according to his duty, he dissolved them.

But the Burgesses would not be silenced. Filing out of the Capitol, they went to the nearby Raleigh Tavern for an un-

[3] CO5-1332, Feb. 18, 1769.
[4] *Virginia Gazette*, P. and D., May 18, 1769.

official session. After they had elected Peyton Randolph moderator, they discussed the serious problems facing the colony. They then appointed a committee to draw up a plan for an association, and adjourned until the next day.

The report of the committee, which was signed by eighty-eight men, is a document of the greatest importance in the history of the clash between the American colonies and Great Britain. It spoke of the " grievances and distresses " with which the people were oppressed, of the evils which threatened their ruin and the ruin of their posterity by reducing them " from a free and happy people to a wretched and miserable state of slavery." They denounced " the restrictions, prohibitions, and ill-advised regulations in several late acts of Parliament," and declared that the " unconstitutional act imposing duties on tea, paper, glass, etc. for the sole purpose of raising a revenue in America is injurious to property, and destructive to liberty." [5] Those who signed the association promised to discourage luxury and extravagance, agreed not to import goods taxed by Parliament or any of a long list of commodities, until the hated duties were removed.

After all had affixed their signatures, they gathered around the punch bowl to drink a series of toasts—to the King, the Queen and the Royal Family, Lord Botetourt, A Speedy and lasting Union between Great Britain and her Colonies, The Constitutional British Liberty in America and all true Patriots, the Supporters thereof, the Duke of Richmond, the Earl of Shelburne, Colonel Barré, the late Speaker, etc. At last, either because the liquor or the toasts gave out, the meeting came to an end.[6]

It was while the Assembly was in session that Secretary Hillsborough wrote Botetourt assuring him that the King's ministers would soon propose the repeal of the obnoxious duties. Whereupon the Governor called an Assembly and laid the joyous news before them. But the Burgesses must have seen the joker in the announcement when they noted that the repeal would be based, not on any illegality in the duties, but on the fact that they had been laid " contrary to the true principles of commerce." [7]

Yet Botetourt was all optimism. " I will be content to be

[5] Ibid.   [7] Journals of the House of Burgesses, 1766-1769: 227.
[6] CO5-1332, Botetourt to Hillsborough, May 19, 1769.

declared infamous if I do not to the last hour of my life . . . exert every power with which I am or ever shall be legally invested . . . to obtain and maintain for the continent of America that satisfaction which I have been authorized to promise by the confidential servant of our gracious sovereign." Some months later, when the Virginians learned just how the Ministry had carried out this promise, Botetourt had reason to think that he had been led into deceiving them. It is true that all the duties had been taken off save that on tea. But so far from considering this a favor, the colonists resented it as a bait to make them acknowledge the right of Parliament to tax them. The resentment of the people was all the greater because of their disappointmnt. Hillsborough's promise had made them lax in enforcing the association, so in June, 1770, they organized a new one. A long list of imported goods were to be boycotted, industry was to be encouraged, prices were not to be advanced. To see that the agreement was carried out committees were to be organized in every county to examine invoices and expose violators.

It was unfortunate for Virginia that Botetourt's administration was short. He died October 15, 1770. "Truly and justly to express the many great virtues and amiable qualities which adorned this noble lord, as well in his public as private character, would demand the skill of the ablest penman," stated the death notice in the *Gazette*. "Virginia, in his fall, sorely laments the loss of the best of Governors and the best of men." [8]

A few days later a sorrowful procession moved from the Palace to Bruton Parish Church, amid the tolling of the bells in the church, the college, and the Capitol. In front of and beside the hearse were eight mourners carrying staffs draped in black, around them were the pallbearers—six Councillors and the Speaker of the House. Then followed the Governor's servants, the clergy, the professors of the college, the Williamsburg officials preceded by the city mace, and many others, all having white hatbands and gloves. After the service in the church the procession moved to the Wren Building where the lead casket, covered with a crimson velvet cloth, was placed in a vault below the floor of the chapel.[9]

As a token of affection the Assembly employed Richard Hayward, of London, to make a marble statue of Botetourt,

[8] *Virginia Gazette*, P. and D. Oct. 18, 1770.   [9] *Ibid.*, Supplement.

which arrived in 1773 and was set up in the piazza of the
Capitol. Later it was mutilated by a crowd of vandals as an
expression of their hostility to all things British. In 1801 the
College of William and Mary acquired it and removed it to the
campus in front of the Wren Building, where it stands today
an object of veneration for faculty, students, and alumni.

The grief of the people at the loss of Botetourt would have
been all the greater had they known who was to be his successor.
At the time John Murray, Earl of Dunmore, was Governor of
New York, where he was regarded with contempt. At a feast
of the Sons of St. Andrew he got drunk, acted like " a damned
fool," and " sank himself " so low with vile language that the
entire company was abashed. When word reached him that he
was to be transferred to Virginia, he expressed resentment.
" Damn Virginia! " he cried. " Why is it forced on me? I asked
for New York. New York I love and they have robbed me of
it." At a farewell dinner given in his honor, " he took too
cheerful a glass," and got into a fight.[10]

The people of Virginia were probably not aware of Dunmore's character, for they greeted him cordially upon his arrival
in Williamsburg, late in September, 1771. In the evening the
city was illuminated, with a candle in every window, as a testimony of joy at his Excellency's safe arrival.[11]

The time was auspicious, for there was a lull in the controversy with the mother country. Though the duty on tea had
not been removed, there was general hope that all differences
could be adjusted. It is true that Dunmore aroused suspicion
by trying to create new fees with which to pay his secretary,
but his promptness in relinquishing them soon dissipated it.
" A ball and elegant entertainment " at the Capitol given by the
Burgesses in his honor testified to a spirit of cordiality.

It was just this lull which alarmed some of the younger
leaders in Virginia. As long as the tax on tea remained they
realized that the danger to liberty persisted. So when the Assembly met in the spring of 1773, Patrick Henry, Thomas
Jefferson, Richard Henry Lee, and others held private consultations in the Raleigh Tavern on how to awaken the people,
not only of Virginia, but of all the colonies, to the need of a
common defense.[12]

[10] William Smith, *Diary*, Dec. 1, 1770; July 9, 1771.
[11] *Virginia Gazette*, P. and D., Sept. 17, 1771.
[12] *The writings of Thomas Jefferson*, ed. A. A. Lipscomb, 1: 7.

A momentous series of meetings they proved to be, for out of them came the intercolonial system of committees of correspondence and the Continental Congress. " We were all sensible that the most urgent of all measures was that of coming to an understanding with all the other colonies to consider the British claims as a common cause to all, and to produce a unity of action," Jefferson stated afterward. " And for this purpose that a committee of correspondence in each colony would be the best instrument for intercommunication. And that their first measure would probably be to propose a meeting of deputies from every colony, at some central place, who should be charged with the direction of the measures to be taken by all." [13]

On March 13, the resolution to appoint the committee of correspondence for Virginia was introduced in the House of Burgesses by Dabney Carr, and adopted unanimously. To the committee were appointed some of the first men in the colony— Peyton Randolph, Thomas Jefferson, Richard Henry Lee, Patrick Henry, Edmund Pendleton, etc.

William Lee, writing from London, said that this action "struck a greater panic into the Ministers" than anything since the passage of the Stamp Act. And well it might, for soon the entire country was covered with committees, who kept in close touch with each other, formulated public opinion, and prepared the way for revolutionary action.

The need for these bodies became glaringly evident when the British Government adopted a policy of repression which aroused the spirt of resistance to the highest pitch. At the time the East India Company was on the verge of bankruptcy. In order to save it the government agreed to remit the long-standing duty of twelve pence a pound on tea entering Great Britain. When the tea was re-exported to America the price, even after the three pence duty there had been paid, would be nine pence less than formerly. George III approved of the plan heartily, and confidently expected the colonists to swallow the pill of Parliamentary taxation, now that it was coated with the sugar of reduced prices.

Never was a man more mistaken. The Americans, after struggling for a century and a half to win liberty, were not going to sell it for a cup of tea. When the East India Company ships arrived, angry mobs forced some to turn back with their

[13] *Ibid.*

cargoes, some were boarded and the tea destroyed. When the brigantine *Mary and Jane* arrived in Norfolk with nine chests of tea, a crowded meeting at the courthouse demanded that they be sent back. When the importers complied they received a vote of thanks.[14] The York County committee, headed by Thomas Nelson, debated whether a ship which came in with two chests of tea should not be burnt, but contented themselves with forcing her to leave without the expected cargo of tobacco.

Tea was banned in every patriotic household. One evening at Nomini Hall, Mrs. Robert Carter made " a dish of tea " for her husband. " He smelt, sipt, looked." " What is this? " he asked. Then " splash " he emptied the cup in the fire.[15] But what chiefly aroused the ire of the British Ministry was the so-called Boston Tea Party, when fifty or sixty men, disguised as Indians, boarded the tea ships and threw box after box in the harbor, while a large crowd looked on and applauded.

This provoked the British Government into making their most serious blunder—the passage of what the Americans called the " Intolerable Acts." The port of Boston was closed; the Massachusetts government was altered to increase the power of the Governor; in certain cases accused persons might be sent to England for trial; the Governors were authorized to requisition buildings for the use of royal troops; the boundaries of the province of Quebec were extended to the Mississippi on the west and the Ohio on the south.

The American patriots now realized that they must act with vigor and firmness or lose all that they held most dear. The King and Parliament were determined to force the issue. When the Virginia Assembly met in May, 1774, Henry, Jefferson, Richard Henry Lee, and several others met in the Council Chamber in the Capitol to agree on some measure to arouse the people to a sense of the danger. After some discussion it was decided to propose to the Burgesses that they make June 1, the date set for the closing of the port of Boston, a day of general fasting and prayer. The resolution was introduced by Robert Carter Nicholas, and passed without opposition.[16]

The resolution stated that it was necessary to have a day of " fasting, humiliation, and prayer, devoutly to implore the

[14] T. J. Wertenbaker, *Norfolk: historic southern port*, 55.
[15] *Journal of Philip Vickers Fithian*, ed. H. D. Farish, 257.
[16] *The writings of Thomas Jefferson*, ed. A. A. Lipscomb, 1: 9.

Lord Dunmore. From the copy in the possession of the Virginia
Historical Society of the original portrait by
Sir Joshua Reynolds.

The Governor's Palace, Williamsburg. Courtesy of Colonial Williamsburg, Inc.

divine interposition for averting the heavy calamity which threatens destruction to our civil rights, and the evils of civil war; to give us one heart and mind firmly to oppose, by all just and proper means, every injury to American rights; and that the minds of his Majesty and his Parliament may be inspired from above with wisdom, moderation, and justice to remove from the loyal people of America all cause of danger from a continued pursuit of measures pregnant with ruin." Dunmore thought the resolution reflected on the King and Parliament, and so made it necessary for him to dissolve the Assembly.[17]

But on June 1, in all parts of Virginia, the people dropped their daily tasks to assemble in the churches. Every face reflected the universal alarm, as the eastern aristocrat, the frontiersman in his buckskin clothes, the great landholder, and the small planter knelt in prayer. In Williamsburg the citizens and as many of the Burgesses as had remained in town, assembled at the courthouse and moved in solemn procession to the church to listen to a sermon by the chaplain of the House.[18] There had been no such solemn occasion since the French and Indian War, and it came as an electric shock to the people.[19]

In the meanwhile, events of great importance were taking place in Williamsburg. When Dunmore dissolved the Assembly, the Burgesses, instead of dispersing, met as they had done five years before in the Raleigh Tavern. Here, as they sat in the beautiful Apollo Room, they renewed the association to boycott English goods; proposed to the committees of correspondence in every colony that they appoint deputies to a continental Congress; and suggested that each county in Virginia should elect representatives to a convention to meet at Williamsburg on August 1.[20]

Despite their revolutionary activities, the members of the Assembly maintained cordial relations with the Governor. When Lady Dunmore joined her husband earlier in the spring, she was greeted with cheers by the people of Williamsburg. On May 26, the Burgesses gave a ball and entertainment in the Capitol in her honor. My lady seems to have been a most graceful dancer. When she and the Governor visited Norfolk where a ball was given them, the city authorities sent to Princess Anne

[17] Journals of the House of Burgesses, 1773-1776: 124.
[18] Virginia Gazette, P. and D., June 2, 1774.
[19] The writings of Thomas Jefferson, ed. A. A. Lipscomb, 1: 11.
[20] Ibid., 10.

County for Colonel Moseley to come "with his famous wig and shining buckles" to dance the minuet with her. So when the fiddles struck up away she went "sailing about the room in her great, fine hoop-petticoat, and Colonel Moseley after her wig and all." [21]

Most of the Burgesses of the Assembly of 1774 had hardly rested from their journey home when they had to repack their saddlebags, mount their horses, and set out again for Williamsburg to attend the provincial convention. When they had assembled they once more renewed the association, and then proceeded to the election of delegates to the Continental Congress. Randolph was chosen because it was thought he would preside, Washington because he might be called on to command the army, Henry and Richard Henry Lee because of their eloquence, Bland, Harrison, and Pendleton because of their ability as political leaders.

As these men turned their faces toward Philadelphia, their minds must have reverted to the series of violations of the rights of the people which had brought on the crisis. The questions George Washington asked himself no doubt were in the minds of all. "Does it not appear as clear as the sun in its meridian brightness that there is a regular, systematic plan formed to fix the right and practice of taxation upon us? . . . Does not the uniform conduct of Parliament for some years past confirm this? . . . Is not the attack upon the liberty and property of the people of Boston . . . a plain and self-evident proof of what they are aiming at? Do not subsequent bills . . . convince us that the administration is determined to stick at nothing to carry its point?" [22]

Congress met in the "plain and spacious rooms" on the lower floor of Carpenter's Hall which had been completed four years before. After some debate they adopted a Declaration of Rights and Grievances, stating the American case against taxation without representation and demanding the repeal of the "unpolitic, unjust, cruel, and unconstitutional" Intolerable Acts. They then framed a "Continental Association" to be enforced by local committees.

The Association proved remarkably successful. To this Dunmore himself bore testimony. To the Earl of Hillsborough he

[21] Lower Norfolk County Antiquary 5: 32-35.
[22] Writings of George Washington, ed. Jared Sparks, 2: 389.

wrote in December, 1774: " The Associations . . . recommended by the people of this colony, and adopted by what is called the Continental Congress, are now enforcing throughout this country with the greatest rigor. A committee has been chosen in every county whose business it is to carry the Association of the Congress into execution, which committee assumes an authority to inspect the books, invoices, and all the secrets of the trade and correspondence of the merchants, to watch the conduct of every inhabitant without distinction, and send for all such as come under their suspicion into their presence, to interrogate them . . . and to stigmatize, as they term it, such as they find transgressing what they are hardy enough to call the laws of Congress." [23]

The American patriots were greatly encouraged by the support they received from many of the ablest men in Great Britain. These men were shocked at the disregard by Parliament of the principle that no man should be taxed without his own consent. Pitt declared that if America fell the British Constitution would fall with her. When troops were sent to Boston, the Duke of Richmond blurted out: " I hope from the bottom of my heart that the Americans may resist and get the better of the forces sent against them."

Today one wonders how the King and Parliament could have turned a deaf ear to the ringing words of Edmund Burke in his famous address on " Conciliation with the Colonies." " As long as you have the wisdom to keep the sovereign authority of this country as the sanctuary of liberty, the sacred temple consecrated to our common faith, wherever the chosen race and sons of England worship freedom, they will turn their faces toward you. The more they multiply, the more friends you will have; the more ardently they love liberty, the more perfect will be their obedience. Slavery they can have anywhere—it is a seed that grows in every soil. . . . But, until you become lost to all feeling of your true interest and your national dignity, freedom they can have from none but you. . . . Deny them this participation of freedom, and you break that sole bond which originally made, and must still preserve, the unity of the Empire. . . . It is the spirit of the English Constitution which, infused through the mighty mass, pervades, feeds, unites, in-

[23] Dunmore papers, No. 22.

vigorates, vivifies every part of the Empire, even down to the minutest members." [24]

In the revolutionary changes in Virginia it was the House of Burgesses, not the Council, who took the lead. Washington, Henry, Jefferson, Pendleton, Richard Henry Lee, George Mason were all Burgesses. In fact the members of the Council were placed in a most embarrassing position. Appointed by the King to aid and advise the royal Governor, they owed a double allegiance—to Crown and country. To them the breach was a tragedy, the choice of allegiance a difficult one. So for the most part they played a negative role. In the Council meetings they usually voted with the Governor. But as the crisis grew more acute they drifted away from him to join their countrymen in resisting the assaults on their liberty.

John Page, Junior, in Council supported Dunmore in dissolving the Assembly in May, 1774; yet he remained in town and joined the Burgesses in the procession to the church on the fast day. [25] On the other hand, Robert Carter, though he had refused to drink a cup of tea, would not permit any of his family to observe the day. " By this I conclude he is a courtier," wrote Fithian in his *Diary*. But he did not long remain a " courtier." " The enemies of government are so numerous and so vigilant over the conduct of every man that the loyalists have been so intimidated that they have entirely shrunk away," wrote Dunmore in July, 1775. " Even the Council . . . approves everything done by the Burgesses." The only members he could rely upon were Ralph Wormeley, Gawin Corbin, and the Reverend John Camm. [26] The rest, while not subscribing to the Association, adhered strictly to it.

But John Randolph, the Attorney General, remained faithful to the King to the end. His opposition to the resolutions denouncing the Stamp Act, the boycott, and the calling of the provincial and Continental Congresses brought down on him the wrath of the patriots. Dunmore stated that he was insulted, his life threatened, and his home destroyed. [27] In 1775 he sailed for England with his family, never to return.

In the fall of 1774 Dunmore brought on himself the hatred of the Virginia frontiersmen by his conduct in a war with the

[24] *Burke's speech*, ed. S. C. Newsom, 105, 106.
[25] Dunmore papers, Dunmore to Dartmouth, March 14, 1775.
[26] *Ibid.*, No. 28.
[27] *Ibid.*, No. 30.

western Indians. Placing himself in command of one force, and General Andrew Lewis of another, he gave the order to advance. Lewis defeated the famous chief Comstock in the bloody battle of Point Pleasant, but Dunmore, ignoring the chance to deliver a crushing blow, made a treaty of peace with the Indians.

The frontiersmen, as they turned their faces homeward, cursed the Governor as a traitor, who spared the Indians because he planned to use them against the Virginians should they go to war with Great Britain. Nor were their suspicions groundless, for a few months later Dunmore wrote the Earl of Dartmouth that if the King would send him " a small body of troops " and arms and ammunition, he could raise " such a force among Indians, Negroes, and other persons " as would soon reduce Virginia to obedience.[28]

But at this moment obedience was far from the minds of the people. On March 20, 1775, the second Provincial Congress met in St. John's Church, Richmond. The place was but a straggling village, but it was more centrally located than Williamsburg, and further away from the British warships in the York River. The delegates were unanimous in approving the proceedings of the Continental Congress, and in thanking the Virginia representatives for their services. But it soon became evident that they were divided on the vital question of preparing for war. When Henry introduced resolutions for putting the colony in a state of defense by arming and disciplining a force of militia, some of the leading members drew back. War was unthinkable, they said. The country was too weak, too defenseless, too open to invasion. The only hope was for reconciliation, for the mediation of America's friends in Parliament.

This brought Henry to his feet. " What has there been in the conduct of the British Ministry for the last ten years to justify hope? Are fleets and armies necessary to a work of love and reconciliation? These are the instruments of subjugation sent over to rivet upon us the chains which the British Ministry have been so long forging. What have we to oppose them? Shall we try argument? We have been trying that for the last ten years. . . . Shall we resort to entreaty and supplication? We have petitioned, we have remonstrated, we have supplicated; and we have been spurned from the foot of the throne. . . . If we wish to be free we must fight! I repeat it, sir, we must

[28] *Ibid.*, No. 26.

fight! . . . Is life so dear or peace so sweet as to be purchased at
the price of chains and slavery? Forbid it, Almighty God. I
know not what course others may take, but as for me, give me
liberty or give me death." [29] Henry's eloquence carried the day,
yet so fraught with danger was the issue, that his motion was
carried by a majority of five only.

A few days later Dunmore wrote to Dartmouth denouncing
the proceedings of the Convention. " The most dangerous, as
well as the most daring attempt is the resolution which is
adopted for raising a body of armed men, horse and foot as
well. The plan for imbodying, arming, and disciplining of
which is by these resolutions published as the final order for
putting the same into execution."

Almost overnight Virginia was converted into an armed camp.
Everywhere there was the sound of drums, the sharp commands
of drillmasters, marching and countermarching. Even in Williamsburg the streets were full of men with arms in their hands.
In the Valley of Virginia, Fithian jotted down in his *Diary* on
June 6: " Here every presence is warlike, every sound is
martial! Drums beating, fifes and bagpipes playing. . . . Every
man had a hunting-shirt, which is the uniform of each company. Almost all have a cockade and bucktail in their hats to
represent that they are hardy, resolute, and invincible natives
of the woods of America." [30]

These warlike preparations drove Dunmore to take a step,
which aroused the fury of the patriots. In Williamsburg there
still stands a little octagonal building which was used as a magazine in colonial days. Here were stored twenty barrels of
powder and several guns. To keep the independent companies
from seizing the powder the Governor ordered a party of sailors
to take it on board an armed schooner nearby in the James
River. Before daybreak, on April 20, they made off with most
of it, and it was later put on board the *Fowey* man-of-war.[31]

Despite the gloom of early dawn the removal of the powder
was observed, and the beating of drums gave the alarm. The
independent companies got under arms, the people assembled,
and the Governor was threatened with violence unless he returned the powder. The mayor and other city officers, leaving

[29] William Wirt, *Life of Patrick Henry*, 139-141.
[30] *Philip Vickers Fithian, journal*, eds. Albion and Dodson, 24.
[31] Dunmore papers, no. 26.

the troops nearby, went to the Palace with an address which Dunmore thought amounted to a peremptory demand for the powder. Should he refuse they could not answer for the dreadful consequences.

The Governor not only refused, but prepared to resist any attack with the aid of several British officers and a few men from the warships. Had not Peyton Randolph and Robert Carter Nicholas persuaded the angry troops to disperse, the war in Virginia would have begun with an assault on the Palace. As it was, parties of armed men continued to pour into Williamsburg, and word came that several hundred cavalry were at Fredericksburg, ready to march, and that Patrick Henry was leading a force up from the south. In alarm the Governor sent Lady Dunmore and his children to one of the warships, and threatened to arm the slaves and reduce Williamsburg to ashes.[32]

The more conservative leaders among the Virginians, who were still hoping for a compromise with Great Britain, were able, though with great difficulty, to restrain the troops. At Fredericksburg the men pledged themselves to be in readiness at a moment's notice to defend the laws, the liberties, and the rights of Virginia and any sister colony, and then dispersed.[33] Henry's force got within fifteen miles of Williamsburg, and halted only when Richard Corbin, the Receiver General, paid for the powder from the royal funds by handing him a bill of exchange for £330.

Fate decreed that hostilities should begin, not in Virginia, but in Massachusetts. The Virginia delegates were just preparing to leave for the second Continental Congress when the news of the skirmish at Lexington and Concord arrived. New England was already at war. The question in everyone's mind was, would the rest of the country follow? Washington's answer was to wear his military uniform. Along the road he and the other Virginia delegates were cheered on by crowds of enthusiastic people, amid the blaring of bands and the firing of guns.

It was with difficulty that some of the conservative members of Congress prevented a declaration of independence. And though a petition to the King was agreed on, the taking over of the New England army around Boston and appointing Washington commander in chief, was in effect a declaration of war.

[32] *Ibid.*
[33] *The Virginia Gazette,* Pinckney, May 11, 1775.

Yet, as Washington was leaving for the east to draw the sword, Pendleton returned to Virginia to resume his post as Speaker in a last attempt to re-establish the old government.

He was welcomed to Williamsburg like a conquering hero. A detachment of cavalry met him at the Pamunkey River and escorted him the rest of the way. Two miles from the city they were joined by a company of infantry. At sunset, as they entered Williamsburg, they were received by the ringing of bells and the cheers of the crowds in the streets. At dark every house was illuminated.

Dunmore thought " this pompous military exhibition " had been planned " to raise the importance of the members of this new created power, the Congress, before the people." And the " appearance of numbers of the Burgesses in the clothes of the American troops, wearing a shirt of coarse linen or canvas over their clothes and a tomahawk by their sides," added fuel to the fire.[34]

The Assembly had been in session but three days when several overzealous young men broke into the magazine to take out some of the arms. They stumbled against a cord which had been attached to a gun pointed at the entrance, which went off wounding two of them. This aroused the people to action, and the next day at noon an angry crowd, among them several Burgesses, entered the mazagine and carried off about 400 stand of arms. A committee of the House of Burgesses persuaded the people to return the arms, and then set a military guard around the magazine. " So the custody of the magazine and public stores is thus wrested out of the hands of the Governor," complained Dunmore.[35]

At the opening of the Assembly the Governor began by urging the acceptance of the resolutions which Lord North had pushed through Parliament in February, as the basis for reconciliation. These resolutions promised that if any colony would raise of its own authority the cost of its own government, Parliament would not tax that colony. In other words, if the Americans guaranteed to pay into the hands of the King's Governors funds sufficient to make them independent of the Assemblies, Parliament would not take their money from them to do so. The Burgesses must have been indignant when Dunmore told

[34] Dunmore papers, No. 28.
[35] *Ibid.*

them that he had strong hopes a consideration of this offer would bring to an end the disputes with the mother country.[36]

The reply of the Burgesses, which was almost certainly written by Jefferson, is notable because of the clearness with which it exposed the unconstitutionality of the British position. They had viewed the proposal with pain and disappointment, for it merely changed the form of oppression without lightening its burden. " The British government has no right to intermeddle with the support of civil government in the colonies. For us, not for them, has government been instituted here. . . . We cannot conceive that any other legislature has a right to prescribe either the number or pecuniary appointment of our officers." The claim of Parliament of the right to tax the people of the colony had no precedent. Even the act of 1680 giving the King a perpetual revenue was passed, not by Parliament, but by his Majesty " with the consent of the General Assembly." [37]

The Burgesses were not willing to purchase exemption from an unjust taxation by saddling the people with a perpetual tax to be disposed of by the King or Parliament. " We have a right to give our money as the Parliament does theirs, without coercion. . . . It is not merely the mode of raising, but the freedom of granting our money for which we have contended, without which we possess no check on the royal prerogative."

Upon receiving assurance that no harm was intended his family, Dunmore had brought them back to the Palace. But on June 8, before daybreak, he, Lady Dunmore, the children, his secretary, and some of the servants stole out and went on board the *Fowey*. " My house was kept in continued alarm and threatened every night with an assault," Dunmore explained. " Surrounded as I was by armed men . . . and situated so far from any place where men-of-war can approach, . . . I could not think it safe to continue in that city." [38]

The Assembly urged the Governor to return, but he refused. So on the night of June 24, a large body of men forced their way into the Palace by bursting open a window, and carried off several hundred stand of arms which had been kept in the hall. Some days later another group entered the building, went

[36] *Journals of the House of Burgesses*, 1773-1776: 174, 175.
[37] *Ibid.*, pp. 219-221.
[38] Dunmore papers, No. 28.

from room to room breaking into cabinets, and carried off arms of various sorts.[39]

And now Williamsburg became an armed camp. Bands of horse and foot, in uniforms and each company displaying their distinctive badge flocked in. Some of them lodged in the Capitol, the cavalry encamped on the Palace Green.[40] One wonders whether these men knew that a century earlier Nathaniel Bacon had assembled his men on or near this spot, or whether any of them realized that they had fought for the same cause as they, the cause of liberty?

With Dunmore on the *Fowey* and the Assembly in Williamsburg, the remainder of the session was rather futile. There was renewed bickering over the removal of the powder, the Burgesses drew up a long address to the Governor criticizing his administration, and accusing him of misrepresenting conditions in Virginia in one of his letters to the Earl of Dartmouth. The Assembly adjourned on June 24, until October 12, and on that date, when only thirty-seven members showed up, adjourned again until March 7, 1776. This time less than a fourth of the Burgesses attended, and immediately adjourned to May 6, when several members met, " but did neither proceed to business nor adjourn, as a House of Burgesses." And so died the Virginia Assembly after more than a century and a half of existence, in which it had fought and won the good battle for liberty. It now remained for other bodies to defend and preserve that liberty for future generations.[41]

Even while the Assembly was in session the government, in reality, had passed into the hands of the conventions and the committees of safety. As early as December, 1774, Dunmore wrote that the royal government had been " entirely overthrown." " There is not a justice of peace in Virginia that acts except as a committeeman. The abolishing of the courts of justice was the first step taken, in which the men of fortune and pre-eminence joined equally with the lowest and meanest. The General Court . . . is in much the same predicament." [42] All that was needed to take the government completely out of the hands of the Governor and the Assembly was an executive head. And this was supplied by the third convention which met in

[39] *Ibid.*

[40] *Ibid.*, No. 29.

[41] *Journals of the House of Burgesses*, 1773-1776.

[42] Dunmore papers, No. 22.

Richmond in July, 1775, by the appointment of a "general committee of safety."

To this body were appointed some of the ablest men in the colony—Pendleton, George Mason, John Page, Richard Bland, Thomas Ludwell Lee, and others. It was given almost dictatorial powers, for it had the supervision of military affairs, appointing officers, collecting supplies, and naming paymasters; it corresponded with the county committees, arrested Loyalists, held inquiries.[43]

The convention, having created a body to take over the functions formerly exercised by the Governor and Council, itself practically replaced the dying Assembly. It prepared for the defense of the colony by raising two regular regiments and several thousand minutemen, reorganizing the militia, and setting up works for the manufacture of arms and powder. It authorized the Treasurer to issue £350,000 of paper money. It levied taxes on tithables, coaches, land, licenses, legal papers, etc.[44]

A state of war now existed. If they could have laid hands on Dunmore, the patriots no doubt would have kept him in confinement. And on one occasion he barely escaped. It was in July that he went in a barge to a farm which he owned on a creek about seven miles from Williamsburg. He and Captain Montague, of the *Fowey*, had just finished dinner when the servants rushed in to warn them that the Americans were coming. They had barely time to run to their boat and push off. Two of their men were captured, and another, jumping into a canoe, paddled desperately with bullets whizzing past his head.[45]

As early as May, 1775, Dunmore wrote Dartmouth that he could not maintain even an appearance of authority without "a force to support it." Dartmouth replied that he was sending him 3,000 stand of arms, 200 rounds of powder and ball for each musket, and four light brass cannon. "I see that Gage has ordered sent you a detachment of the Fourteenth Regiment. I hope with the Negroes, Indians, etc., you can reduce Virginia. ... It is the King's firm resolution that the most vigorous efforts should be made, by sea and land, to reduce his rebellious subjects to obedience."[46]

[43] *Proceedings of the Convention*, etc.; C. R. Lingley, *Transition in Virginia*.
[44] *Ibid*.
[45] *Dunmore papers*, No. 29.
[46] *Ibid*., No. 22.

Dunmore was soon in control of Virginia waters. The sloop of war *Otter* arrived late in June, the *Mercury*, carrying twenty guns, on July 10, to be followed by the *Liverpool*, a frigate of twenty-eight guns; the *Kingfisher*, and the *Dunmore*. But the Governor was never able to raise a land force capable of contending with the Virginians. With the arrival of seventy men from St. Augustine and one company from Rhode Island to add to the marines, he could muster about 200 men. This small force he hoped would be a nucleus for an army of Tories and Negroes, and on November 7 he issued a proclamation declaring martial law, summoning all " loyal " citizens to join him, and offering freedom to any slaves who would take up arms for the King.[47]

In the meanwhile, he had moved with his little fleet into the Elizabeth River. It was necessary for him to find provisions, and he counted upon the Scottish merchants of Norfolk and other Tories in the lower counties to supply him. When the local committee of safety denounced all who sent food out to the ships as enemies of liberty, he threatened to bombard the city.

The Norfolk printer, John Holt, ignoring the guns of the warships which pointed out over the town, continued to issue his gazette and to urge the people not to give up their liberty. On September 30 a party of British rowed ashore, marched to the printing office, and carried off the press, the type, the ink, the paper, and two of the printers. As they embarked they gave three huzzas, in which a crowd of Negroes joined. " I am now going to have a press for the King," Dunmore said.[48]

On November 16, Dunmore took possession of Norfolk, where he raised the royal standard. To his great satisfaction the Scottish merchants and their clerks, some Negroes, and others took the oath. He then began to fortify the city with earthworks.[49] He would have done better to build forts at different points on the long, circuitous road by which alone Norfolk could be approached, between the Dismal Swamp and the heads of several branches of the Elizabeth River. Not until it was too late did he fortify Great Bridge where the Southern Branch flowed between two marshes, each crossed by a long causeway.

[47] T. J. Wertenbaker, *Norfolk: historic southern port*, 57, 67.
[48] Dunmore papers, No. 32.
[49] *American Archives*, Fourth Ser. 4: 343.

In the meanwhile, the Virginia troops had been concentrating at Williamsburg, under the command of Colonel Woodford. They now crossed the James, marched through Suffolk, and headed for the Great Bridge. Many of the men were from the western counties, and were armed, not with muskets, but with rifles. They were deadly shots, as the British soon found to their sorrow. When the Virginians reached Great Bridge, the British, instead of waiting for them to attack their almost impregnable position, themselves took the initiative. The regulars led the way over the causeways and the bridge, followed by the Tories and Negroes.[50] " Reserve your fire until they are within fifty yards," the Virginia officers ordered. Then the shirtmen, aiming as coolly as though they were shooting deer, let fly. The regulars were cut to pieces, the Tories and Negroes refused to fight, so with the coming of darkness the British left their posts and streamed back to Norfolk.[51]

When Dunmore heard of this defeat he raved like a madman, and even threatened to hang the boy who brought the news. With the shirtmen advancing on the city, flight was all that was left him. Soon the streets were jammed with panicky soldiers, men, women, and children, hastening to the wharves to take refuge on the warships or the fleet of merchantmen. They were none too soon, for on December 11, the Virginians, reinforced by a body of North Carolinians under Colonel Howe, entered the city.

But having gained Norfolk, the two commanders now debated what they should do with it. If a large force of British attacked it by land and sea it could not be defended, and the garrison would be captured.[52] On the other hand, for the enemy it would be invaluable as a base for attacks on any point in eastern Maryland, Virginia, or North Carolina. Howe wrote the Virginia convention, hinting for permission to burn the city.

Dunmore's folly gave him an excuse for doing so without waiting for a reply. Food and water were becoming scarce on the crowded ships in the river, many of the refugees became ill, several died. So Dunmore threatened to bombard the city if the patriots cut off supplies, and moved the warships to a position close by. But now the riflemen, firing from warehouses

[50] *Richmond College historical papers* 1: 101.
[51] *Ibid.*, 115-121.   [52] *Ibid.*, 138, 139, 148.

near the wharves, began picking off his men whenever they appeared on deck. On the afternoon of January 1, 1776, the warships opened fire, and several boatloads of soldiers rowed up to the wharves and set fire to the adjacent buildings.[53]

It was a striking evidence of the sacrifices which the colonial Virginians were willing to make in the cause of liberty that twice they applied the torch to one of their towns to prevent the enemy from using it as a base. The burning of Jamestown by Bacon and his men foreshadowed the burning of Norfolk by the revolutionary troops a century later. Seizing upon the fires set by the British as an excuse, the soldiers went from house to house to spread the flames. In all nearly nine hundred houses were destroyed. A month later, by command of the convention, the Americans burned down what was left of the city, 416 houses in all.[54]

The burning of Norfolk was a drastic step indeed. All who witnessed the plight of the people as they trudged along the roads leading out of the city to seek refuge in nearby farms must have condemned it as an act of useless cruelty. But in the end it probably saved more suffering than it entailed. Had the city been spared, the British would almost certainly have occupied it and held it throughout the remainder of the war, just as they held New York. It would have been a haven for Tories from all the adjacent states, the British would have made it a great naval and military base, from it expeditions would have been launched up the great Virginia rivers as Berkeley had launched expeditions from the Eastern Shore.

Since the Virginians had no fleet of warships capable of driving Dunmore out of their waters, they decided to starve him out. They even threatened to move the entire population of parts of Norfolk and Princess Anne Counties to prevent provisions from reaching him. In May he gave orders for the fleet to leave the Elizabeth River and proceed to Gwynn's Island, in the Chesapeake Bay, near the mouth of the Rappahannock River. Here he established a camp. But when General Andrew Lewis set up batteries on the mainland and opened fire, the place became untenable. One shot struck the *Dunmore* and wounded the Governor. " Good God! that ever I should come to this! " he shouted. A few days later his fleet sailed down the

[53] *Lower Norfolk County Antiquary* 2: 80.
[54] *American Archives*, Fourth Ser. 4: 540; *Virginia Magazine* 23: 414.

bay and out through the capes. With it went the last vestige of British authority in Virginia.[55]

Now the question of independence was in the minds of all. The small planter as he set out his tobacco crop debated it with himself; the blacksmith talked it over with his client as he shod his horse; it was the topic of conversation in the church yard before the sermon began; the members of the convention debated it as they rode along the muddy roads. In May, 1775, Dunmore wrote: "It is no longer to be doubted that independence is the object in view."[56] But in this he was wrong. The colonists did not want independence. They were Englishmen, most of them, speaking the English language, living under English law, attached to English institutions. They had hardly ceased to speak of England as "home." They looked to the British navy for protection, they were keenly alive to their economic dependence upon the mother country, they were weak and disunited. The colonies went into the war hugging the hope that there might yet be reconciliation, with Washington referring to the British soldiers as the Ministerial troops, and the American chaplains, in public services, praying for the King.

The colonies, in taking up arms, sought only to maintain existing conditions. The King and the Ministry were the real revolutionists, not the Americans. It was Washington who wrote in 1769, that "at a time when our lordly masters in Great Britain will be satisfied with nothing less than the deprivation of American freedom, something should be done to avert the stroke and maintain the liberty which we have derived from our ancestors." Washington by no means considered himself a rebel. He was championing the British constitution and American rights under it against the illegal aggressions of a reactionary Ministry.

But the war had not been long in progress before the people saw that they must preserve their freedom at the bayonet's point, or make abject submission. When, in the summer of 1775, Richard Penn and Arthur Lee went to England with the last effort of Congress for reconciliation, the so-called Olive Branch, they were rebuffed. The King and his Ministers refused to see them. While they were in London a proclamation

[55] *Ibid.*, Fifth Ser. 1: 150, 151, 431, 432.
[56] Dunmore papers, No. 27.

was read at Palace Yard and Temple Bar by heralds, prohibiting all intercourse with the colonies.

Moreover, the ties of reverence and affection gave way rapidly before the anger and bitterness of war. The news that the King was purchasing troops from certain German rulers for use against them aroused the Americans to fury. Angry men gathered everywhere, in the coffee houses, on the village greens, or around the courthouses to discuss the burning of Portland in the midst of a Maine winter, or the arming of the slaves by Dunmore.

It was at this moment that Tom Paine's *Common Sense* made its appearance. Although this pamphlet was bombastic, radical, and filled with absurdities, it fell in with the trend of the day, and so tended to crystallize thought in favor of independence. More than 100,000 copies were sold, and it was estimated that every third person in the colonies read it. " Where, some say, is the King of America? I'll tell you friend. He reigns above, and doth not make havoc of mankind like the royal brute of England. A government of our own is our natural right. Ye who oppose independence now, ye know not what ye do: ye are opening a door to eternal tyranny."

Reluctantly the leaders of thought in Virginia came to the conclusion that the British government was forcing them into independence. Jefferson wrote John Randolph in November, 1775, that he loved the union with Great Britain, " but by the God that made me I will cease to exist before I yield to a connection on such terms as the British Parliament propose, and in this I think I speak the sentiments of America."

Yet the Virginia convention, in August, 1775, had declared: " We again and for all, publickly and solemnly declare, before God and the world, that we do bear faith and true allegiance to his Majesty George the Third, our only lawful and rightful King." [57]

But before the meeting of the convention of May 6, 1776, sentiment had changed. Jefferson said that nine out of every ten persons were now for independence.[58] In February, Benjamin Harrison had hinted strongly that the time was ripe for separation. In January Washington had written Joseph Reed that " a few more such flaming arguments " as Falmouth and

[57] *American Archives* 4: 391.
[58] *The writings of Thomas Jefferson*, ed. A. A. Lipscomb, 4: 255.

Norfolk would not leave many to oppose a separation. On April 12 John Page predicted that independence would be voted in the approaching convention; two days later Carter Braxton expressed the opinion that independence was not only desirable but inevitable; Pendleton, though greatly disturbed at the prospect of separation, thought that no other course was possible.

There was great excitement in Williamsburg when the delegates arrived to take their seats in the Hall of Burgesses for the opening of the convention. The crowds which filled the gallery must have pointed out each distingiushed member as he entered—the aged Richard Bland; George Mason, his black hair now showing a touch of gray; Patrick Henry, in the plain garb he always wore; Richard Henry Lee, who had been called from Congress by the illness of his wife; James Madison, a small delicate young man, widely known as a scholar and political thinker; Edmund Pendleton, six feet in height, lithe, and handsome; Robert Carter Nicholas, Henry Lee, Edmund Randolph.[59]

On the question of independence there were three opinions. Nicholas was opposed to separation, for he thought there was still hope for conciliation. Henry wished Congress to establish independence through a declaration. Pendleton argued for a statement by the convention and by Congress that independence already existed by the action of King and Parliament.

In the end Pendleton was directed to prepare a resolution on independence. So, on May 15, Thomas Nelson, Junior, rose and read two resolutions which Pendleton had drawn up:

Forasmuch as all the endeavors of the United Colonies, by the most decent representations and petitions to the King and Parliament of Great Britain to restore peace and security to America under the British government, and a reunion with that people upon just and liberal terms, instead of a redress of grievances, have produced, from an imperious and vindictive administration, increased insult, oppression, and a vigorous attempt to effect our total destruction. By a late act, all these colonies are declared to be in rebellion, and out of the protection of the British Crown; our properties subjected to confiscation; our people, when captivated, compelled to join in the murder and plunder of their relations and countrymen; and all former rapine and oppression of Americans declared legal and just. Fleets and armies are raised, and the aid of foreign troops engaged to assist in these destructive purposes.

[59] H. B. Grigsby, *The Virginia convention of 1776.*

The King's representative in this colony hath not only withheld all the powers of government from operating for our safety, but, having retired on board an armed ship, is carrying on a piratical and savage war against us, tempting our slaves by every artifice to resort to him, and training and employing them against their masters. In this state of extreme danger, we have no alternative left but an abject submission to the will of those overbearing tyrants, or a total separation from the Crown and government of Great Britain, uniting and exerting the strength of all America for defence, and forming alliances with foreign powers for commerce and aid in war: Wherefore, appealing to the SEARCHER OF HEARTS for the sincerity of former declarations, expressing our desire to preserve the connection with that nation, and that we are driven from that inclination by their wicked councils, and the eternal laws of self-preservation:

Resolved, unanimously, That the delegates appointed to represent this colony in the General Congress, be instructed to propose to that respectable body to declare the United Colonies free and independent states, absolved from all allegiance to, or dependence upon the Crown or Parliament of Great Britain; and that they give the assent of this colony to such declaration, and to whatever measures may be thought proper and necessary by the Congress for forming foreign alliances, and a confederation of the colonies, at such time, and in the manner as to them shall seem best; Provided, the power of forming government for, and the regulations of the internal concerns of each colony, be left to the respective colonial legislatures.

Resolved unanimously, That a committee be appointed to prepare a DECLARATION OF RIGHTS, and such a plan of government as will be most likely to maintain peace and order in this colony, and secure substantial and equal liberty to the people.

The people of Virginia everywhere applauded this final breach with Great Britain. In Williamsburg the " Union flag of the American states " was raised over the Capitol. The troops, under General Lewis, wheeled and marched in a nearby grove in the presence of the members of the Committee of Safety and of the convention and a crowd of citizens. After the resolutions of the convention had been read to the troops, a toast was proposed to " The American Independent States," which was drunk to the shouts of the crowd and the firing of the artillery. Then followed toasts to " The Grand Congress of the United States and their Respective Legislatures," and to " General Washington and Victory for the American Arms."

With coming of night the people illuminated the town amid demonstrations of joy " that the domination of Great Britain was now at an end." [60]

The resolutions of the convention were tantamount to a Virginia declaration of independence. Though it was thought wise to act in concert with the other colonies, the convention did not wait for Congress, but proceeded to draw up a constitution for an independent state, with Governor, Senate, House of Delegates, and judiciary. One hundred and sixty-nine years, almost to a day, after Captain Christopher Newport planted the English flag on the Jamestown peninsula, English authority in Virginia was overthrown.

As the delegates rode home after the convention had concluded its work, the minds of some must have gone over the developments of those seventeen decades, the heritage of self-government which their ancestors had brought with them from England, the struggle to defend their liberty against the assaults of despotic Kings and despotic Governors, the spirit of self-reliance fostered by life in the New World, and now the attempts of a reactionary government in Great Britain to turn back the hands of the clock and deprive them of the rights they had won. It had been James I and Charles I, and even George III who, in their dealings with the colonies, had insisted upon " obedience," but the colonists insisted upon another word, the word " liberty." Now that they had won liberty, it remained to be seen whether they could preserve it against the attacks of the British armies and navy. And none could foresee that at Yorktown, but a few miles away, British armed might in America was destined to be broken, as its political power had already been broken at Williamsburg.

[60] *Virginia Gazette*, Purdie, May 17, 1776.

ESSAY ON SOURCES

Any political history of Virginia in the colonial period must be based chiefly on the documents in the British Public Record Office. During many months of work in this office the author made more than eight hundred pages of notes and transcripts which he has used freely in the writing of this volume. The notations CO1-3, CO5-1318, etc., in the footnotes all refer to the Public Record Office.

It is especially fortunate that these documents have been preserved, since of the copies left in Virginia, when there were copies, most have been destroyed. Among the scores of manuscript volumes on Virginia in the Record Office, thirty-two are devoted to the correspondence of the Board of Trade, seventeen to the correspondence of the Secretary of State, twenty-two to Entry Books, letters, commissions, warrants, etc., for the period from 1680 to the American Revolution alone.

In this vast collection are found the instructions to governors; memorials concerning the clergy, the revenue, the College of William and Mary; addresses of the Assembly to the Throne; reports of special agents of the Crown; accusations against governors; nominations to office; the journals of the Council and of the House of Burgesses.

During the second half of the nineteenth century William Noel Sainsbury, Assistant Keeper of the Records, made no less than twenty volumes of abstracts of these documents, which have been deposited in the Virginia State Library. They cover the long period from the founding of the colony to 1730. The McDonald Papers, also transcribed from the documents in the Public Record Office, and also deposited in the Virginia State Library, parallel the Sainsbury abstracts, but they are fuller and give some papers overlooked by Sainsbury. The author spent the summer of 1908 in Richmond to study these papers, but they merely whetted his desire to see the original collection. So June, 1910, found him in the chilly old building off Chancery Lane, London, immersed in the musty but fascinating mass of documents.

Virginia historians today no longer have to make the journey across the Atlantic, for the United States Government has had transcriptions made of the papers relating to our colonial history for the Library of Congress. Moreover, the journals of the House of Burgesses and the journals of the Council have been published. Many other documents in the Public Record Office have been published in part or in full in the *Calendar of State Papers, Colonial Series, America and West Indies*, and in historical magazines.

The Coventry papers relating to Virginia, Barbados, and other colonies, at Longleat, the magnificent residence of the Marquess of Bath, which have been microfilmed by the American Council of Learned Societies, throw a flood of light on Virginia history, especially upon Bacon's Rebellion. They contain letters from Bacon to Berkeley, from Berkeley to Bacon, and from Philip Ludwell to Lady Berkeley, reports from the Virginia agents who were seeking a charter for the colony, Berkeley's account of the evacuation of Jamestown, and many other valuable documents. They give new and overwhelming evidence that Bacon and his followers rose in arms, not only to protect the people from the Indians, but to right their wrongs under Berkeley's government.

The American Council of Learned Societies was also responsible for the microfilming of the Sackville manuscripts belonging to the Earl of Dorset. They contain letters to the British Government from the Virginia House of Burgesses and from the Council in 1631, and throw a gleam of light on an obscure period.

The correspondence of Lord Dunmore and Lord Dartmouth, in the British Public Record Office, is vital to any account of the early years of the Revolution in Virginia. In his letters Dunmore reports on the committees of correspondence, the boycott, the plight of the Tories, his conflict with the Assembly, the arming of the patriots, his flight from Williamsburg, his seizure of Norfolk, etc. This correspondence is available to scholars in microfilm in the Library of Congress.

W. W. Hening (ed.), *The Statutes at Large* (1809-1823), in thirteen volumes, are indispensable to the historian. In addition to the Virginia laws it publishes a few extremely important documents.

The county records throw light on local government and the use of the patronage by the governors to control the Assembly. It is unfortunate that many documents in the county courthouses were destroyed in the Revolution and the War between the States. Yet the records of Surry, York, Essex, Rappahannock, Accomac, Elizabeth City, and other counties have been preserved.

Peter Force (ed.), *Tracts and Other Papers* (1836), has many valuable documents relating to early Virginia history. The accounts of Bacon's Rebellion are of especial interest. Edward Arber (ed.), *The Works of Captain John Smith* (1910), is a main source for the founding and early history of Jamestown. But Smith's tendency to glorify himself and the probability that he colored his account to further the designs of King James I and the court party have caused many historians to distrust much that he has written.

Alexander Brown, *Genesis of the United States* (1890), gives many documents on early Virginia history which had long been inaccessible to scholars. Other publications of documents or early histories are Susan M. Kingsbury (ed.), *The Records of the Virginia Company of London* (1906-1935); J. C. Hotten (ed.), *Original Lists of Emigrants to America, 1606-1700* (1874); *Lower Norfolk County* Antiquary; Lyon G. Tyler (ed.), *Narratives of Early Virginia* (1907); Charles M. Andrews (ed.), *Narratives of Insurrections* (1915); Clayton C. Hall (ed.), *Narratives of Early Maryland* (1910); and Edmund Goldsmid (ed.), *Hakluyt's, The Principal Navigations* (1885-1890).

R. A. Brock (ed.), *The Official Records of Robert Dinwiddie* (1883-1884); while of great value, is incomplete, since many letters in the British Public Record Office have been omitted. R. A. Brock (ed.), *The Original Letters of Alexander Spotswood* (1882-1885), from the manuscript collection in possession of the Virginia Historical Society, is also far from complete.

Among the historical magazines which have published documents relating to Virginia the most important are *The Virginia Magazine of History and Biography, William and Mary College Quarterly, Tyler's Quarterly Historical and Genealogical Magazine*, and the *Massachusetts Historical Society, Proceedings*.

Three narratives, Henry Hartwell, James Blair, and Edward Chilton, *The Present State of Virginia and the College*; Robert Beverley, *The History and Present State of Virginia*; and Hugh Jones, *The Present State of Virginia*, have all the value of primary sources. The Hartwell, Blair, and Chilton history was written in 1697 and first published by John Wyat at the Rose, in St. Paul's churchyard, London, in 1727. It was republished in 1940, with an able introduction by Hunter D. Farish. Beverley's volume appeared in 1705, and a new edition was published in 1947. Hugh Jones' history came out in 1724, was reprinted in 1865 in a limited edition, and republished in 1956. The last edition, edited by Richard L. Morton, has a valuable introduction, and more than a hundred pages of illuminating notes.

There are a number of histories of Virginia. William Stith, *The History of the First Discovery and Settlement of Virginia* (1747), is little more than a rehash of Captain John Smith's story. John Burk, *The History of Virginia* (1822), though more critical, is out of date since the author did not have access to a mass of documents now available to the historian. The same criticism applies to Charles Campbell, *History of the Colony and Ancient Dominion of Virginia* (1860). Henry Howe, *Historical Collections of Virginia* (1845), brings together many facts, traditions, and biographical sketches. It also gives brief descriptions of contemporaneous life in the various counties. John Fiske's *Old Virginia and her Neighbors* (1900), is interesting, but untrustworthy. Edward D. Neill, *Early Settlement of Virginia and Virginiola* (1878), *The English Colonization of America during the Seventeenth Century* (1871), *History of the Virginia Company of London* (1869), *Virginia Vetusta* (1885), *and Virginia Carolorum* (1886), are based on primary sources and are still valuable. John Esten Cooke, *Virginia: A History of the People* (1884), is interesting but full of mistakes.

Other works on early Virginia history are Alexander Brown, *The First Republic in America* (1898), T. J. Wertenbaker, *Virginia under the Stuarts* (1914); Mary Newton Stanard, *The Story of Virginia's First Century* (1928); Matthew Page Andrews, *The Soul of a Nation* (1943), and *Virginia, the Old Dominion* (1937); William Foote, *Sketches of Virginia* (1850); Robert R. Howison, *A History of Virginia* (1848); Conway W. Sams, *The Conquest of Virginia* (1924); and Wesley Frank Craven, *Dissolution of the Virginia Company* (1932).

In 1957 the Virginia 350th Anniversary Celebration Corporation published a series of booklets on seventeenth-century Virginia history under the able editorship of Dr. Earl G. Swem.

Among them are E. G. Swem and John M. Jennings, *A Selected Bibliography of Virginia*, 1607-1699; William W. Abbot, *A Virginia Chronology*, 1585-1783; Samuel M. Bemiss (ed.), *The Three Charters of the Virginia Company of London*; Wesley Frank Craven, *The Virginia Company of London*; Charles E. Hatch, Jr., *The First Seventeen Years at Jamestown*, 1607-1634; Thomas J. Wertenbaker, *Bacon's Rebellion* and *The Government of Virginia in the Seventeenth Century*; Richard L. Morton, *Struggle against Tyranny and the Beginning of a New Era*; Martha W. Hiden, *How Justice Grew*. Dr. Wilcomb E. Washburn, *Virginia under Charles I and Cromwell*, takes issue with most Virginia historians by coming to the defense of Governor John Harvey who was kicked out of Virginia because of his despotic rule, abuse of the courts, and disregard of law.

Among the special studies relating to the political history of Virginia are Philip A. Bruce, *The Institutional History of Virginia* (1910); Julian A. C. Chandler, *The History of Suffrage in Virginia* (1901); Oliver P. Chitwood, *Justice in Colonial Virginia* (1905); Percy S. Flippin, *Financial Administration of the Colony of Virginia* (1915); Armistead C. Gordon, *The Laws of Bacon's Assembly* (1914); Albert O. Porter, *County Government in Virginia* (1947); Mary N. Stanard, *The Story of Bacon's Rebellion* (1907); R. T. Barton, *Colonial Decisions* (1909); Edward Ingle, *Virginia Local Institutions* (1885); Elmer I. Miller, *The Legislature of the Province of Virginia* (1907); Lyon G. Tyler, *The Cradle of the Republic* (1906); Moncure D. Conway, *Omitted Chapters* (1888); H. J. Eckenrode, *The Revolution in Virginia* (1916); Hugh Blair Grigsby, *The Virginia Convention of 1776* (1855); Charles R. Lingley, *The Transition in Virginia from Colony to Commonwealth* (1910); Charles S. Sydnor, *Gentlemen Freeholders, Political Practices in Washington's Virginia* (1952); Curtis P. Nettels, *George Washington and American Independence* (1951).

Biographies of prominent Virginians seem to come in pairs. There are two biographies of William Claiborne, Norton C. Hale, *Virginia Venturer* (1951), and John H. Claiborne, *William Claiborne of Virginia* (1917); two biographies devoted to the Lee family, Burton J. Hendrick, *The Lees of Virginia* (1935), and Cazenove G. Lee, Jr., *Lee Chronicle* (1956); two short studies of James Blair, Daniel E. Motley, *Life of Com-*

missary *James Blair* (1901), and Edgar L. Pennington, *Commissary Blair* (1936); two biographies of Edmund Pendleton, Robert L. Hilldrup, *The Life and Times of Edmund Pendleton* (1939), and David J. Mays, *Edmund Pendleton* (1952); there are several biographies of Captain John Smith.

Philip A. Bruce, *The Virginia Plutarch* (1929), gives brief biographies of Sir William Berkeley, Nathaniel Bacon, Alexander Spotswood, William Byrd II, Patrick Henry, and others. Among other biographies are Richmond C. Beatty, *William Byrd of Westover* (1932); Thomas J. Wertenbaker, *Torchbearer of the Revolution, The Story of Bacon's Rebellion and Its Leader* (1940); Leonidas Dodson, *Alexander Spotswood* (1932); Louis K. Koontz, *Robert Dinwiddie* (1941); Louis Morton, *Robert Carter of Nomini Hall* (1941); Kate Mason Rowland, *Life and Correspondence of George Mason* (1892); William Wirt Henry, *Patrick Henry* (1891); A. T. S. Goodrick, *Edward Randolph* (1898-1909); Thomas Jefferson, *Autobiography.*

There are numerous Virginia local histories, among them W. Asbury Christian, *Richmond, Her Past and Present* (1912); (1931); Ralph T. Whitelaw, *Virginia's Eastern Shore* (1951); John B. Bodie, *Seventeenth Century Isle of Wight County, Virginia* (1938); Marshall Wingfield, *A History of Caroline County, Virginia* (1924); and Herbert C. Bradshaw, *History of Prince Edward County, Virginia* (1955).

The Virginia Gazette is a major source for the history of Virginia in the eighteenth century. The scattered numbers still in existence have been photostated and copies deposited in some of the larger libraries. Their usefulness has been greatly enhanced by the preparation of an Index by Lester J. Cappon and Stella F. Duff.

Virginia historians will always be grateful to Dr. Earl G. Swem for his *Virginia Historical Index*, covering *The Virginia Magazine of History and Biography*, volumes 1-38; *William and Mary College Quarterly*, first series, volumes 1-27; second series, volumes 1-10; Hening's *Statutes at Large*, and other publications.

Index